2025

Abitur

Original-Prüfungsaufgaben
mit Lösungen

W0192194

Berlin · Brandenburg

Englisch

STARK

© 2024 STARK Verlag GmbH, St.-Martin-Straße 82, 81541 München
20. ergänzte Auflage
www.stark-verlag.de

Inhalt

Abiturprüfungsaufgaben Berlin/Brandenburg

Abiturprüfungsaufgaben 2024 .... **www.stark-verlag.de/mystark**

Sobald die Original-Prüfungsaufgaben 2024 freigegeben sind, können sie als PDF auf der Plattform MySTARK heruntergeladen werden (Zugangscode vgl. Umschlaginnenseite).

Autorinnen und Autoren

Holtwick, Birgit (Übungsaufgabe 1: Prüfungsteil 1; Übungsaufgabe 2: Prüfungsteil 1 Aufgabe 1, 2, 3.1)

Jacob, Rainer (Lösungen GK 2021 1.1 und 2.2)

Klewitz, Bernd (Lösungen LK 2021 Aufgabenstellung 1.1 und 2.1)

Klimmt, Robert (Die wichtigsten Stilmittel zur Textanalyse; Lösungen 2023 2.1)

Lemke, Frank und Nussdorf, Kathryn (Lösungen GK 2022)

Nussdorf, Kathryn (Lösungen GK 2021 2.1, GK 2023, GK 2024)

Redaktion (digitale Kurzgrammatik, Lernvideos zur Textaufgabe; Übungsaufgabe 1: Prüfungsteil 2)

Ressel, Johanna (Lösungen GK 2021 1.2)

Schulz, Katrin (Lösungen LK 2021 1.2 und 2.2, LK 2022, LK 2023 1.1, 1.2 und 2.2, LK 2024)

Warlimont, Peter (Übungsaufgabe 2: Prüfungsteil 1 Aufgabe 3.2, Prüfungsteil 2)

Vorwort

Liebe Schülerinnen, liebe Schüler,

mithilfe der folgenden Informationen, Aufgaben und Lösungen haben Sie verschiedene Möglichkeiten, sich auf das Abitur im Fach Englisch vorzubereiten:

– Der erste Teil des Buches enthält **Hinweise und Tipps** zur schriftlichen Abiturprüfung im Fach Englisch in Berlin und Brandenburg. Hier finden Sie Informationen zu häufigen Aufgabenstellungen, wichtigen Stilmitteln und zu einer geschickten Vorgehensweise in der Abiturprüfung.

– Die **Übungsaufgaben** gliedern sich in zwei Teile: Zunächst finden Sie die Aufgabenstellungen zu den **Lernvideos**. Lesen Sie die Texte und Aufgaben, bevor Sie sich die Videos ansehen. Im zweiten Teil finden Sie zwei **Übungsaufgaben** mit Lösungen, die sich an den aktuellen Vorgaben zum **Abitur in Berlin und Brandenburg** orientieren. Der Schwierigkeitsgrad ist dabei ansteigend.

– Im Anschluss folgt eine Auswahl von **Original-Prüfungsaufgaben der Grund- und Leistungskurse** der letzten Jahre.

– Lernen Sie gerne am PC, Tablet oder Smartphone? Auf den nächsten Seiten finden Sie Hinweise zu den digitalen Inhalten in diesem diesem Band.

Wir wünschen Ihnen viel Erfolg bei der Abiturprüfung,

Ihre Autorinnen und Autoren

Hinweise zu den digitalen Inhalten

Auf alle digitalen Inhalte können Sie online über die Plattform MySTARK zugreifen. Ihren persönlichen Zugangscode finden Sie auf der Umschlaginnenseite (vorne im Buch).

PDF der Original-Prüfungsaufgaben 2024

Um Ihnen die Prüfung 2024 schnellstmöglich zur Verfügung stellen zu können, bringen wir sie in digitaler Form heraus.

Sobald die **Original-Prüfungsaufgaben 2024** zur Veröffentlichung freigegeben sind, können sie als PDF auf der **Plattform MySTARK** heruntergeladen werden.

Kurzgrammatik

Mit der Kurzgrammatik können Sie sich eine knappe und verständliche Übersicht über die wichtigsten Themenfelder der englischen Grammatik herunterladen. Schlagen Sie hier die Grammatikregeln zu Fehlern nach, die Sie noch häufig machen.

Lernvideos

Textaufgaben sind Teil vieler Prüfungen und Klausuren – und machen oft einen Großteil der Prüfungsleistung aus. Mithilfe der **Lernvideos zum richtigen Umgang mit Textaufgaben** können Sie sich optimal auf die Anforderungen in diesem Bereich vorbereiten. Am Beispiel von zwei Texten mit je drei Aufgabenstellungen wird gezeigt, wie man an eine Textaufgabe herangeht und sie erfolgreich löst.

Die Lernvideos beinhalten:
- **Schritt-für-Schritt-Anleitungen** zum richtigen Vorgehen in der Prüfung
- **Sachtext** und **literarischer Text** als Grundlage
- nützliche Hinweise zu **häufigen Operatoren** und **Zieltextsorten**

Die im Video behandelten Übungsaufgaben sind im Kapitel „Lernvideos zur Textaufgabe" abgedruckt. Lesen Sie sich die Texte und Aufgabenstellungen zunächst durch, bevor Sie sich die Videos auf MySTARK ansehen.

Interaktives Training

Im **Online-Training „Basic Language Skills"** erhalten Sie Zugriff auf zahlreiche **interaktive Aufgaben** zu Grundlagen wie **Hörverstehen, Leseverstehen** und **Sprachverwendung im Kontext**. Dies sind ganz wichtige „Basics", die Sie für eine gute Sprachbeherrschung brauchen.

Das interaktive Training bietet Ihnen:

- **„Listening"** – authentische Hörtexte mit vielfältigen Aufgaben, die Ihr Hörverstehen testen
- **„Reading"** – abwechslungsreiche Lesetexte und dazugehörige Aufgaben
- **„English in Use"** mit gemischten Aufgaben rund um den Gebrauch der englischen Sprache
- Alle Aufgaben sind interaktiv, d. h., Sie können sie direkt am PC oder Tablet bearbeiten und erhalten sofort eine Rückmeldung zu Ihren Antworten.

Web-App „MindCards"

Mit der Web-App **„MindCards"** können Sie am Smartphone Vokabeln lernen. Auf diesen interaktiven Karteikarten finden Sie hilfreiche Wendungen, die Sie beim Schreiben von Texten oder im mündlichen Sprachgebrauch einsetzen können.

Scannen Sie einfach die QR-Codes oder verwenden Sie folgende Links, um zu den „MindCards" zu gelangen:
https://www.stark-verlag.de/mindcards/writing-2
https://www.stark-verlag.de/mindcards/speaking-2

Writing

Speaking

Hinweise und Tipps

Allgemeine Hinweise und Tipps

Im Folgenden finden Sie alle wichtigen Informationen zu den zentralen Abiturprüfungen 2025 in Berlin und Brandenburg im Fach Englisch. Sollten nach Erscheinen dieses Bandes noch entscheidende Änderungen in der Abiturprüfung bekannt gegeben werden, finden Sie aktuelle Informationen dazu auf der Plattform MySTARK (Zugangscode vgl. Umschlaginnenseite).

Ablauf der Prüfung

Der Ablauf der Abiturprüfung in Berlin und Brandenburg erfolgt nach demselben Muster. Zu Beginn der Prüfung werden Ihnen pro Prüfungsbereich zwei Aufgabenstellungen vorgelegt (zwei im Bereich **„Leseverstehen und Schreiben"**, zwei im Bereich **„Sprachmittlung"**). Anschließend haben Sie 30 Minuten Zeit, um alle Aufgabenstellungen zu lesen und sich jeweils für eine der beiden Aufgaben zu entscheiden. Die gesamte Prüfungszeit beträgt im **Leistungskurs 285 Minuten**, im **Grundkurs 255 Minuten**. Sie können sich die Auswahl- und Bearbeitungszeit frei einteilen. Als Richtlinie gilt, dass Sie etwa 60 Minuten für die Bearbeitung der Sprachmittlungsaufgabe nutzen sollten, die übrige Zeit für die Schreibaufgabe.

Tipp

Lesen Sie nicht nur die Texte, sondern auch die Aufgabenstellungen sehr genau. Es ist möglich, dass Ihnen das Thema eines Textes zusagt, Sie jedoch mit der Aufgabenstellung nicht zurechtkommen, oder dass Ihnen die Analyseaufgabe leichtfällt, die Erörterung sich jedoch als besonders komplex erweist. Berücksichtigen Sie dies bei Ihrer Auswahl. Da die Zeit in der Prüfung knapp bemessen ist, sollten Sie gleich zu Beginn eine Aufgabe fest auswählen und sich nicht während der Prüfung noch einmal umentscheiden.

Sie dürfen bei der Bearbeitung jeweils ein einsprachiges und ein zweisprachiges Wörterbuch Englisch sowie ein Nachschlagewerk zur deutschen Sprache verwenden.

Kursart	Auswahlzeit	Leseverstehen/ Schreiben	Mediation	gesamt
GK	30 Min	195 Min	60 Min	255 Min
LK	30 Min	225 Min	60 Min	285 Min

Inhaltliche Schwerpunkte

Die Prüfungsschwerpunkte für das Abitur werden basierend auf dem Rahmenlehr-
plan und den bundesweiten Bildungsstandards für die fortgeführte Fremdsprache
festgelegt. Für die Prüfung 2025 wurden folgende **Themenbereiche** für Grund- und
Leistungskurs ausgewählt:

Individuum und Gesellschaft (1. Kurshalbjahr): *Aims and ambitions* – Ziele und Ambitionen	Hier geht es um die **Vielfalt der Gesellschaft** und unsere unterschiedlichen Lebensentwürfe. Verschiedene Bildungswege, Herausforderungen, soziokulturelle Unterschiede und Generationen-unterschiede können thematisiert werden. Quer-bezüge ergeben sich insbesondere zu den Themen, die in Q 2 behandelt werden (z. B. *American Dream*).
Nationale und kulturelle Identität (2. Kurshalbjahr): *Nations between tradition and change* – mit Fokus auf die USA als Bezugskultur	In diesem Bereich geht es um historische und aktuelle Entwicklungen in den USA (insbesondere die amerikanischen Ideale **Freiheit, Gleichheit** und das **Streben nach Glück**). Hier hilft Ihnen ein Wissen zu den wichtigsten Inhalten des *U.S. Constitution*, zum Begriff des **American Dream** und eine grundlegende Kenntnis zum Bereich Black History (z. B. *Declaration of Independence, Segregation, Brown vs. Board of Education, Montgomery Bus Boycott, Black Lives Matter*).
Eine Welt – globale Fragen (3. Kurshalbjahr): *Saving the planet* – Umwelt- und Klimaschutz	Das Thema **Klimawandel** wird im Kontext von **Klimagerechtigkeit** behandelt. Es wird hinterfragt, wie in Zeiten von **Globalisierung** fair mit dem Thema Nachhaltigkeit umgegangen werden kann und wie sich das Verhalten der westlichen Zivi-lisation auf das Klima in verschiedenen **Regionen der Welt** auswirkt (Dürren, Hungersnöte, Stürme etc.).
Herausforderungen der Gegenwart (4. Kurshalbjahr): *The impact of the media on society* – Rolle und Wirkungsweise der Massenmedien	Hier stehen nicht die Medienerfahrungen Einzelner im Mittelpunkt, sondern die **Auswirkung von Medien auf unsere Gesellschaft**. Neben positiven Aspekten *(information, entertainment)* werden auch problematische Bereiche thematisiert *(manipulation, fake news)*.

Es wird kein Detailwissen abgeprüft und die Prüfungsthemen sind weit gefasst. Für
die Bearbeitung der Schreibaufgabe ist es dennoch hilfreich, wenn Sie zu einigen
häufig behandelten Themen Vorwissen und einen passenden Wortschatz mitbringen.
Konzentrieren Sie sich in der Prüfungsvorbereitung auf die im Unterricht behandel-
ten Materialien und erarbeiteten Sie sich den Wortschatz in den prüfungsrelevanten
Bereichen. Wenn Sie sich gerne noch einen kurzen Überblick über die wichtigsten
Themen der Oberstufe verschaffen wollen, können Sie diese in unserem **Abitur-
Skript Englisch** nachschlagen (Bestellnr. 10546S2).

Die Prüfung besteht aus zwei Teilen, **Leseverstehen und Schreiben** (Teil 1) und **Sprachmittlung** (Teil 2). Für jeden Teil können Sie aus zwei Aufgabenstellungen diejenige auswählen, die Ihnen mehr zusagt.

– **Teil 1:** Der **Kompetenzbereich Leseverstehen und Schreiben** besteht aus 1–2 Texten mit Arbeitsanweisungen, die alle drei Anforderungsbereiche (**Zu-**

Anforderungsbereich I	Textverstehen / Zusammenfassung
Anforderungsbereich II	Textanalyse
Anforderungsbereich III	Diskutieren / Gestalten

sammenfassung, Analyse und **Schreibaufgabe**; siehe auch „Hinweise zu den Aufgabenstellungen") abdecken. In der Regel werden in einer Aufgabenstellung ein oder mehrere **literarische Texte,** in der anderen ein oder mehrere **Sachtexte** vorkommen. Diese können durch **Bilder** und **Grafiken** (schwarzweiß) ergänzt werden, auf die Sie in der Schreibaufgabe Bezug nehmen müssen.

– **Teil 2:** Der **Kompetenzbereich Sprachmittlung/Mediation** umfasst ein oder zwei deutsche Ausgangstexte, aus denen wesentliche Inhalte in die Zielsprache Englisch transportiert werden sollen. Welche Informationen aus den deutschen Texten relevant sind, hängt von der **Zielgruppe** ab, an die sich der Text richtet, sowie von dem **Kontext**, in den die Aufgabe eingebettet ist. Häufig wird als Zieltext ein (Online-) **Artikel**, eine **E-Mail** oder ein **Blogeintrag** gefordert.

Teil 1: Leseverstehen und Schreiben

Der **erste Arbeitsauftrag** bezieht sich weitgehend auf den **Anforderungsbereich I (Textverstehen)**. Sie sollen unter Beweis stellen, dass Sie die Textvorlage(n) verstanden haben und in der Lage sind, eine Zusammenfassung zu erstellen und sich auf bestimmte Aspekte zu konzentrieren.

Die **zweite Aufgabe** bezieht sich auf den **Anforderungsbereich II (Textanalyse)**. Im Zentrum steht hier die Analyse des Informationsgehalts des Textes oder der Texte in Zusammenhang mit der Textgestaltung. Durch die Aufgabenstellung ist festgelegt, auf welche Aspekte der Textgestaltung Sie sich konzentrieren sollen. Im Bereich „Hinweise zu den Aufgabenstellungen" finden Sie weitere Informationen dazu, nach welchen Gestaltungsmitteln im Konkreten gefragt werden kann.

In der **dritten Aufgabe (Diskutieren und Gestalten)** stehen zwei Aufgabenstellungen zur Auswahl. Erwartet wird eine Form der **Stellungnahme (Erörterung/Kommentar)**. Es kann eine situationsgebundene Textart (z. B. **Brief, Blogeintrag, Rede** etc.) mit dem dazugehörigen **Register** verlangt werden. In der Schreibaufgabe ist Ihr Vorwissen gefragt. Die Thematik des Textes wird weitergeführt. Einige Aufgabenstellungen erfordern, dass Sie den Ausgangstext, ein (teils daraus entnommenes) Zitat oder eine ergänzte Grafik in Ihre Argumentation mit einbeziehen. Wenn die Aufgabe ein **Zitat** oder **Bildmaterial** enthält, müssen Sie dies zunächst kurz erläutern und explizit darauf Bezug nehmen. Es ist nicht ausreichend, lediglich auf die enthaltene Thematik zu verweisen. Umgekehrt wird auch keine ausführliche Bildbeschreibung von Ihnen erwartet. Konzentrieren Sie sich auf die wesentlichen Aussagen.

Teil 2: Sprachmittlung

Bei der **Sprachmittlungsaufgabe** müssen Sie Informationen aus dem Textmaterial kohärent, strukturiert, **situations-** und **adressatengerecht zusammenfassen**.

Hinweise zu den Aufgabenstellungen

1 Textzusammenfassung

Die erste Aufgabe im Bereich des Leseverstehens und Schreibens prüft, ob Sie den Text verstanden haben und wesentliche Inhalte in gekürzter Form wiedergeben können. Dabei kann allgemein erwartet werden, dass Sie den gesamten Text zusammenfassen. Häufiger noch wird eine **gelenkte Inhaltszusammenfassung** gefordert, bei der Sie sich auf einzelne Aspekte des Textes konzentrieren sollen. Im Folgenden finden Sie **Operatoren**, die in der Aufgabenstellung enthalten sein können:

Operatoren	Erläuterungen	Beispiele
Gelenkte Zusammenfassung		
outline	Give the main features, structure or general principles of a topic in your own words omitting minor details. Do not include your opinion or interpretation.	• Outline the information the narrator/author provides on … • Outline the situation of … • Outline what … says about …
give an account of		• Give an account of … (as described in …).
sum up		• Sum up the main ideas on … as presented in …
describe	Give an accurate account of sth in your own words.	• Describe … as depicted in …
state, point out	Present the main aspects of sth using your own words.	• State the information the author gives on …
Zusammenfassung		
summarise/ summarize/ sum up	Give a concise account of the main aspects/points in your own words.	• Summarise the content of the article. • Sum up the content of the excerpt.

Warum wird eine Zusammenfassung geschrieben?

Die Zusammenfassung hat eine Schlüsselfunktion in der Vorbereitung der Textanalyse und der Interpretation. Zunächst muss man sicher sein, dass auch wirklich erfasst worden ist, worum es in dem Text geht. Dann ist es möglich, den Text auf Aufbau, Argumentationsweise, Sprache und Stilmittel, d. h. in Bezug auf seine Gestaltungsmittel hin, zu untersuchen. Nachdem die Textaussage und die Textgestaltung klar erfasst sind, können Sie sich der Textauslegung, der Interpretation und der Analyse der Bedeutung des Textes zuwenden.

Wie wird eine Zusammenfassung vorbereitet?

Lesen Sie zunächst noch einmal die **Aufgabenstellung** und **markieren** Sie, welche Elemente Sie aus dem Text herausarbeiten sollen. Gehen Sie dann den **gesamten Text durch und markieren Sie die entsprechenden Textstellen** farbig. In vielen Fällen ist es in der Zusammenfassung sinnvoll, von der **Textreihenfolge abzuweichen**, um zusammengehörende Aspekte entsprechend zu organisieren. Dies hilft auch dabei, unnötige Wiederholungen zu vermeiden. Entscheiden Sie für Ihre Zusammenfassung:
– Was ist zentral und wichtig?
– Was ist eher ausschmückendes Beiwerk? Welche Beispiele kann man abstrahieren und zusammenfassen?
– Was könnte man erwähnen, muss es aber nicht?

Bei der Entscheidung, was man weglassen kann, helfen Überlegungen wie „Könnte ich den Text verstehen, wenn mir diese Information nicht zur Verfügung gestellt würde?".

Tipp

Wie genau Sie von der Vorbereitung in den Schreibprozess übergehen, ist auch eine Typsache. Verschiedene Techniken haben sich bewährt. Testen Sie in der Abiturvorbereitung, welche davon Ihnen helfen, Ihren Text klar zu strukturieren und die Zusammenfassung in eigenen Worten wiederzugeben:
– Notieren Sie schon beim Lesen die Kerninhalte der markierten **Textpassagen in eigenen Worten am Rand**.
– **Nummerieren** Sie die markierten Inhalte / Stichworte im Anschluss an den Leseprozess, um die Reihenfolge für Ihre Zusammenfassung festzulegen.
– Schreiben Sie eine **kurze Gliederung** auf einem Schmierblatt, die alle wichtigen Aspekte erfasst und bereits abstrahiert.

Was ist beim Schreiben zu beachten?

Ihre inhaltliche Zusammenfassung kann mit einem *umbrella sentence* beginnen, der Angaben zur Autorin/zum Autor, zum Titel, zur Textsorte, zum Zeitpunkt des Entstehens und zum thematischen Schwerpunkt des Textes enthält. Berücksichtigen Sie das, was Sie im Unterricht zum Einstieg in die Textzusammenfassung besprochen haben. Für die formale und sprachliche Gestaltung gelten folgende Punkte:
– **Textlänge:** Der Umfang der Zusammenfassung liegt bei etwa **einem Drittel** der Länge der Textvorlage.
– **Tempus:** Eine Zusammenfassung wird im **Präsens** verfasst. Im Text vorkommende Vor- bzw. Nachzeitigkeit bleibt erhalten.
– **Bezüge:** Personen-, Zeit- und Ortsbezüge werden wie in der indirekten Rede umgeformt, also wird *I* zu *he* oder *she*; *yesterday* zu *the day before*; *here* zu *there* usw.
– **Tabus:** Die Zusammenfassung enthält keine direkte Rede und **keine Zitate**. Die Zusammenfassung enthält **keine wertende persönliche Stellungnahme** und ist in jedem Fall in **eigenen Worten** zu formulieren.

Tipp

Nutzen Sie **allgemeine Begriffe** (wie z. B. *means of transport* anstelle von *car, bike and underground*), um zusammenhängende Aspekte knapp darzustellen. Aufzählungen sollten vermieden werden und stattdessen in einem Oberbegriff zusammengefasst werden.

Sprachlich tendiert die Zusammenfassung zu einem gehobenen Niveau und Abstraktionsgrad. Sie stellt das dem Ursprungstext zugrunde gelegte Konzept dar und lässt ausschmückende Details und konkrete Beispiele weg. Dies und die Textlänge unterscheidet sie von der Nacherzählung.

2 Analyse

In der Analyseaufgabe wird ein tiefer gehendes Textverständnis von Ihnen erwartet. Sie erfassen den oder die Texte nicht mehr nur auf inhaltlicher Ebene, sondern verknüpfen Inhalt und Form miteinander. In der Aufgabenstellung ist in der Regel vorgegeben, auf welche **Gestaltungsmittel** Sie sich beziehen sollen. Dies erleichtert Ihnen die Analyse und die Strukturierung Ihrer Lösung. Berücksichtigen Sie, dass die Gestaltungsmittel nicht nur erkannt und aufgelistet, sondern auch in Ihrer Funktion erläutert werden sollen.

Operatoren	Erläuterungen	Beispiele
Textanalyse		
analyse/ analyze	Name and explain the meaning of specific aspects and/or features of the text and their effect on the reader/audience.	• Analyse how the author's use of language helps to convey her message. • Analyse how the narrative technique employs the message of the text. • Analyse how the reader's interest in the text is attracted by its content and structure.
examine		• Examine the problems the protagonist faces and how the narrative technique is used to bring them across …
compare/ contrast	Point out similarities and differences./Emphasize the differences between two or more things.	• Compare/contrast the communicative strategies the authors of the material (Text A and B) use to convey their opinion on artificial intelligence.
characterize/ give/write a characterization of	describe and analyse how a person is presented in a literary text	• Write a characterisation of Mae, also taking into account the effect the narrative perspective has on the reader's perception of her character.

Auf welche Gestaltungsmittel bezieht sich der Arbeitsauftrag?

Im Bereich der Textanalyse wird in der Regel die Aufgabenstellung bereits einen Hinweis darauf enthalten, welche **Gestaltungsmittel** für die Analyse besonders wesentlich sind.

Bei **Sachtexten** könnte es sich um einen der folgenden Bereiche handeln:
- **structure:** Hier geht es im Wesentlichen um den Aufbau des Textes. Wie steigt der Autor oder die Autorin ins Thema ein? Womit beendet er oder sie seinen Artikel? Wie arrangiert er oder sie die Argumente?
- **use of language:** In diesem Bereich können Sie ganz klassisch auf Stilmittel (*stylistic devices*) eingehen. Oft spielt auch allgemein die Wahl der Wörter (positiv oder negativ besetzt; mit Bezug zu einem bestimmten Wortfeld o. Ä.) und der

Tonfall (z. B. ironisch, sachlich, emotional, besorgt ...) für diesen Bereich eine wichtige Rolle. Ist der Text eher faktenbasiert oder appelliert er an die Emotionen der Lesenden? Ist er berichtend oder argumentativ? Eine Auswahl von rhetorischen Mitteln finden Sie am Ende des Hinweiskapitels.

- **communicative strategies:** Wie versucht der Autor oder die Autorin von der eigenen Perspektive zu überzeugen? Werden Zitate von Expertinnen und Experten oder Betroffenen eingesetzt? Werden die Lesenden direkt angesprochen? Werden Beispiele oder Statistiken angeführt? Wie ausgewogen wird das Thema dargestellt?

In **literarischen Texten** wird meist nach folgenden Gestaltungsmitteln gefragt:

- **use of language:** Auch hier geht es um Stilmittel, Satzkonstruktionen, Wortfelder und die Wortwahl allgemein. Welcher Tonfall wird eingeschlagen (*humorous, ironic, sarcastic, pleasant, depressing, dark, forboding, tense ...*)?
- **narrative techniques:** Welche Erzählperspektive verwendet der Autor oder die Autorin im Text (*third-person vs. first person; omniscient vs. personal vs. neutral*)? Wie werden die Figuren charakterisiert? Gibt es Besonderheiten bei der zeitlichen Struktur des Textes (Zeitraffung oder Zeitdehnung, Zeitsprünge)? Wie wird der Text präsentiert (Beschreibungen vs. direkte Rede / Dialoge)?

Meist werden in einem Arbeitsauftrag verschiedene Gestaltungsmittel genannt. Hierbei können Oberkategorien und Teilaspekte gemischt werden ("Focus on use of language *(Oberkategorie)* and the narrative perspective *(Teilaspekt)* ...").

Was ist beim Schreiben zu beachten?

Beginnen Sie Ihre Textanalyse mit einem kurzen **Einleitungssatz**. Dieser sollte sich auf die Aufgabenstellung beziehen und kann ein mögliches **Fazit der Analyse** bereits vorwegnehmen. Im Folgetext können Sie diese Annahme dann anhand der verschiedenen Textelemente belegen.

Achten Sie darauf, sich nicht darin zu verlieren, möglichst viele Stilmittel oder Textelemente, die Sie erkannt haben, aufzulisten. Konzentrieren Sie sich auf die **Gestaltungsmittel, die Ihre These am besten** belegen. Achten Sie auch darauf, nur auf solche Gestaltungsmittel einzugehen, die in der **Aufgabenstellung** gefordert werden. Einige Elemente, wie Stilmittel, müssen Sie mithilfe von Textstellen belegen. Hierbei können Sie **direkt zitieren** oder **indirekt zitieren**. Mehr dazu finden Sie im nächsten Abschnitt.

Bemühen Sie sich insgesamt um eine **fokussierte Betrachtung**. Die Zeit in der Prüfung ist knapp bemessen und eine gelungene Analyse einiger wichtiger Punkte wirkt im Kern überzeugender als eine lange, unstrukturierte Beschreibung vieler Aspekte. Falls die Lehrkraft im Unterricht Richtlinien in Bezug auf die **Wortzahl** der Analyse vorgegeben hat, sind diese einzuhalten.

Wie zitiere ich richtig?

Achten Sie beim Zitieren darauf, sich auf das **Wesentliche zu begrenzen**. Es reichen zwei oder drei Beispiele, um ein Stilmittel zu belegen. Auch müssen nicht immer ganze Sätze oder Passagen wiedergegeben werden. Kürzen Sie, wo es möglich und sinnvoll ist, und verweisen Sie bei einigen Gestaltungsmitteln, etwa bei Expertenzitaten oder Statistiken, einfach auf die entsprechende Textstelle. Grundsätzlich unterscheidet man zwischen **direkten** und **indirekten Textzitaten.**

Direkte Zitate:
- Sie geben Textpassagen in Ihrem genauen Wortlaut wieder. Dabei verwenden Sie **Anführungszeichen.** Berücksichtigen Sie, dass im Englischen sowohl die öffnenden als auch die schließenden Anführungszeichen oben stehen.
- Wenn Sie **vom Wortlaut abweichen (Textänderungen)**, etwa um ein Zitat in einen Satz einzubauen, müssen Sie dies durch **eckige Klammern** kennzeichnen. **Textkürzungen (Auslassungen)** kennzeichnen Sie durch **drei Punkte in eckigen Klammern.** Beispiel:
  His outward appearance also contributes to it. His ill-fitting clothes that "squeeze[] his upper arms and his neck" (ll. 6/7) and the "corduroy jacket [...] that [seems] as permanent as a turtle's scuffed shell" (ll. 9/10) support the feeling that Manuel is too weak.

Indirekte Zitate:
- Sie geben Textpassagen sinngemäß wieder.
- In Klammern verweisen Sie auf die Textstellen, damit die Leser*innen Ihres Aufsatzes sehen, auf welchen Textabschnitt Sie sich beziehen.

Die **Textstelle** geben Sie am Ende des Zitats **in Klammern** an. Hier gibt es verschiedene Varianten:
- „l." nutzen Sie für ein Zitat, das aus nur einer Textzeile entnommen ist.
- „ll." bezieht sich auf ein Zitat, dass sich über mehrere Textzeilen erstreckt. In diesem Fall können Sie entweder alle Zeilen mit angeben (Beispiel: **ll. 5–8**; bei zwei aufeinanderfolgenden Zeilen **ll. 5/6**) oder mit der Bezeichnung „f." bzw. „ff." für „following" arbeiten (Beispiel: **ll. 5 ff.**; bei zwei aufeinanderfolgenden Zeilen **ll. 5 f.**)
- Bei indirekten Zitaten nutzen Sie die Bezeichnung „cf." („confer"), was in etwa so viel bedeutet wie „vgl." („vergleiche"). Beispiel:
  *In the first part of the text, Barkham conveys Kate Milman's background (**cf. ll. 1– 18**), so the reader can understand why she founded the forest school.*
  (Hier wird auf die Struktur des Textes eingegangen).

Tipp

Auch wenn sich die Aufgabenstellung im Detail je nach Text unterscheidet, bleibt die grundsätzliche Vorgehensweise bei den jeweiligen Operatoren gleich. In den **Videos** auf der Plattform **MySTARK** (Zugangscode vgl. Umschlaginnenseite) erklären wir Ihnen, wie Sie bei den wichtigsten Operatoren im Bereich Schreiben vorgehen müssen. Außerdem erfahren Sie etwas zu häufigen Zieltextformaten wie z. B. Leserbrief oder Blogartikel.

---

3 Persönliche Stellungnahme/Kommentar und kreatives Schreiben

In der dritten Aufgabe im Bereich Textanalyse und Schreiben haben Sie in der Regel die Wahl zwischen einem eher traditionell angelegten **Kommentar** bzw. einer klassischen **Erörterung** und einem kontextgebundenen argumentativen Text, der zum Beispiel in Form eines **Blogartikels**, eines **Zeitungsartikels** oder in Form einer **Rede** verfasst sein muss.
Der grundsätzliche Aufbau ist dabei gleich. In beiden Aufgabenformen wird eine **kurze, zielgerichtete Einleitung** von Ihnen erwartet.

Kommentar	Erörterung
eigene Meinung	Diskussion aus verschiedenen Perspektiven
meist wird nur eine Seite (pro oder kontra) beleuchtet	verschiedene Bereiche (z. B. pro und kontra) werden betrachtet
4–6 Argumente	2–3 Argumente
Ihre eigenen Erfahrungen und Wertvorstellungen werden im gesamten Text reflektiert.	Die Argumentation erfolgt sachlich, erst im Schluss kann die eigene Meinung dargelegt werden.

Angeschlossen folgen **Argumente**, die einer klaren Struktur folgen und **Erläuterungen** und **Beispiele oder Belege** enthalten. Bei der Reihenfolge der Argumente gibt es verschiedene Varianten. In einem Kommentar können Sie mit dem schwächsten Argument beginnen und dann bis zum besten Argument steigern. Eine andere Variante ist es, mit einem stärkeren Argument zu beginnen, dann mittelstarke Argumente anzuführen und mit dem stärksten Argument zu enden. In einer Diskussion beginnt man mit dem stärksten Argument der Gegenseite, auf das die schwächeren Argumente folgen, bei der Seite, die man vertritt, steigert man vom schwächeren Argument zum stärksten. Es ist auch möglich, im Wechsel Argumente von Pro und Kontra zu präsentieren, die Gegenseite also immer gleich zu widerlegen. Diese Variante ist jedoch anspruchsvoller und sollte nur dann von Ihnen gewählt werden, wenn Sie sich in Ihrer Argumentation sehr sicher fühlen. **Wiederholungen oder Abschweifungen vom Thema müssen vermieden werden.** Falls Ihre Lehrkraft Ihnen Vorgaben zur Länge des Aufsatzes gemacht hat, sollten Sie sich daran halten. Bei dem kontextgebundenen argumentativen Text finden Sie am häufigsten eine der folgenden drei Textformen:

Zeitungsartikel/Artikel für ein Magazin oder eine Webseite:
– Durch das Medium, bei dem der Artikel erscheint, ist klar, welche **Zielgruppe** angesprochen wird. Der Stil, der von Ihnen gefordert wird, ist tendenziell gehoben und **sachlich**.
– Zusätzlich zu Einleitung, Hauptteil und Schluss verfassen Sie hier eine **geeignete Überschrift**, die dazu animiert, den Text zu lesen.

Blogartikel:
– Der Blogartikel ist dem Zeitungsartikel oder Webartikel sehr ähnlich. Häufig steht er in einer Reihe, sodass auf (fiktive) vorangegangene Artikel verwiesen werden kann. Denken Sie auch hier an eine passende **Überschrift**.
– Die Sprache kann etwas **persönlicher** sein und sich an ein vertrautes Publikum richten. Auch hier ist ein zu umgangssprachlicher Ton jedoch nicht zu empfehlen.

Rede:
- Eine Rede ist insofern besonders, als es sich um einen Text handelt, der für den **gesprochenen Gebrauch** gedacht ist.
- Typisch ist, dass das **Publikum direkt angesprochen** wird. Auch der Kontext (der in der Aufgabe vorgegeben ist) kann zu Beginn der Rede angesprochen werden.
- Reden enthalten in der Regel **rhetorische Mittel**, die den Text strukturieren und interessanter machen. Besonders häufig findet man Alliterationen, Wiederholungen, *rule of three*, Ironie, rhetorische Fragen, Klimax und Vergleiche. Auch die Art der Syntax (kurze Sätze, Parallelismen) unterscheidet sich oft von anderen Textformen.

Operatoren	Erläuterungen	Beispiele
assess/ evaluate	Decide on the value or the state of something and give reasons for your decision.	• With reference to the quotation, assess the impact of …
comment on	Based on arguments express your personal view on a problem/certain behaviour, attitudes or viewpoints.	• Comment on the impact of globalisation on families. • Comment on the author's thesis/view "…" (l. …).
discuss	Examine/analyse, give reasons for and against and come to a justified conclusion. Present arguments with supporting evidence and conclude with your personal view.	• Discuss whether the difficulties and chances illustrated in Text A are typical phenomena of globalization. • Discuss if the protagonist has coped with the problem in an adequate way. • Discuss the relevance/chances of …
explain	Describe in detail and give reasons for/refer to causes/effects.	• Explain the quote and discuss the advantages and disadvantages of …
interpret	Establish the meaning of something in a wider context and give your own view.	• Interpret the quotation …
justify	Show adequate grounds for decisions or conclusions.	• Justify the protagonist's behaviour in the light of …

4 Sprachmittlung

Warum wird eine Sprachmittlung geschrieben?
Sprachmittlungen (auch Mediationen genannt) haben einen sehr hohen Realitätsbezug. Früher war es in Fremdsprachen üblich, wörtliche Übersetzungen fremdsprachlicher Texte anzufertigen. Da diese spezielle Form der Mediation jedoch selten dem entspricht, was im heutigen (Arbeits-)Leben von uns verlangt wird, wird jetzt eine sinngemäße Übertragung der fremdsprachlichen Texte gefordert. Es handelt sich um eine (meist gelenkte) Zusammenfassung eines deutschen Textes in der Fremdsprache.

Wie bereitet man die Mediation vor?

Je öfter Sie das Aufgabenformat der Sprachmittlung geübt haben, desto eher gewöhnen Sie sich an den Ablauf und können die Ihnen zur Verfügung stehende Bearbeitungszeit optimal für sich nutzen.

- Sie haben durch die Aufgabenstellung einen konkreten **Schreibanlass** genannt bekommen. Markieren Sie im Arbeitsauftrag den **Kontext** und **den Adressaten/die Adressatin**. Meist wird für die Lösung die Form des **Zieltextes (E-Mail, Blogartikel** o. Ä.) vorgegeben.

- Häufig wird im Arbeitsauftrag auch, wie bei einer **gelenkten Zusammenfassung**, vorgegeben, welche Aspekte des Ausgangstexts/der Ausgangstexte Sie in Ihrer Lösung zusammenfassen müssen. Markieren Sie auch dies in der Aufgabenstellung.

- Bestimmen Sie nun die **zentrale Aussage des Textes**.

- Markieren Sie als Nächstes inhaltlich relevante Passagen im Ausgangstext/in den Ausgangstexten, die für die Bearbeitung der Aufgabe wesentlich sind. Auch unbekannte Begriffe können Sie sich markieren, wenn diese für das Textverständnis notwendig sind. Es kann hilfreich sein, die Punkte am **Rand** oder auf einem gesonderten **Schmierpapier** bereits **in der Zielsprache** festzuhalten. Überlegen Sie, welche Aspekte man zusammenfassen kann und ob und wie man die **Reihenfolge** verändern sollte, um einen möglichst schlüssigen Zieltext zu formulieren.

Tipp

Sie haben in der Prüfung ein ein- und ein zweisprachiges Wörterbuch zur Verfügung. Diese können Ihnen eine große Hilfe sein. Bedenken Sie jedoch, dass es viel Zeit in Anspruch nimmt, diese zu nutzen.

- Gibt es Konzepte, Ereignisse oder Organisationen, **die im englischsprachigen Raum nicht bekannt sind**? Markieren Sie sich diese gesondert und überlegen Sie, wie Sie sie für jemanden aus Großbritannien oder Amerika **umschreiben** können.

Operatoren	Erläuterungen	Beispiele
outline/give an account of/sum up	Give the relevant information on the topic. Use paraphrases. Do not quote from the text.	• You are part of a youth project that is trying to protect wild bees in your area. A partner project in London has asked you for tips how to protect wild bees in public areas. Outline the information the article contains on concrete activities …

Worauf muss man beim Ausformulieren der Sprachmittlung achten?

- Berücksichtigen Sie das **geforderte Textformat**, d. h., beginnen Sie eine E-Mail mit einer Anrede und schließen Sie mit einer geeigneten Floskel, ergänzen Sie bei Artikeln eine geeignete Überschrift usw.

- Formulieren Sie (je nach Kontext) einen **Basissatz**, der die Kernaussage des Textes enthält sowie Informationen zu Autorin/Autor, Titel, Quelle und ggf. situativem Rahmen des Textes gibt.
- Berücksichtigen Sie bei der Sprachwahl auch die in der Aufgabenstellung genannten Adressaten und Adressatinnen.
- Umschreiben Sie Ausdrücke, die keine Entsprechung im Englischen haben, in eigenen Worten, wenn deren Verständnis für die Aufgabenstellung notwendig ist (kulturspezifische Erläuterungen).
- Verwenden Sie **Konjunktionen**, um logische und zeitliche Bezüge herzustellen.
- Bedenken Sie, dass Ihre *mediation* nur etwa **ein Drittel des Ausgangstextes** umfassen sollte. Fokussieren Sie sich daher auf das Wesentliche, fassen Sie wo möglich zusammengehörige Aspekte in der Lösung zusammen.

Tipp

Nutzen Sie die Web-App „**MindCards**" zum Lernen und Wiederholen **hilfreicher Wendungen** für verschiedene Aufgabenstellungen in der schriftlichen Prüfung. Diese interaktiven Karteikarten können Sie bequem am Smartphone nutzen.

Hinweise zur Bewertung

Die Korrektur der Abituraufgaben erfolgt durch die Lehrkraft, von der Sie unterrichtet wurden, sowie durch einen Zweitkorrektor oder eine Zweitkorrektorin. Der erteilte Unterricht kann somit bei der Bewertung der Abituraufgaben berücksichtigt werden. Darüber hinaus existieren zentrale Bewertungsvorgaben.

Bei allen Aufgabenarten wird zwischen **inhaltlicher** und **sprachlicher Leistung** unterschieden. Bei der Festlegung der Gesamtnote kommt der sprachlichen Leistung im Vergleich zur inhaltlichen die größere Bedeutung zu. Sie werden im Verhältnis 60:40 gewertet.

Genauere Informationen zu Kriterien bei der Begutachtung finden Sie unter https://berlin.klausurgutachten.de/ bzw. https://brandenburg.klausurgutachten.de/

Beide Prüfungsteile werden zunächst separat nach deren inhaltlichen und sprachlichen Leistung bewertet. In die **Gesamtbewertung** fließen **Teil 1** (Leseverstehen und Schreiben) mit stärkerer Gewichtung als **Teil 2** (Sprachmittlung) ein.

Die Arbeit mit dem Buch

Es gibt verschiedene Möglichkeiten, wie Sie mit dem vorliegenden Buch arbeiten können. Entscheidend ist, dass es Ihnen nützt, z. B. indem Sie Ihre **sprachlichen Leistungen verbessern**, die **Prüfungssituation** trainieren, ein Gefühl für die **Zeiteinteilung** in der Prüfung bekommen und damit Ihre Kompetenz und Ihr **Selbstvertrauen** stärken.

Variante 1: Einzelne Aufgaben auswählen und lösen

Wissen Sie bereits, welche Aufgabenformen Ihnen besonders schwerfallen? Gibt es Themengebiete, in die Sie sich noch einarbeiten möchten? Sind es bestimmte Zieltextformate oder Operatoren, die Sie vor der Prüfung noch einmal üben möchten? Dann gehen Sie die Prüfungen im Band durch und wählen Sie entsprechende Aufgaben zur Bearbeitung aus. Schauen Sie sich diese zunächst selbstständig an und versuchen Sie sie zu lösen. Die Hinweise aus dem vorangegangenen Kapitel können Ihnen hier bei der Bearbeitung helfen. Berücksichtigen Sie auch gleich, wie viel Zeit Ihnen in der Prüfung für die jeweilige Aufgabe zur Verfügung stehen wird, und bedenken Sie, dass Sie Zeit zum Einlesen und zum Korrigieren Ihrer eigenen Lösung einplanen müssen.

Tipp	
	Eine grobe Zeiteinteilung könnte wie folgt aussehen:

Eine grobe Zeiteinteilung könnte wie folgt aussehen:
- – Auswahlzeit: ca. 15 Minuten (LK und GK)
- – Zusammenfassung und Textanalyse (Aufgabe 1 und 2): ca. 120 Minuten (LK) bzw. 100 Minuten (GK)
- – Argumentation (Aufgabe 3): ca. 60 Minuten (LK) bzw. 50 Minuten (GK)
- – Mediation/Sprachmittlung: ca. 60 Minuten (LK und GK)
- – Korrekturzeit: ca. 30 Minuten

Falls Sie sich noch unsicher fühlen, können Sie, bevor Sie Ihre Lösung ausarbeiten, bereits einen kurzen Blick auf die Hinweise hinter den Rauten im Lösungskapitel werfen. Hier finden Sie wichtige Stichpunkte für die Lösung zusammengefasst (ab dem Prüfungsjahrgang 2022). Diese Stichpunkte können Ihnen auch bei der Beurteilung Ihrer eigenen Lösung helfen: Haben Sie alle wichtigen Informationen erfasst? Gibt es Aspekte, auf die Sie beim nächsten Mal genauer achten sollten?

Im Anschluss können Sie sich die Beispiellösung ansehen. Wie wird hier die Lösung strukturiert? Gibt es besonders geeignete Formulierungen, die Sie sich markieren und für die Abiturprüfung lernen können? Gibt es Aspekte im Bereich der Textanalyse, die für Ihre Prüfung relevant sein könnten, zum Beispiel Wirkungsweisen bestimmter Stilmittel und Textelemente? Gibt es im Bereich der Argumentation besonders gelungene Argumente, die man aufgreifen könnte, falls in der Prüfung ein ähnliches Thema auftaucht?

Variante 2: Ganze Prüfungsaufgaben am Stück lösen

Besonders hilfreich ist es, vor der Prüfung eine Art Probeklausur zu schreiben. Nehmen Sie sich genau so viel Zeit für die Aufgaben, wie Ihnen auch im Abitur selbst zur Verfügung steht. Legen Sie alle Hilfsmittel bereit, wählen Sie eine Aufgabe aus und bearbeiten Sie sie, genau wie in der Abiturprüfung. Diese Art der Vorbereitung ist gut geeignet, um das eigene Zeitmanagement zu überprüfen. Anschließend können Sie Ihre eigenen Lösungen wie in Variante 1 mit den Lösungen aus diesem Buch überprüfen.

Variante 3: Mit den digitalen Inhalten arbeiten

Nutzen Sie die Möglichkeit, multimedial zu arbeiten. Auf der Umschlaginnenseite finden Sie den Zugangscode zum digitalen Bereich dieses Buches. In den Videos erhalten Sie wertvolle Tipps zum Bearbeiten der Schreibaufgabe. Mithilfe der Webapp „MindCards" können Sie wichtige englische Ausdrücke für die Prüfung auswendig lernen. Schauen Sie auch in das interaktive Training, um Ihre Sprachkenntnisse weiter zu vertiefen.

Variante 4: Das vorliegende Buch als „Lesebuch"

Wenn der Kopf mal etwas träge ist und das Lernen nicht gut klappen will, können Sie das Buch auch einfach als Lesebuch nutzen. Das Lesen in der Fremdsprache verbessert Ihre Sprachkenntnisse und auch inhaltlich können Sie viel mitnehmen. Haben Sie die allgemeinen Hinweise und Tipps zur Prüfung schon gelesen? Wenn nicht, dann nutzen Sie doch jetzt die Gelegenheit und holen das nach.

Die wichtigsten (Stil-)Mittel zur Textanalyse

1. **Alliteration**

   Definition: An alliteration is a figure of speech in which words start with the same consonant sound.

   Examples: Literary characters such as Tiny Tim (Dickens), Donald Duck (Disney), Peter Parker (Spiderman), brand names like Coca-Cola, Best Buy or tongue twisters like "Betty Botter bought some butter."

   "So we beat on, boats against the current, borne back ceaselessly into the past."
   F. Scott Fitzgerald: *The Great Gatsby* (1925)

   Here the repetition of the "b" sound helps to create a sense of rhythm that evokes the beating of waves against a boat.

   Function: Alliterations and assonance help to emphasize a point, attract attention and make an expression (or scene) more memorable.

2. **Allusion**

   Definition: Allusion is a reference to a character, historical or political event or a piece of art or literature the reader is likely to know or be familiar with.

   Example: "Her color is a cross she will always carry. But it's not my fault. It's not my fault. It's not my fault. It's not."
   Toni Morrison: *God Help the Child* (2015)

   Function: The cross Lula Ann, the protagonist of the story, has to carry is an allusion to the Bible. Jesus had to carry the cross when he died and took on the sins of mankind. In this scene Lula Ann's mother, a light-skinned Black woman, describes the shock, when her daughter was born. Lula Ann is born with a very dark skin colour. The baby is innocent (Jesus), but her mother feels appalled by her darkness. She reflects that her own feelings are a result of the way Black people have to suffer in society (sins of mankind).

   Function: Allusions create associations (see **connotation**) in the reader's mind and thereby either have an emotional impact or stimulate the reader's intellect.

3. **Anaphora**

   Definition: Anaphora is the **repetition** of an expression at the beginning of successive clauses.

   Example: "I still have a dream. […] I have a dream that one day this nation will rise up and live out the true meaning of its creed: 'We hold these truths to be self-evident; that all men are created equal.' I have a dream that one day on the red hills of Georgia the sons of former slaves and the sons of former slave owners will be able to sit down together at the table of brotherhood."
   Martin Luther King: "I have a dream"-speech (1963)

Function: Anaphora is used to give prominence to ideas by adding rhythm and thereby making the text more pleasurable to read/listen to and easier to remember. This way it appeals to the emotions of the audience in order to persuade, inspire, motivate and encourage.

4. **Antithesis (contrast, opposite)**

   Definition: Antithesis (which literally means "opposite") is a rhetorical device in which two opposite ideas (a thesis and an opposing antithesis) are put together.

   Example: "It was the <u>best</u> of times, it was the <u>worst</u> of times, it was the age of <u>wisdom</u>, it was the age of <u>foolishness</u>, it was the epoch of <u>belief</u>, it was the epoch of <u>incredulity</u>, it was the season of <u>Light</u>, it was the season of <u>Darkness</u>, it was the spring of <u>hope</u>, it was the winter of <u>despair</u>, we had <u>everything</u> before us, we had <u>nothing</u> before us, we were all going direct to <u>Heaven</u>, we were all going direct <u>the other way</u> […]."
   Charles Dickens: *A Tale of Two Cities* (1859)

   Function: Antithesis is used to create emphasis by exposing the reader to often stark and unexpected contrast. Thus, it conveys opinions and emotions more vividly and emphatically.

5. **Characterisation** (direct/indirect)

   Definition: Characterisation refers to the presentation of characters (literary figures) in a text. There are two different ways of characterisation:

   a) Direct (or explicit) characterisation: A character can be characterised directly (explicitly) which means the audience is given direct information about the character:

   Example: "Oh! But he was a tight-fisted hand at the grindstone, Scrooge! a squeezing, wrenching, grasping, scraping, clutching, covetous, old sinner! Hard and sharp as flint, from which no steel had ever struck out generous fire; secret, and self-contained, and solitary as an oyster."
   Charles Dickens: *A Christmas Carol* (1843)

   Function: Direct characterisation provides straightforward information about a character. There is no need to "read between the lines" and draw one's own conclusion.

   b) Indirect characterisation: Here the audience has to find out about the character's qualities by observing his or her actions, behaviour, thoughts, language, appearance, and his/her way of relating and responding to other characters or problems.

   Function: Characterisation aims at informing the audience helping them to make sense of the events taking place. Indirect characterisation is the more subtle way of allowing and encouraging the reader to draw his or her own conclusions which makes the reading (or viewing) process more demanding and challenging but also more rewarding and pleasurable.

6. **Connotation**

Definition: Connotations (or standardized associations) are ideas or emotions associated with an expression.

Example: The term "Route 66" is often associated with ideas of freedom and adventure. The term "shark" is frequently connected with images of danger and death. The expression "life sciences" might connote (negative) concepts of genetic modification and/or the successful fight against diseases.

Function: Many expressions, but especially figurative language, generate various connotations (associations) in the readers' mind, addressing their feelings as well as their understanding.

7. **Ellipsis**

Definition: Ellipsis is the omission of one or more words which are necessary to make a complete sentence but which can be supplied by the reader.

Elliptical sentences are typical of oral communication.

Example: "Got it?", "Seen it?"

Function: Ellipsis can be used as a literary device to indicate casual speech. Thus, in a speech, ellipsis could create a sense of community or familiarity between the speaker and his or her audience or help to highlight important keywords.

8. **Euphemism**

Definition: A euphemistic expression describes a rather harsh or unpleasant fact in gentler and friendlier terms and is often used to sound more indirect and polite.

Examples: "Our cat was very ill. We had her put to sleep."

"'For the time being,' he explains, 'it had been found necessary to make a readjustment of rations.'"

George Orwell: *Animal Farm* (1945)

Here, the word "readjustment" replaces the word "reduction", but the impression given is that there is only a change taking place, with "readjustment" being a rather positively connoted expression.

Function: Euphemism helps to convey ideas which are not supposed to be mentioned directly. Euphemisms can also have an ironic (even sarcastic) effect depending on the context.

9. **Figurative/metaphorical language**

Definition: "Figurative" or "metaphorical language" are general terms to describe language that differs from everyday "literal language" in order to intensify comparison, emphasis, clarity, or originality of expression. Metaphor and simile are the two most frequently used, but figurative language also includes hyperbole and puns.

Examples: See metaphor, simile, hyperbole, pun

Function: In general, figurative language appeals to our senses as well as to our intellectual curiosity as the reader has to "decipher" its meaning and message within the given context.

10. **Hyperbole** (exaggeration/over-statement)

Definition: Hyperbole is a form of figurative/metaphorical language and involves an unreal exaggeration of ideas.

Examples: "I will die of shame."

Function: Hyperbole can be used to either achieve a humorous effect or in order to emphasize the importance or intensity of an experience.

11. **Imagery** (figurative/metaphorical language)

Definition: Imagery involves the usage of figurative/metaphorical language such as similes and metaphors, expressions which must be "translated" by the reader to make sense.

Examples: see metaphor, simile

Function: The use of imagery aims at making expressions more colourful than everyday speech and thus raises greater awareness in the reader.

12. **Irony** (and Sarcasm)

Definition: The expressed meaning is the opposite of what the author wants to say.

Example: "Wonderful. I have just dropped my favourite cup."

Function: The contrast between what is said and what is meant, the literal and the intended meaning, emphasizes the point made by the speaker. The use of irony can also detect a certain detachment of the speaker from his or her subject.

Example: "It is a truth universally acknowledged, that a single man in possession of a good fortune, must be in want of a wife."
Jane Austen: *Pride and prejudice* (1813)

Function: The beginning of Jane Austen's novel *Pride and Prejudice* is meant to be seen as ironic or sarcastic. While society at the time expects a wealthy man who is single to be looking for a wife, this must not necessarily be the case. Sarcasm has the additional function of criticizing a person or a concept, in this case the concept of marriage.

Dramatic irony: describes the contrast between what the protagonist and the audience knows, e.g. in the first act of Shakespeare's *Romeo and Juliet* (1597):

"Go ask his name: if he be married.
My grave is like to be my wedding bed."

In this simile, Julia says that if Romeo were already married, her wedding bed would turn out to be her grave. Here, the dramatic irony unfolds because the audience already knows (from the prologue) that at the end of the play she will die.

Function: Dramatic irony reflects the limited understanding of man (e. g. the limitations and shortcomings of Shakespeare's tragic heroes). By putting the readers in a superior position, dramatic irony evokes their curiosity, their hopes, and their fears concerning the characters' fate and therefore applies to their emotions.

13. Metaphor

Definition: A metaphor, a form of figurative/metaphorical language, is a comparison where something is represented by an expression that normally occurs in a very different context. Unlike similes metaphors **do not** contain direct terms such as "like" or "as".

Example:
"All the world's a stage,
And all the men and women merely players:
They have their exits and their entrances;
And one man in his time plays many parts,"
William Shakespeare: *As You Like It* (1600)

Here, the theatre ("stage"/"players") serves as a metaphor for human life.

Function: Metaphors appeal directly to the senses of listeners or readers. They make the language colourful and challenge our imaginations, thereby providing new and original ways of looking at the world from a different perspective.

14. Onomatopoeia

Definition: Onomatopoeic expressions imitate the sounds of things, animals or people.

Examples: The words "whisper", "roar" or "splash" imitate the actual sounds they stand for, e. g. the sound when something hits the water.

"He saw nothing and heard nothing but he could feel his heart pounding and then he heard the clack on stone and the leaping, dropping clicks of a small rock falling."
Ernest Hemingway: *For Whom the Bell Tolls* (1940)

Function: Onomatopoeic expressions have an emotional effect on the reader as they appeal directly to his or her senses.

15. Personification

Definition: Personification refers to the technique of presenting animals or objects as if they possessed human qualities.

Example:

"Because I could not stop for Death –
He kindly stopped for me –"
Emily Dickinson: "Because I could not stop for Death" (published in 1890 after her death)

Function: In this poem death is personified as a kind gentleman. He accompanies the speaker on her path to (Christian) immortality, making a normally frightening experience (death) peaceful and calm.

A genre that uses personification as a guiding principle is the **fable**, where animals take on human qualities.

Function: The use of personification helps to relate animals or things closer to human life and behaviour, appealing to our experiences and emotions.

16. **Paradox** (contradiction)

Definition: A paradox is a statement that embodies two opposing statements or ideas and therefore appears to be contradictory in itself.

Examples:
"I can resist anything except temptation."
Oscar Wilde: *Lady Windermere's Fan: A Play About a Good Woman* (1892)

"All animals are equal, but some are more equal than others".
George Orwell: *Animal Farm* (1945)

Function: The usage of paradox causes the reader to reflect on the message which is often witty, ironic, playful and therefore achieves a humorous effect which in turn makes the text more enjoyable.

17. **Parallelism**

Definition: The same sentence structure is used in two or more sentences. Often it is found in combination with repetition and short sentences.

Example:
"The Jews cry for the Jews. The Russians cry for the Russians. We cry for Africa, because we are Africans"
Zadie Smith: "The Embassy of Cambodia" (2013)

Function: As it attracts the attention of the audience parallelism can be used to stress the importance of something that is said. It is also often used to compare different things, situations or ideas. Anaphora and antithesis (see above) are special forms of parallelism.

18. **Pun** (play on words)

Definition: Puns or plays on words use language in order to create two or more meanings, or they use an expression in a different, unfamiliar context.

Examples:
"Ask for me tomorrow and you shall find me a grave man."
William Shakespeare: *Romeo and Juliet* (1597)

Here, "grave" can mean "serious and solemn", or it can be taken literally, as meaning "dead in one's grave". As Mercutio has just been fatally stabbed, this pun implies a rather sarcastic undertone, but fits Mercutio's witty character well.

Function: Puns (or plays on words) make deliberate use of ambiguity, revealing the cleverness and creativity of both the writers and their characters. Puns cause the reader to think about what is being said, thus demanding more concentration but also providing more intellectual and aesthetical pleasure. As many puns create a humorous effect, plays on words are also used for comic relief, for example in Shakespeare's tragedies.

19. **Rhetorical question**

Definition: A rhetorical question is a question that is raised by the author but does not require an answer as the answer is either obvious, or the question cannot/is not supposed to be answered at all.

Examples:
"How many deaths will it take till he knows
that too many people have died?"
Bob Dylan: "Blowing in the Wind" (1962)

Function: Rhetorical questions are often used as means of persuasion as the answer often corresponds with the argumentation of the speaker implying that the listener understands the intended message and agrees with it.

20. **Simile** (Comparison)

Definition: A simile is a comparison between objects, persons and ideas using "like", "as" or "as if".

Example:
"I am only thirty.
And like the cat I have nine times to die.
This is Number Three."
Sylvia Plath: "Lady Lazarus" (1962)

The author refers to the famous proverb that cats have nine lives. The speaker of the poem "Lady Lazarus" is currently dead, but, like Lazarus in the Bible, she has been brought back to life (allusion; see above) and she will be brought back to life again as she still has six lives left "like the cat". Sylvia Plath processes her depressive episodes in the poem.

Function: Like metaphors, similes appeal to our senses and imagination and therefore make a speaker's speech more colourful and memorable.

21. **Tone**

Definition: The tone reflects how the writer uses language to create a certain mood, revealing the emotional attitude towards the topic, the characters and the reader. The tone may for instance be formal, informal, ironic, sarcastic, playful, humorous, angry, emotional or neutral.

Function: The tone helps to convey the atmosphere, the mood and the intention of a text. Furthermore, it can be used for implicit characterisation.

Lernvideos zur Textaufgabe
Step-by-Step – Textaufgaben bearbeiten

Es gibt Aufgabenstellungen, die in Englischprüfungen immer wieder auftauchen. Grundlage für diese Aufgabenstellungen sind sogenannte **Operatoren** wie „describe", „analyse", „comment on" und viele mehr. Auch wenn sich die Aufgabenstellung für die Textarbeit im Detail je nach Text unterscheidet, bleibt die grundsätzliche Vorgehensweise bei den jeweiligen Operatoren gleich.

In den Videos auf der Plattform **MySTARK** (Zugangscode vgl. Umschlaginnenseite) erklären wir Ihnen, wie Sie bei den wichtigsten Operatoren in Textaufgaben vorgehen müssen. Außerdem erfahren Sie etwas zu häufigen **Zieltextformaten** wie Leserbriefen, Blogeinträgen und Reden.

TIPP

Lesen Sie die Aufgaben und die dazugehörigen Texte, **bevor Sie sich die Videos ansehen**! Sie können auch schon überlegen, wie Sie selbst bei der Aufgabenstellung vorgehen würden und welche inhaltlichen Aspekte für die Lösung interessant wären – und im Anschluss Ihre Lösung/Vorgehensweise mit den Videos vergleichen. Viel Spaß!

Ausgangstext: *newspaper article*
Operatoren: *outline, analyse, write*
Themen: *social media, the impact of the media on society*
Zieltextformate: *letter to the editor, blog entry, speech*

Aufgabenstellung

1. **Outline** the author's view on social media. *(Video 1)*

2. **Analyse** the means he uses to convey his attitude and the effect they have on the reader. *(Video 2)*

3. **Write** a **letter to the editor/blog entry/speech** expressing your own opinion on the chances and dangers of social media. *(Video 3)*

Text: "I used to think social media was a force for good. Now the evidence says I was wrong" by Matt Haig

More and more, it's clear these platforms create divisions, exploit our insecurities and risk our health. They're as bad as the tobacco industry.

1   I used to think social media was essentially a force for good, whether it was to initiate the Arab spring of 2011, or simply as a useful tool for bringing together like-minded people to share videos of ninja cats. Having spent a lot of time thinking about mental health, I even saw social media's much-maligned potential for anonymity as a good
5   thing, helping people to open up about problems when they might not feel able to do so in that physical space we still quaintly call real life. [...]
    Yes, I would occasionally feel that maybe staring at my Twitter feed near-continuously for seven hours wasn't that healthy [...]. Yes, I'd see articles warning of the dangers of excessive internet use, but I dismissed these as traditional, reactionary takes.
10 I saw social media naysayers as the first reviewers of Technicolor movies, who felt the colour distracted from the story, or were like the people who walked out on Bob Dylan at Newport folk festival for playing an electric guitar, or like those who warned that radio or TV or video games or miniskirts, or hip-hop or selfies or fidget spinners or whatever, would lead to the end of civilisation. [...]
15 Then I started the research for a book I am writing on how the external world affects our mental health. I wanted to acknowledge the downsides of social media, but to argue that far from being a force for ill, it offers a safe place where the insanities of life elsewhere can be processed and articulated.
    But the deeper into the research I went, the harder it was to sustain this argument.
20 Even the internet activist and former Google employee Wael Ghonim – one of the initiators of the Arab spring and one-time poster boy for internet-inspired revolution – who once saw social media as a social cure – now saw it as a negative force. [...]: "The same tool that united us to topple dictators eventually tore us apart." Ghonim saw social

V 2

media polarising people into angry opposing camps – army supporters and Islamists –
25 leaving centrists such as himself stuck in the middle, powerless.

And this isn't just politics. It's health too. A survey conducted by the Royal Society of Public Health asked 1,500 young people to keep track of their moods while on the five most popular social media sites. Instagram and Snapchat came out worst, often inspiring feelings of inadequacy, anxiety and self-loathing. […]

30 Kurt Vonnegut said: "We are what we pretend to be, so we must be careful who we pretend to be." This seems especially true now we have reached a new stage of marketing where we are not just consumers, but also the thing consumed. If you have friends you only ever talk to on Facebook, your entire relationship with them is framed by commerce. When we willingly choose to become unpaid content providers, we com-
35 mercialise ourselves. And we are encouraged to be obsessed with numbers (of followers, messages, comments, retweets, favourites), as if operating in a kind of friend economy, an emotional stock market where the stock is ourselves and where we are encouraged to weigh our worth against others.

Of course, humans comparing themselves to others isn't new. But when the others
40 are every human on the internet, people end up comparing themselves – their looks, their relationships, their wealth, their lives – to the carefully filtered lives of people they would never meet in the real world – and feeling inadequate.

Reading first-hand accounts by people with bulimia and anorexia who are convinced that social media exacerbated or even triggered their illnesses, I began to realise
45 something: this situation is not the equivalent of Bob Dylan's electric guitar. It is closer to the tobacco or fast-food industries, where vested interests deny the existence of blatant problems that were not there before. […]

We are traditionally far better at realising risks to physical health than to mental health, even when they are interrelated. If we can accept that our physical health can
50 be shaped by society – by secondhand smoke or a bad diet – then we must accept that our mental health can be too. And as our social spaces increasingly become digital spaces, we need to look seriously and urgently at how these new, business-owned societies are affecting our minds. We must try to see how the rising mental health crisis may be related to the way people are living and interacting.

55 Facebook's Mark Zuckerberg says that "by giving people the power to share, we're making the world more transparent". But what we really need to do is make social media transparent.

Of course, we won't stop using it – I certainly won't – but precisely for that reason we need to know more about what it is doing to us. To our politics, to our health, to
60 the future generation, and to the world around us. We need to ensure we are still the ones using the technology – and that the technology isn't using us. *(842 words)*

From: Matt Haig: "I used to think social media was a force for good. Now the evidence says I was wrong", https://www.theguardian.com/commentisfree/2017/sep/06/social-media-good-evidence-platforms-insecurities-health, 06.09.2017, Copyright Guardian News & Media Ltd 2020

Annotations
l. 2 *Arab spring*: series of protests and rebellions against authoritarian regimes, e. g. in Tunisia, Egypt and Libya fidget spinner: a popular toy
l. 30 *Kurt Vonnegut:* famous American writer (1922 – 2007)

V 3

Ausgangstext: *extract from a novel*
Operatoren: *describe, characterise, discuss*
Themen: *ethnic minorities in the US, police violence*

Aufgabenstellung

1. **Describe** the night of the shooting as it is presented in the interview and as Starr remembers it. *(Video 1)*

2. **Characterise** the police officer as he is presented in this extract. Take the narrative perspective into account. *(Video 2)*

3. "'His life always matters more!' […] 'That's the problem!'"
   Discuss the statement referring to the general situation of African Americans in the US. *(Video 3)*

Text:
The Hate U Give by Angie Thomas (extract from the novel)

Starr, who lives in the fictional, Black* neighborhood of Garden Heights, is the only witness of a police shooting in which her childhood friend Khalil got killed. She goes to a school in a different district, which is mainly attended by White kids. For fear of being singled out she does not talk to her school-friends about her life in Garden Heights, not even about the shooting.

1   "Back up, back up," I tell Maya. She flicks through the channels, and when he appears again, I say, "Right there!"
     I've pictured his face so much. Actually seeing it again is different. My memory is pretty spot-on – a thin, jagged scar above his lip, bursts of freckles that cover his face
5   and neck.
     My stomach churns and my skin crawls, and I wanna get away from One-Fifteen. My instinct doesn't care that it's a photograph being shown on TV. A silver cross pendant hangs from his neck, like he's saying Jesus endorses what he did. We must believe in a different Jesus.
10   What looks like an older version of him appears on the screen […].
     "My son was afraid for his life," he says. "He only wanted to get home to his wife and kids."
     Pictures flash on the screen. One-Fifteen smiles with his arms draped around a blurred-out woman. He's on a fishing trip with two small, blurred-out children. They show
15   him with a smiley golden retriever, with his pastor and some fellow deacons who are all blurred out, and then in his police uniform.
     "Officer Brian Cruise Jr. has been on the force for sixteen years," the voice-over says, and more pics of him as a cop are shown. He's been a cop for as long as Khalil

was alive, and I wonder if in some sick twist of fate Khalil was only born for this man
20 to kill.

"A majority of those years have been spent serving in Garden Heights," the voice-over continues, "a neighborhood notorious for gang and drug dealers."

I tense as footage of my neighborhood, my home, is shown. It's like they picked the worst parts – the drug addicts roaming the streets, the broken-down Cedar Grove pro-
25 jects, gangbangers flashing signs, bodies on the sidewalks with white sheets over them. What about Mrs. Rooks and her cakes? Or Mr. Lewis and his haircuts? Mr. Reuben? The clinic? My family?

Me?

I feel Hailey's and Maya's eyes on me. I can't look at them.
30 "My son loved working in the neighborhood," One-Fifteen's father claims. "He always wanted to make a difference in the lives there."

Funny. Slave masters thought they were making a difference in black people's lives too. Saving them from their "wild African ways." Same shit, different century. I wish people like them would stop thinking that people like me need saving.
35 One-Fifteen Sr. talks about his son's life before the shooting. How he was a good kid who never got into trouble, always wanted to help others. […]

The interviewer asks about that night.

"Apparently, Brian pulled the kid over 'cause he had a broken taillight and was speeding."
40 Khalil wasn't speeding.

"He told me, 'Pop, soon as I pulled him over, I had a bad feeling,'" says One-Fifteen Sr.

"Why is that?" the interviewer asks.

"He said the kid and his friend immediately started cursing him out –"
45 We never cursed.

"And they kept glancing at each other, like they were up to something. Brian says that's when he got scared, 'cause they could've taken him down if they teamed up."

I couldn't have taken anyone down. I was too afraid. He makes us sound like we're superhumans. We're kids.
50 "No matter how afraid he is, my son's still gonna do his job," he says. "And that's all he set out to do that night."

"There have been reports that Khalil Harris was unarmed when the incident took place," the interviewer says. "Has your son told you why he made the decision to shoot?"
55 "Brian says he had his back to the kid, and he heard the kid say, 'I'm gon' show your ass today.'"

No, no, no. Khalil asked if I was okay.

"Brian turned around and saw something in the car door. He thought it was a gun –"
It was a hairbrush. […]
60 "Brian's a good boy," he says, in tears. "He only wanted to get home to his family, and people are making him out to be a monster."

That's all Khalil and I wanted, and you're making us out to be monsters. […]

"How has your son's life changed since this happened?" the interviewer asks.

"All our lives have been hell, honestly," his father claims. "Brian's a people person,
65 but now he's afraid to go out in public, even for something simple as getting a gallon
of milk. There have been threats on his life, our family's lives. His wife had to quit her
job. He's even been attacked by fellow officers." […]

"This is awful," Hailey says. "That poor family."

She's looking at One-Fifteen Sr. with sympathy that belongs to Brenda and Ms.
70 Rosalie.

I blink several times. "What?"

"His son lost everything because he was trying to do his job and protect himself.
His life matters too, you know?"

I cannot right now. I can't. I stand up or otherwise I will say or do something really
75 stupid. Like punch her.

"I need to … yeah." I say all that I can and start for the door, but Maya grabs the
tail of my cardigan. […]

"Maya," I say, as calmly as possible. "Please let me go. I cannot talk to her. Did
you not hear what she said?"

80 "Are you serious right now?" Hailey asks. "What's wrong with saying his life matters too?"

"His life always matters more!" My voice is gruff, and my throat is tight. "That's
the problem!"

(969 words)

Thomas, Angie: The Hate U Give. *London: Walker Books Ltd, 2017. pp. 243–247.*

Annotations
l. 6   *One-Fifteen:* One-Fifteen is the badge number of the police officer who shot Khalil
ll. 69/70 *Brenda and Ms. Rosalie:* Khalil's mother and grandmother

Prüfungsteil 1: Leseverstehen und Schreiben   (75 %)

Aufgabenstellung 1 – Tasks

Themenschwerpunkte: *Aims and ambitions, The impact of the media on society*

1   Describe the situation the characters find themselves in.   (25 %)

2   Write a characterisation of Mae, also taking into account the
    effect the narrative perspective has on the reader's perception
    of her character.   (40 %)

3   Choose **one** of the following tasks.   (35 %)

3.1 Discuss whether modern communication via smartphones and the like is
    a blessing or a curse.

OR

3.2 Mercer has left the house without an explanation, so he feels obliged to
    explain his behaviour to Mae. Write his personal letter to her in which he
    offers this explanation and tells Mae what he thinks about her initiative to
    post the photo.

Text (excerpt from the novel)

The Circle
by Dave Eggers

Note: *Mae Holland works for a very powerful Internet company and rarely sees her parents. One day, however, she visits her parents at their home and there she also meets Mercer, her former boyfriend. Mercer has given her parents a self-made chandelier. Mae likes it very much and, without informing anyone, posts a photo of the chandelier and links to Mercer's website in different Internet forums. While she is doing so upstairs, the others are waiting for her downstairs so they can have dinner together.*

1   When she was finished, Mercer was sitting with her parents at the kitchen table, which
    was crowded with salad and stir-fried chicken and vegetables. Their eyes followed her
    down the stairs. "I called up there," her father said.
       "We like to eat when it's hot," her mother added.
5   Mae hadn't heard them. "Sorry. I was just – Wow, this looks good. Dad, don't you
    think Mercer's chandelier* is awesome?"

1

"I do. And I told you, and him, as much. We've been asking for one of his creations for a year now."

"I just needed the right antlers," Mercer said. "I hadn't gotten any really great ones
10 in a while." He went on to explain his sourcing, how he bought antlers only from trusted collaborators, people he knew hadn't hunted the deer, or if they had, had been in-
structed to do so by Fish and Game to curb overcrowding.

"That is fascinating," her mother said. "Before I forget, I want to raise a toast …
What's that?"

15 Mae's phone had beeped. "Nothing," she said. "But in a second I think I'll have
some good news to announce. Go on, Mom."

"I was just saying that I wanted to toast having us –"

Now it was Mercer's phone ringing.

"Sorry," he said, and maneuvered his hand outside his pants, finding the off button.
20 "Everyone done?" her mother asked.

"Sorry Mrs. Holland," Mercer said. "Go on."

But at that moment, Mae's phone buzzed loudly again, and when Mae looked to
its screen, she saw that there were thirty-seven new zings and messages.

"Something you have to attend to?" her father said.

25 "No, not yet," Mae said, though she was almost too excited to wait. She was proud
of Mercer, and soon she'd be able to show him something about the audience he might
have outside Longfield. If there were thirty-seven messages in the first few minutes,
in twenty minutes there would be a hundred.

Her mother continued. "I was going to thank you, Mae, for all you've done to im-
30 prove your father's health, and my own sanity. And I wanted to toast Mercer, too, as
part of our family, and to thank him for his beautiful work." She paused, as if expecting
a buzz to sound any moment. "Well, I'm just glad I got through that. Let's eat. The
food's getting cold."

And they began to eat, but after a few minutes, Mae had heard so many dings, and
35 she'd seen her phone screen update so many times, that she couldn't wait.

"Okay, I can't stand it anymore. I posted that photo I took of your chandelier,
Mercer, and people love it!" She beamed, and raised her glass. "That's what we should
toast."

Mercer didn't look amused. "Wait. You posted them where?"
40 "That's great, Mercer," her father said, and raised his own glass.

Mercer's glass was not raised. "Where'd you post them, Mae?"

"Everywhere relevant," she said, "and the comments are amazing." She searched
her screen. "Just let me read the first one. And I quote: Wow, that is gorgeous. That's
from a pretty well-known industrial designer in Stockholm. Here's another one: Very
45 cool. Reminds me of something I saw in Barcelona last year. That was from a designer
in Santa Fe who has her own shop. She gave your thing three out of four stars, and had
some suggestions about how you might improve it. I bet you could sell them there if
you wanted to. So here's another –"

Mercer had his palms on the table. "Stop. Please."

2

"Why? You haven't even heard the best part. On DesignMind, you already have 122 smiles. That's an incredible amount to get so quickly. And they have a ranking there, and you're in the top fifty for today. Actually, I know how you could raise that –" […]

"Mae. Stop. Please stop." Mercer was staring at her, his eyes small and round. "I don't want to get loud here, in your parents' home, but either you stop or I have to walk out."

"Just hold on a sec," she said, and scrolled through her messages, looking for one that she was sure would impress him. She'd seen a message come in from Dubai, and if she found it, she knew, his resistance would fall away.

"Mae," she heard her mother say. "Mae."

But Mae couldn't locate the message. Where was it? While she scrolled, she heard the scraping of a chair. But she was so close to finding it that she didn't look up. When she did, she found Mercer gone and her parents staring at her. *(763 words)*

Excerpt(s) from The Circle *by Dave Eggers, copyright © 2013 by Dave Eggers. Used by permission of Alfred A. Knopf, an imprint of the Knopf Doubleday Publishing Group, a division of Penguin Random House LLC. All rights reserved.*

* Mercer's chandelier is made of antlers (= horn of a male deer). As he is very careful to buy antlers only from trusted suppliers, he only produces very few of them.

Annotation
l. 6   chandelier: round frame for holding candles or lights that hangs from the ceiling and is decorated with small pieces of glass

Aufgabenstellung 2 – Tasks

Themenschwerpunkte: *Aims and ambitions, The impact of the media on society*

You are taking part in an international youth project on "The Impact of Digitisation and AI".

Using the information from the text, write an article for the English project website in which you present the drawbacks of digital language assistants such as Alexa.

Text (Auszug aus dem Artikel)

Experten warnen vor Sprachassistenten: Diese Risiken birgt Alexa für Kinder

Minderjährige geben Alexa, Siri und ähnlichen Sprachassistenten zu viel von sich preis, zeigt ein Gutachten. Auch Datenschützer äußern Kritik.

1 Ein Junge, sechs Jahre alt, wünscht sich ein Kinderlied, ruft „play Digger, Digger" ins Mikrofon. Und was tut Amazons Sprachassistentin „Alexa"? Sie schlägt ihm verschiedene Porno-Titel vor. Diese Geschichte ist nicht die einzige Panne vergangener Jahre, die Eltern schockiert. Zu sehen auf Youtube. Jetzt warnt sogar der Wissenschaftliche
5 Dienst des Bundestags.

In einem Gutachten wird bemängelt, dass Kinder und Jugendliche persönliche Informationen von sich preisgeben oder eben Inhalte abrufen können, die sie nicht hören sollten. Außerdem stelle sich die Frage, was eigentlich mit Besuchern sei, die nicht wüssten, dass die Software gerade ihre Sätze aufzeichnet. Amazon dürfte der Pflicht
10 zur Informationsvermittlung bei der Datenerhebung von Nutzern zwar ausreichend nachkommen, heißt es – „offen bleibt jedoch, wie unbeteiligte Dritte und Minderjährige von der Datensammlung ausgeschlossen werden können".

Mit Blick auf die USA sei außerdem unklar, „zu welchen weiteren Zwecken Amazon seine Daten zukünftig nutzen könnte". Dass sich Kriminelle Zugriff zu den Daten
15 in der Cloud verschaffen könnten, sei ebenfalls nicht auszuschließen.

Eine Reihe von Kritikpunkten. Das Bundesinnenministerium fühlt sich in der Sache aber nicht zuständig. Ein Sprecher erklärte auf Anfrage der Deutschen Presse-Agentur: „Die Nutzung der Sprachassistenten betrifft Datenverarbeitungen durch nichtöffentliche Stellen." Für diese lasse die Datenschutz-Grundverordnung der EU
20 den nationalen Gesetzgebern so gut wie keinen Regelungsspielraum.

„Wir müssen darauf dringen, dass die Einwilligungserklärung für den Nutzer auf die Gefahren und Möglichkeiten hinweist, die mit der Übertragung und Nutzung der Daten sowie der Daten von Dritten, die sich zufällig im Raum befinden, hinweist", meint hingegen der fraktionslose Bundestagsabgeordnete Uwe Kamann. Dies müsse
25 detailliert erfolgen, „und nicht indem man nur einmal ein Häkchen für alles setzt".

Kamann war es, der die Frage aufgeworfen hatte, ob es zulässig ist, dass Amazon die Spracheingaben der „Alexa"-Nutzer auswertet. […]

Der Hamburgische Datenschutzbeauftragte Johannes Caspar ist ebenfalls empört. Er teile die Befürchtungen des Wissenschaftlichen Dienstes des Bundestags. Probleme
30 würden sich „aus der hohen Zahl von Fehlaktivierungen bei automatischen Sprachassistenten" ergeben.

Diese führten dazu, dass Gespräche immer wieder übertragen werden, weil das System das Aktivierungswort fälschlicherweise verstehe. „Von diesen Datenerhebungen sind ausnahmslos alle Personen im Haushalt betroffen, ohne dass die relevanten
35 rechtlichen Vorgaben vorliegen dürften", sagte Caspar zu Tagesspiegel Background Digitalisierung & KI.

Insbesondere dürften „Kinder kaum einwilligungsfähig sein". Ein weiteres Problem ist aus seiner Sicht „die fehlende Zugriffskontrolle durch eine personalisierte Steuerung, mit der eine Nutzung des Sprachsystems durch dritte unbefugte Personen
40 verhindert werden könnte".

Amazon bietet den Nutzern zwar neuerdings mit dem Befehl „Alexa, lerne meine Stimme" die Möglichkeit, ein persönliches Stimmprofil einzurichten. Diese werden nach Angaben eines Amazon-Sprechers aber nur genutzt, „um das individuelle Nutzererlebnis zu verbessern". Auf den Befehl „Computer, spiele Musik!" hin würden für
45 verschiedene Profile unterschiedliche Titel abgespielt. Das Gerät für Kinder zu sperren, erlaubt die neue Stimmerkennung nicht. […]

Der Sprachassistent wird nicht zum ersten Mal als Übel für Kinder angesehen. Im vergangenen Jahr veröffentlichte die britische Childwise Agency eine Untersuchung mit dem Ergebnis: Da Alexa Anweisungen ohne Wörter wie „bitte" oder „danke" aus-
50 führt, fürchten Experten, dass Kinder zu unhöflichen Wesen heranwachsen, die bloß noch befehlen.

Alexa, lies mir eine Gute-Nacht-Geschichte vor! Alexa, ich will …! Im April 2018 brachte Amazon tatsächlich eine Version für Kinder auf den Markt. Diese formuliert ihre Antworten kindgerechter, sagt der Hersteller. Außerdem bekamen Kinder ein Lob,
55 wenn sie bitten und sich bedanken.

Ein anderes Alexa-Problem untersucht nun die Otto-von-Guericke-Universität Magdeburg. Nicht einmal jede vierte KI-Fachkraft sei eine Frau. Daraus ergebe sich die Frage, ob sich dies auch in Denkmustern bei der Künstlichen Intelligenz widerspiegele. Die Unesco hatte bemängelt, dass Siri und Alexa Gender-Stereotype repro-
60 duzieren.

Demnach seien sie unterwürfig, gehorsam und stets freundlich. Vor dem Hintergrund, dass Kinder mit der Technologie aufwüchsen und Sprache ein Geschlechtsmarker sei, bestehe die Gefahr, dass bestimmte Vorstellungen von Frauen transportiert würden – als dienende Maschinen.

(614 Wörter)

Sonja Álvarez, Marie Rövekamp: Experten warnen vor Sprachassistenten – Diese Risiken birgt Alexa für Kinder, Tagesspiegel vom 09.07.2019, https://www.tagesspiegel.de/wirtschaft/experten-warnen-vor-sprachassistenten-diese-risiken-birgt-alexa-fuer-kinder/24573516.html

Lösungsvorschläge

Prüfungsteil 1: Leseverstehen und Schreiben

1   *In der ersten Aufgabe müssen Sie die Situation in eigenen Worten beschreiben. Versuchen Sie alle W-Fragen zu beantworten, zum Beispiel, wo sich die Szene abspielt, wer teilnimmt, was die Figuren machen, wie sie miteinander umgehen und weshalb sie sich so verhalten.*
   – *Mercer, Mae und ihre Eltern sitzen am Küchentisch beim Essen.*
   – *Mae kommt zu spät, da sie damit beschäftigt war, ein Foto von Mercers Kronleuchter zu posten (allerdings, ohne ihn um Erlaubnis zu fragen).*
   – *Maes Mutter möchte einen Toast aussprechen, aber jedes Mal, wenn sie zu sprechen beginnt, klingelt ein Telefon.*
   – *Mae erhält zahlreiche Reaktionen auf das Bild, das sie geposted hat.*
   – *Sie erzählt den anderen von den Nachrichten.*
   – *Mercer ist davon nicht begeistert und droht zu gehen.*
   – *Mae ignoriert ihn und liest weiter die ankommenden Nachrichten.*
   – *Selbst als Mercer tatsächlich geht, nimmt sie dies nicht wahr.*
   – *Als sie aufblickt, ist Mercer verschwunden.*
   – *Ihre Eltern starren sie ungläubig an.*

The excerpt from Dave Eggers' novel *The Circle*, published in 2013, is set in the kitchen of Mae's parents. *(reference to source)*

Her parents and her former boyfriend Mercer have been waiting for her so they can have dinner together. Mae comes in late because she has posted a photo of the chandelier Mercer gave to her parents. The other characters do not know about her posting the photo and Mae intends to surprise them with it. *(description of the situation)*

Mae's mother wants to propose a toast but she is interrupted several times by either Mae's or Mercer's phone ringing, so she gets a little upset. Whereas Mercer turns off his phone, Mae's phone keeps receiving messages in response to the photo she has posted. Finally, she cannot wait any longer and tells everybody what she has done. While Mae is proud of herself, Mercer himself seems to be appalled and threatens to leave if she does not stop. However, Mae ignores him and does not even realise his departure because she is too busy checking her phone for a message from Dubai. When she finally looks up from her phone, she only sees her parents staring at her.   *(193 words)*

6

Zunächst müssen Sie sich Notizen dazu machen, was Mae sagt und wie sie spricht. Zusätzlich sollten Sie festhalten, wie die anderen Figuren sie behandeln. Interpretieren Sie anschließend, was das über ihre Figur aussagt. In Ihrer Analyse sollten Sie außerdem darauf eingehen, welche Rolle die Erzählperspektive spielt. Daher müssen Sie prüfen, aus wessen Perspektive die Geschehnisse dargestellt werden und wie das die Informationen, die wir erhalten, beeinflusst. Bedenken Sie auch, dass die Erzählperspektive Einfluss darauf hat, mit wem sich die Leser*innen am ehesten identifizieren.

- *Mae hat gute Absichten. Sie postet das Bild, um Mercers tolle Arbeit zu zeigen.*
- *Sie handelt allerdings sehr unsensibel und nimmt nicht wahr, dass Mercer nicht einverstanden mit ihrer Handlung ist.*
- *Sie ist so eingenommen von ihrem Smartphone und der Welt, mit der das Gerät sie verbindet, dass sie die Fähigkeit verloren hat, mit den Menschen, die sie direkt umgeben, in Kontakt zu treten.*
  - *Weder nimmt sie wahr, dass Mercer den Tisch verlassen hat, noch dass ihre Eltern sie anstarren. Stattdessen gilt ihre ganze Aufmerksamkeit den Nachrichten aus der ganzen Welt. (vgl. Z. 60–62)*
  - *Sie lässt die gesamte Familie am gedeckten Tisch auf sie warten und geht nicht wirklich darauf ein, als ihr Vater sie darauf hinweist. (vgl. Z. 3–6)*
  - *Sie verhält sich unhöflich, da sie ihr Telefon nicht leise stellt, obwohl es ihre Mutter mehrmals unterbricht. (vgl. Z. 15/16, 22–25, 34/35)*
- *Die Geschichte ist aus Maes Sicht erzählt. Zunächst teilt der Leser oder die Leserin ihre Begeisterung für Mercers Arbeit. Erst später nimmt man wahr, dass sie den Kontakt zu ihrer Umwelt verloren hat.*

Mae is the protagonist in Dave Eggers' novel. At first sight she seems to be a nice girl who cares for others but throughout the excerpt the reader realises that Mae is very insensitive and much too concerned with her smartphone than to empathise with the people sitting with her at the table.

introduction: thesis

At first Mae seems to be quite likeable because she appears to care for others. Thus she apologises for coming in late and praises the food her parents have prepared as well as Mercer's handicraft (cf. ll. 5/6). She is "proud of Mercer" (ll. 25/26) and wants to promote his chandeliers for him. When she realises how many messages she receives in answer to the photo she has posted, she actually beams and wants to celebrate what she perceives as Mercer's success (cf. ll. 36–38).

main part: characterisation of Mae
→ likeable, cares for others

While Mae certainly has good intentions, she is utterly insensitive and, therefore, incapable of putting herself into Mercer's position. Mae should have known that she was not doing Mercer a favour by promoting his handicraft because he cannot produce his chandeliers quickly enough for online sale. Her parents had to wait "for one of his creations for a year" (ll. 7/8) because it is very important

→ insensitive, superficial

to Mercer to get "the right antlers" (l. 9) "from trusted collaborators" (ll. 10/11). The fact that Mae does not take this into account underlines how little interest she really has in her former boyfriend and how little she knows him. Even when he does not "look amused" (l. 39) she still believes that learning about a message from Dubai will make his resistance crumble (cf. ll. 57/58) because "she [is] sure [it will] impress him" (l. 57).

In this context the narrative perspective is relevant. The story is told from Mae's point of view. The readers perceive everything through her eyes, e.g. the readers know that a chair has been moved but only when Mae looks up, do they learn that Mercer has left the room (cf. ll. 60–62). This has the effect that the readers first tend to identify with Mae because of her positive traits described above. They are invited to share Mae's excitement (cf. l. 35) and only realise later on that they have been misled.

narrative perspective
→ Mae's perspective

→ reader is misled

Once this becomes clear, certain remarks by the characters acquire a greater significance. For example, at the beginning her parents mildly reproach Mae for being late. Her mother should not have to point out, "We like to eat when it's hot" (l. 4), as this is a habit Mae should be well aware of. So this incident hints at her lack of empathy.

characterisation
→ lack of empathy

This lack of empathy seems to arise from her obsession with her smartphone and the world it connects her to. She is too impressed with the number of messages her post has provoked and with the distant places some of these messages come from to even notice that the person she thinks she is doing all this for is first "staring at her, his eyes small and round" (l. 53) and then leaves (cf. l. 62).

All in all, Mae seems to be too caught up in the digital world to be really interested in the people surrounding her in person. Her relation to them seems very superficial because she does not really know what is important to the people she should be close to. Thus, she herself appears to be superficial and insensitive.   *(577 words)*

conclusion

3.1 *In Ihrer Erörterung müssen Sie beide Seiten darstellen, bevor Sie zu einem Ergebnis kommen. Berücksichtigen Sie sowohl die positiven als auch die negativen Aspekte moderner Kommunikation. Sie müssen darauf eingehen, wie Mae moderne Kommunikationsmittel nutzt, andererseits aber auch weitere Argumente und Aspekte mit einbringen. Versuchen Sie auch Texte einzubeziehen, die Sie im Unterricht gelesen haben. Diese können zusätzliche Argumente und Belege liefern.*
   – *Argumente dafür, dass moderne Kommunikationsmittel ein Segen sind:*
      • *Ein Leben ohne sie ist in einer globalisierten Welt nicht vorstellbar.*
      • *Sie ermöglichen es uns, mit Menschen auf der ganzen Welt in Kontakt zu treten, ohne zu reisen.*

- *Menschen können leichter in Kontakt bleiben. Kommunikation wird einfacher.*
- *Gegenargumente:*
  - *Zwar kommunizieren Menschen mehr, dafür auch oft oberflächlicher.*
  - *Menschen lassen sich im direkten Gespräch mit anderen von ihren Smartphones ablenken (vgl. Mae).*
  - *Viele Menschen sind geradezu abhängig von ihren Smartphones.*
  - *Kommunikation wird schneller. → Druck schnell zu reagieren*
  - *Kommunikation wird anonymer. → Cyberbullying*

These days, in many countries smartphones, tablets and other portable devices are very common. Especially among teenagers they are widely distributed. Most teenagers could not imagine living without a smartphone; they are so-called smart natives and feel their mobile is a blessing. On the other hand, one often hears that the device is a curse. So which perspective is right?

introduction: topic, reference to task

Modern ways of communication certainly have many advantages. For one, communication has become much quicker than it was some thirty years ago. This saves a lot of time and also money, especially as we live in a globalised world. Transnational companies could not work that efficiently if they still had to rely on landlines and the postman.

main part: advantages – first argument

Additionally, research has shown that people communicate more because of smartphones and the like. People tend to talk less to each other but communicate in written form via instant messenger applications. For teenagers, these applications are the most important ones on their smartphones and more than 80 % of them have them installed.

second argument

However, one must not forget the drawbacks. It is very common for teenagers to meet friends but instead of talking to each other they are all occupied with their smartphones. Mae, the protagonist of Dave Eggers' novel *The Circle,* is a good example. Although she is sitting with her parents and her former boyfriend at the table, she has her smartphone turned on and checks incoming messages. What is more, she does not seem to know any longer that there are people around her. Communication seems to become more indirect and superficial, which leads to relations becoming more shallow.

disadvantages – first argument

→ reference to novel

The fact that communication has become quicker definitely has its advantages as shown above but the disadvantages are considerable, too. People are expected to react instantly to incoming messages, which may lead to spontaneous but wrong decisions and to words better left unsaid. An example is the widespread phenomenon of cyberbullying.

second argument

In the end, it depends on the users if mobile devices are a blessing or a curse. If they use their mobile devices cleverly, they can save a lot of time and get in touch with others if it is really necessary, for instance in cases of emergency. In order to prevent these devices from becoming a curse, users must decide to ignore them, or even turn them off in certain situations, such as when they meet friends. *(398 words)*

conclusion

3.2 *Bevor Sie zu schreiben beginnen, müssen Sie sich in Mercer hineinversetzen. Lesen Sie den Text noch einmal und konzentrieren Sie sich auf die Informationen, die Sie über Mercer erhalten. Wie reagiert er auf Mae und ihren Post? Was lernen wir über seine Werte? Nachdem Sie sich darüber Gedanken gemacht haben, können Sie überlegen, was Sie in Ihren Brief mit aufnehmen sollten und wie Ihr Tonfall sein sollte. Denken Sie daran, dass Sie einen persönlichen Brief schreiben und dass es sich bei Mercer (vermutlich) um einen jungen Erwachsenen handelt. Daher sollten Sie Alltagssprache verwenden. Obwohl Sie verleitet sein könnten, einen sehr informellen Sprachstil einzuschlagen und eventuell sogar Schimpfworte zu nutzen, sollten Sie sich im Kontext der Abiturprüfung damit zurückhalten.*

– *Mercer erklärt, warum er gegangen ist.* → *Wut, Unglaube über Maes fehlende Empathie*
– *Mercer ist wütend darüber, dass Mae ihn nicht um Erlaubnis gebeten hat, bevor sie sein Werk gepostet hat (allerdings können Sie selbst entscheiden, wie wütend er tatsächlich ist oder ob er auch bereit ist, ihre positiven Intentionen wahrzunehmen).*
– *Mercer interessiert sich nicht für materiellen Erfolg.*
– *Er nutzt nur Geweihe von Anbieter*innen, denen er vertraut.*
– *Er ist enttäuscht darüber, wie wenig Mae über ihn weiß.*
– *Möglicherweise kommentiert er die Art, in der Mae ihr Smartphone nutzt.*
– *Vermutlich wird er Mae bitten, das Bild zu entfernen.*

6 May, 2013   date

Dear Mae,   form of address

Yesterday, I left your parents' house without a word. Hopefully you know that this is not like me but it only goes to show how furious I was and still am. You posted a photo of my chandelier without asking me about it first. I would like to believe that you meant well but I'm really shocked at how little you know me after all the years we spent together.

reason for writing: furious at Mae

she does not know him

Your parents had waited for the chandelier for one year for a good reason. I only get the antlers from suppliers I trust because I don't want any deer to be shot just for the sake of my chandeliers. So how am I to satisfy the demand of people from all over the world? Plus, money is not important to me. I like my work and like to be independent. What you have done puts far too much pressure on

reasons he is not happy with Mae's posts

10

me. My phone starts ringing as soon as I turn it on and I get orders from all over the world. If I wanted to answer them all, I wouldn't be doing anything else.

That's not the way I work or communicate, so please, remove this photo straight away to undo at least some of the damage you've done.

asks Mae to remove the post

I'd also like to tell you that I was horrified by your obsession with your smartphone. Your parents see so little of you and when you visit them, you keep your eyes on the screen. For heaven's sake, Mae, talk to the people who are sitting face-to-face with you and do not constantly interrupt the conversation because there is a message on your phone.

advice for Mae

I've shut down my mobile for good because I can no longer stand the pressure you've put me under and I advise you to do so, too, at least when you visit your parents.

Whatever you do, Mae, remove that photo. Quickly and for good! You had no right to post it in the first place.

closing sentence: repeats demand

Mercer *(337 words)*

name

Prüfungsteil 2: Sprachmittlung

Bevor Sie mit dem Schreiben Ihrer Lösung beginnen, sollten Sie sich die Aufgabenstellung genau durchlesen. Diese enthält Informationen dazu, welches Zieltextformat gefordert ist und welche Leserschaft angesprochen werden soll. Zusätzlich enthält sie meist Informationen dazu, auf welche Aspekte Sie sich in Ihrer Lösung konzentrieren sollen. In diesem Fall schreiben Sie einen Artikel für die Homepage eines Projektes. Sie müssen eine interessante Überschrift formulieren und Ihren Text in klar strukturierte Absätze gliedern. Ihr Publikum besteht aus den Teilnehmerinnen und Teilnehmern eines internationalen Projektes, das sich an Jugendliche richtet. Daher sollte Ihr Text nicht zu formell klingen, dabei aber dennoch Expertise zu den Bereichen Digitalisierung und künstliche Intelligenzen aufweisen. Inhaltlich sollten Sie sich auf die Nachteile und Probleme konzentrieren, die im Text im Zusammenhang mit Alexa, Siri und anderen digitalen Sprachassistenten auftauchen.

Die folgenden Aspekte könnten Teil Ihrer Lösung sein:
- *Zwei Hauptkritikpunkte: Datenschutzaspekte und Gefahren, die Alexa und andere Sprachassistenten für Kinder darstellen*
- *Kinderschutz und pädagogische Aspekte:*
  - *Kinder können nicht altersgerechten Themen begegnen. (vgl. Z. 1–3, 7/8)*
  - *Daten von Kindern werden gespeichert und genutzt, ohne dass diese eingewilligt haben. (vgl. Z. 6/7, 11/12, 37, 45/46)*
  - *Kinder lernen, in Befehlsform zu sprechen. (vgl. Z. 49–51)*

- Kinder erwerben Genderstereotype, da Sprachassistenten weibliche Stimmen und Namen haben und das Bild von folgsamen Dienerinnen reproduzieren. (vgl. Z. 59–64)
- Generelle Datenschutzprobleme:
  - Alle werden aufgezeichnet, unabhängig davon, ob sie die Einwilligung gegeben haben (insbesondere auch, da die Technik anfällig für Fehler ist). (vgl. Z. 8–12, 32–35)
  - Unsicherheit dazu, was mit den Daten geschieht (vgl. Z. 13–15)
  - Fehlender Datenschutz in Deutschland für private Anbieter (vgl. Z. 16–20)

Is Alexa a danger for children as well as for data security?   heading

In many German households, digital language assistants like Siri or Alexa have become a part of everyday life. While they might make some tasks easier, some experts also regard them with growing suspicion.   introduction

One of the most pressing issues is data protection. A voice assistant records thousands of pieces of information and so far there are no clear-cut rules as to what happens with these. Criminals potentially accessing the data are only the tip of the iceberg. With a private company involved in the data collection, many of Alexa's potentially unauthorised uses are not even considered in European data protection laws.   data protection issues: no legal framework, potentially criminal uses of data

Voice assistants do not limit their data collection to those who have explicitly given their permission. Instead, as soon as the assistant is activated – a process that despite experiments with voice recognition is still prone to errors –, everyone in the vicinity is recorded indiscriminately.   lack of consent of those being recorded

In connection with child protection laws, this is especially relevant. Children cannot be considered to have given their permission to be taped. Additionally, Alexa might inadvertently provide them with content that is inappropriate to their age.   child protection and educational issues: inappropriate content

There are further concerns when it comes to Alexa's educational side effects: Alexa does what you want her to do without being asked politely. This might lead to children becoming used to a commanding and impolite language. Secondly, Alexa, Siri and co. could reproduce harmful gender stereotypes: with their female names and their obedient behaviour, they could convey an image of women as docile servants.   communicating by giving commands; gender stereotypes

Thus, for all her alleged progressiveness and user-friendliness, Alexa might also be a danger lurking in your living room.   *(278 words)*   conclusion

Prüfungsteil 1: Leseverstehen und Schreiben (75 %)

Aufgabenstellung 1 – Tasks

Themenschwerpunkte: *Aims and ambitions, Saving the planet*

1   Summarise what happened in Vanuatu and why (Text A). Also
     summarise the conclusions the author draws from the event.   (30 %)

2   Analyse how the author tries to convince the readers that they need to
     "live within [their] overall environmental thresholds" (ll. 56/57). In doing
     so, focus on structure, argumentative techniques and the language used.   (35 %)

3   Choose **one** of the following tasks.   (35 %)

3.1 Discuss if it makes sense for individuals to act in a more environmentally
     friendly way if they are likely "to suffer chronically due to someone
     else's bad habit" (l. 15) anyway.

OR

3.2 You come across the website of an American blogger who often
     complains about the ungrateful young generation, which, in her view, is
     in fact a gilded generation. She asks her readers for their opinion on the
     topic.

     Nobody likes being told they live a carefree, easy-going life – young
     people included. Her constant complaint inspires you to write an article
     for her blog in which you discuss her claim that "Young people have
     never had it so good". Use the material (Text B) provided.

Text A (excerpt from the article)

Developed nations have sown the wind, Vanuatu has reaped the whirlwind
by Andrew Simms

 1 When the president of Vanuatu said that years of progress had been wiped out by a
   single extreme weather event, it was both a warning and an echo. Hurricane Mitch did
   the same to Nicaragua and Honduras in 1998; and in 2005 political failure combined
   with the collapse of sea defences under the onslaught of Hurricane Katrina to wreck
 5 the rich, vibrant culture of New Orleans. Climatic extremes in a warming world stand
   to reverse human progress and expose broken social contracts.

But in the case of Vanuatu there seems to be a crueller twist. Vanuatu is distinguished by having come top of a global index that measures how ecologically successful (low in impact) nations are at producing good lives for their people – so-called "happy life years". Vanuatu beat all other nations through treading lightest on the Earth for the quality and length of life its people enjoyed. Now it sits in the pathway of a giant climatic steamroller, fuelled by the energy-intensive lifestyles of nations much further down that index.

Its people are the national equivalent of the individual who leads an exemplary, healthy life only to suffer chronically due to someone else's bad habit – innocent, global victims of passive smoking. Vanuatu's president, Baldwin Lonsdale, was quick to point the finger of blame at manmade climate change for the severity of Cyclone Pam, saying that "the cyclone seasons, the warm, the rain, all this is affected".

Many may think it's too soon to jump to such conclusions. For years cautious scientists have balked at attributing the effect of warming to individual events. Attribution can sometimes be hard to prove, either for methodological reasons of complexity or due to lack of data. While trepidation remains, things have changed rapidly. Instead of simple claims of cause and effect, climate scientists now readily discuss how the probability of any particular event has been raised by the existence of warming.

Hence joint work in 2011 by the National Oceanic and Atmospheric Administration in the US and the UK's Met Office concluded that a Texas heatwave was 20 times more likely to be caused by climate change than by natural weather variation. A winter warm spell in Britain the same year was 62 times more likely than in the 1960s. The Met Office's Hadley Centre now confidently states that it "can identify any changed risk of such events".

In time, more analysis will be done on Cyclone Pam, but Lonsdale's personal experience and gut reaction fits a pattern of expectations described in the most recent and most comprehensive collation of science on extreme events in the IPCC's Fifth Assessment Report. It concluded that: "The frequency of the most intense storms will more likely than not increase in some basins. More extreme precipitation near the centres of tropical cyclones making landfall is projected in North and Central America, east Africa, west, east, south and southeast Asia as well as in Australia and many Pacific islands."

So, while the present is pretty bad for Vanuatu, in a warming world the future looks set to worsen. For this island nation, that is bitterly ironic. Vanuatu is an archipelago in the western Pacific, famous for having no regular military. When it topped the index in 2006 its ecological footprint per person was no higher than those in non-industrialised countries like Mali and Swaziland, life expectancy matched that in Turkey, and life satisfaction levels were considered as high as New Zealand's. It is democratic, rich in natural wealth but, being remote, exports little, avoiding the scramble of competing in global markets. It is also hugely culturally diverse with more than 100 languages spoken across its islands.

Small island states tend to do very well in the index topped by Vanuatu. Over countless generations and in the face of geographical isolation, many Pacific islands developed more cooperative economies and highly resilient farming methods. In a warming world they are bellwethers, and carry lessons for us all. If climate change

14

renders small island states unliveable, the international community will sooner or later have to learn to accept and support environmental refugees. Though this would be tragic, remote island populations can, at least, relocate. However, blue island-planet populations cannot.

We will seal our own fate if we fail to learn to share and live within our overall environmental thresholds. […]

(717 words)

Simms, Andrew: *"Developed nations have sown the wind, Vanuatu has reaped the whirlwind".*
In: The Guardian, *Copyright Guardian News & Media Ltd 2018*

Annotations
l. 1   *Vanuatu:* archipelago in the South Pacific consisting of about 82 islands.
l. 17   *Pam:* Cyclone Pam hit Vanuatu and damaged large parts of the archipelago in March 2015.
l. 33   *IPCC*: Intergovernmental Panel of Climate Change
l. 51   *bellwether:* something that is used as an indicator of what will happen in the future

Text B (picture)

My children will be an endangered species

Barcroft Media / getty images

Aufgabenstellung 2 – Tasks

Themenschwerpunkte: *Aims and ambitions, Saving the planet*

Die Debatten um die „freie Fahrt für freie Bürger" oder ein generelles Tempolimit auf Deutschlands Autobahnen sind fast so alt wie die Bundesrepublik selbst.
Sie machen ein Praktikum im Stab der EU-Kommissarin für Verkehr. Im Rahmen von Überlegungen zur Harmonisierung europäischer Verkehrsvorschriften steuern Sie in der Amtssprache Englisch Positionen und Fakten aus der Tempolimit-Diskussion in Deutschland bei. Als Grundlage für Ihre Email und das Team dienen Ihnen die beiden untenstehenden Texte.

Text 1: Sind Autobahnen mit Tempolimit sicherer? von Simon Haas

1 […] Nicht immer geht es in dieser sehr deutschen Diskussion um Fakten. […] Hier wichtige Fragen und Antworten zum Thema:

Wie viele Autobahnkilometer sind überhaupt noch frei befahrbar?
Nach einer Erhebung der Bundesanstalt für Straßenwesen (BASt) gilt auf fast jedem
5 dritten Autobahnkilometer bereits ein generelles Tempolimit. Zwei Drittel sind jedoch weiterhin ohne Geschwindigkeitsbegrenzung befahrbar. Auf den restlichen Strecken gibt es lediglich temporäre Beschränkungen, etwa nachts oder bei Nässe.

Sind Autobahnen mit Tempolimit nun sicherer?
Statistisch lässt sich tatsächlich ein Zusammenhang zwischen Tempolimit und weniger
10 Verkehrstoten herstellen: 2016 sind auf deutschen Autobahnen mit Geschwindigkeitsbegrenzung pro Autobahnkilometer 26 Prozent weniger Menschen tödlich verunglückt als auf Autobahnen ohne Tempolimit. 2015 waren es 13 Prozent. Dieser Trend lässt sich auch bei der Anzahl der Schwerverletzten feststellen. Das geht aus einer Auswertung des Deutschen Verkehrssicherheitsrates (DVR) hervor.

15 **Hilft ein Tempolimit der Umwelt?**
Ein Tempolimit von 120 Stundenkilometern auf deutschen Autobahnen würde einer Untersuchung des Umweltbundesamts zufolge pro Jahr rund drei Millionen Tonnen CO_2 einsparen. Das entspricht einem Rückgang um neun Prozent. Drei Millionen Tonnen CO_2 sind allerdings gerade einmal drei Prozent dessen, was der Pkw-Verkehr 2016
20 insgesamt an Treibhausgasen freigesetzt hat.

Verhindert ein Tempolimit Staus?
Diese Frage ist unter Experten umstritten. Der Verkehrsclub Deutschland (VCD) argumentiert: „Ein Tempolimit bedeutet weniger Staus, denn es mindert die hohen Geschwindigkeitsunterschiede auf Autobahnen, die eine wichtige Ursache bei der Stau-

25 entstehung sind." Laut ADAC führt ein generelles Tempolimit von 120 Stundenkilometern hingegen zu keiner nennenswerten Verbesserung der Leistungsfähigkeit von Autobahnen. Verkehrsabhängig gesteuerte Anzeigen reichten demnach aus, um die optimale Geschwindigkeit bei hohem Verkehrsaufkommen zu erreichen.

(253 Wörter)

Erschienen auf der Webseite der Schwäbischen Zeitung https://www.schwaebische.de/sueden/baden-wuerttemberg_artikel,-sind-autobahnen-mit-tempolimit-sicherer-_arid,10784485.html
Gekürzt und leicht adaptiert

Text 2: Sind Autobahnen mit Tempolimit sicherer?

1 Ein generelles Tempolimit auf deutschen Autobahnen machte die Straßen sicherer, wenn sich auch die Fahrkultur ändere, meint Prof. Justin Geistefeldt.

Der Bochumer Verkehrswissenschaftler hofft, dass dann auch weniger hektisch gefahren werde und es weniger unnötige Fahrstreifenwechsel gibt. […]

5 […] Es gibt keine von der Bundesregierung finanzierten Studien zur Verkehrssicherheit durch ein Tempolimit. „Wir haben es hier mit einem forschungspolitischen Loch zu tun, und zwar ist das beabsichtigt", meint Gerd Lottsiepen vom ökologisch ausgerichteten Verkehrsclub Deutschland (VCD). „[…] Die Autoindustrie freut sich, dass es keine neuen Untersuchungen gibt, weil die immer wieder von der Regierung ver-
10 langen, kein Tempolimit einzuführen."

[…] Automobilverbände halten Verkehrsbeeinflussungsanlagen für effizienter als ein starres Tempolimit: Sie geben eine an die jeweilige Verkehrssituation angepasste Höchstgeschwindigkeit vor, die etwa bei schlechtem Wetter anders sein kann als bei gutem. Auf zehn Prozent des 12 200 Kilometer umfassenden Autobahnnetzes sind sol-
15 che Systeme bereits installiert. Laut einer Studie des „Auto Clubs Europa" (ACE) kann ein Geschwindigkeitsmanagement zu einem Rückgang von bis zu 30 Prozent der Unfälle auf Autobahnen führen und die Umwelt entlasten, weil Staus und unnötige Schadstoffemissionen vermieden würden.

(174 Wörter)

Erschienen auf der Webseite des 3sat-Wissenschaftsmagazins „nano"
https://www.3sat.de/nano/umwelt/171852/index.html, 20.09.2017

Prüfungsteil 1: Leseverstehen und Schreiben

1   *Sie sollen kurz die Ereignisse in Vanuatu darstellen und die Ursachen für die Ereignisse darlegen. Zudem sollen Sie die Schlüsse, die der Autor daraus zieht, darstellen.*
   – *Was ist passiert:*
   • *Vanuatu wurde im März 2015 von einem Zyklon getroffen.*
   • *Das Land wurde verwüstet.*
   – *Gründe:*
   • *Vanuatu ist selbst nicht für das Naturereignis verantwortlich, da die Menschen dort sehr umweltbewusst leben.* → *Sie bezahlen für den energieintensiven Lebensstil anderer Nationen.*
   • *Der Präsident von Vanuatu macht die globale Erwärmung verantwortlich.*
   • *Während dieser Schluss nicht von allen akzeptiert wird, zitiert der Autor einen Bericht, der die Sichtweise des Präsidenten bestärkt.*
   – *Schlüsse:*
   • *Die Zahl der Umweltflüchtlinge wird ansteigen.*
   • *Die Erde könnte eines Tages unbewohnbar werden.*
   • *Wir müssen uns alle bewusster werden, welche Auswirkungen unser Verhalten auf das Klima hat, und umweltbewusster leben.*

In his article "Developed nations have sown the wind, Vanuatu has reaped the whirlwind" published in *The Guardian*, the journalist Andrew Simms briefly describes what happened in Vanuatu. He then gives reasons for the event and draws conclusions from it.

introduction: reference to source, topic

In March 2015, Vanuatu was hit by Cyclone Pam and its islands were completely devastated. The president of Vanuatu blames global warming for what happened and although Simms admits that not everybody agrees with the president's analysis, he also quotes a report that supports it. Furthermore, the author mentions that Vanuatu itself is not to blame because this nation lives in a very environmentally friendly way. According to him, developed nations who have more energy-intensive lifestyles are to blame but Vanuatu has to pay the price.

main part: events reasons

Simms predicts that the number of environmental refugees will increase and that one day the earth might no longer be inhabitable. He concludes that we all need to be more conscious of the effect we are having on our planet and its climate and that we need to live in a more environmentally friendly way.   *(181 words)*

conclusions

2   *Diese Aufgabe verlangt, dass Sie analysieren, wie der Autor seine Leserschaft von seiner Meinung überzeugen möchte. Sie müssen sich dabei auf die Struktur des Textes, die Art der Argumentation und die Sprache konzentrieren.*

– *Struktur:*
- *Überschrift: gibt die Stimmung vor → Vanuatu bezahlt für das Fehlverhalten der wirtschaftsstarken Staaten*
- *Text zeigt zunächst, dass Vanuatu kein Einzelfall ist (vgl. Z. 1–6)*
- *Autor greift Überschrift wieder auf → wirtschaftsstarke Staaten und ihr Lebensstil sind für Erderwärmung verantwortlich (vgl. Z. 7–18)*
- *Autor beschreibt Reaktionen auf die Analyse, dass die globale Erwärmung für den Zyklon verantwortlich ist, der Vanuatu getroffen hat (vgl. Z. 19–38)*
- *Aussichtslose Vorhersage für Inseln wie Vanuatu, unseren Planeten und seine Bewohner (vgl. Z. 34–55)*
- *Schlussfolgerung, dass unser Lebensstil weniger energieintensiv werden muss (vgl. Z. 56/57)*

– *Techniken bei der Argumentation:*
- *Beispiele (vgl. Z. 1–5)*
- *Fakten (vgl. Z. 7–11, 41/42)*
- *Zahlen (vgl. Z. 26, 28)*
- *Expertenmeinungen und ein Zitat aus einer Studie (vgl. Z. 19–38)*

– *Sprache:*
- *Bibelstelle, die leicht angepasst wurde, um zu betonen, dass andere den Schaden verursacht haben, den Vanuatu ausbaden muss (vgl. Überschrift)*
- *Wörter mit positiver Konnotation werden genutzt, um Vanuatu und seine Einwohner*innen zu beschreiben, z. B. „distinguished" (Z. 7/8), „ecologically successful" (Z. 8/9), „exemplary, healthy" (Z. 14/15), „innocent" (Z. 15)*
- *Im Kontrast dazu negativ konnotierte Wörter, die wirtschaftsstarke Länder und den Klimawandel beschreiben, z. B. „giant climatic steamroller" (Z. 12), „energy-intensive lifestyles" (Z. 12)*
- *Bildliche Sprache, um zu betonen, dass Vanuatu in der Situation das Opfer vom Fehlverhalten anderer ist (vgl. Z. 10–16)*
- *Aufzählung, die Vanuatus Errungenschaften betont (vgl. Z. 41–44)*

The author's intention in writing this article is to convince the readers that they need to "live within [their] overall environmental thresholds" (ll. 56/57). He tries to achieve his aim by using a structure that leads to the conclusion quoted above, by employing different argumentative techniques and by making use of words that underline both the difference between Vanuatu and developed nations and the author's interpretation that Vanuatu is suffering instead of these developed countries.

introduction: thesis / reference to assignment

This interpretation is introduced right in the headline. The author then shows that Vanuatu is not an isolated case but that other countries have been hit by extreme winds, too (cf. ll. 1–6). In the second and third paragraph, the journalist takes up the headline again

main part: structure

and describes in more detail that developed nations are to blame for global warming and, therefore, climate change (cf. ll. 7–18). In the following three paragraphs he presents reactions to the analysis of Vanuatu's president, who claims that global warming is responsible for the cyclone that hit his country. The author briefly mentions doubts (ll. 19–22) but then dwells on experts, organisations and numbers that support the president's view (cf. ll. 22–38). This indicates that he favours this interpretation of the events himself. In the seventh and eighth paragraph he makes dire predictions about the future of islands like Vanuatu, our planet and its inhabitants to emphasise that we need to take action (cf. ll. 39–55), which leads him to his final conclusion that we have to have less energy-intensive lifestyles (cf. ll. 56/57). Thus, the article's structure leads very logically to the final conclusion that appears to be convincing.

The language employed stresses the view that developed nations are to blame for Vanuatu's misfortune. The differences in lifestyles and their consequences are emphasised. Vanuatu's inhabitants are "ecologically successful" (ll. 8/9) and therefore "distinguished" (ll. 7/8). They lead "an exemplary, healthy life" (ll. 14/15). All these words have a positive connotation and therefore underline that Vanuatu's people are "innocent" (l. 15). They are contrasted with developed nations, which are accused of causing "a giant climatic steamroller, fuelled by […] energy-intensive lifestyles" (ll. 11/12). Thus, developed nations are depicted as villains.

language

→ choice of words
Vanuatu: positive connotation

developed nations: negative connotation

This contrast is already introduced in the headline, which is an adapted proverb from the Bible. The original proverb "they that sow wind shall reap whirlwind" is applied to people who start trouble that grows larger than planned. In this case, however, someone else, namely the developed countries, started the trouble that another party, namely Vanuatu, has to suffer from. This stresses the injustice of the situation.

→ proverb

Additionally, the author uses figurative speech to stress this idea. He compares Vanuatu to "the individual who leads an exemplary, healthy life only to suffer chronically due to someone else's bad habit – innocent, global victims of passive smoking" (ll. 14–16). Furthermore, developed nations, as mentioned above, are blamed for having set free a "steamroller" (l. 12), which ruthlessly destroys other nations. The intended effect of the language used is that people in developed countries should have a guilty conscience and realise that their lifestyle needs to be changed.

→ figurative speech

The argumentative techniques employed support that view. The journalist argues that now extreme weather events happen regularly as Cyclone Pam is an "echo" (l. 2) of preceding hurricanes. To prove this assertion Simms gives several examples (cf. ll. 2–5). The claim that Vanuatu's people lead an exemplary life is backed up by a global index in which Vanuatu excelled (cf. ll. 7–11, 41/42). Thus, the journalist bases his argument on facts, which makes him more trustworthy.

argumentative techniques

→ examples, facts

When Simms supports the analysis of Vanuatu's president that Cyclone Pam was caused by global warming, he refers to unnamed climate scientists who "now readily discuss how the probability of any particular event has been raised by the existence of warming" (ll. 23/24). Furthermore, he quotes from the IPCC's Fifth Assessment Report (ll. 34–38), refers to organisations that share his view (cf. ll. 25–30) and uses their numbers (cf. ll. 26, 28) and thus bases his argument on experts' views, which adds authority to his reasoning.

→ reference to experts, numbers

All in all, Simms makes it clear that people in developed nations need to change their lifestyles if they do not want to live at the expense of somebody else's well-being. He achieves this by using language in a way that clearly contrasts the victim and the perpetrator, by using structure purposefully to make it lead to his final conclusion and by basing his arguments on examples, facts and experts' reports.   *(773 words)*

conclusion:
reference to task

3.1 *Bei dieser Aufgabe müssen Sie argumentieren, ob wir als Individuen umweltfreundlich leben sollten, obwohl das Verhalten eines Einzelnen die globale Erwärmung nicht verhindern kann. Sie müssen Pro- und Contra-Argumente abwägen und am Schluss zu einer Schlussfolgerung kommen.*

  – *Einleitung: Stellen Sie das Thema dar und gehen Sie auf das Dilemma für jeden Einzelnen ein.*
  – *Pro:*
    • *Es hilft nicht, einfach nur den Kopf in den Sand zu stecken.*
    • *Jeden Tag, den wir nichts tun, wird es schwerer das Zwei-Grad-Ziel zu erreichen, daher können wir nicht warten, bis andere beginnen, etwas zu verändern.*
    • *Ein gutes Beispiel könnte andere dazu animieren, zu folgen, etwa eine 10:10 Initiative, die Menschen zusammenbringt, die eine sauberere Welt mit weniger CO_2 Ausstoß wünschen.*
  – *Contra:*
    • *Das Beispiel der Menschen in Vanuatu zeigt, dass das Verhalten des Einzelnen nicht ausreicht.*
    • *Der Einfluss von Individuen ist im Vergleich zu dem großer Unternehmen zu vernachlässigen.*

- *Die USA und China sind für 40 % der weltweiten Treibhausgasemissionen ver-antwortlich. 2016 haben sie endlich das Klimaabkommen in Paris unterzeich-net. Die geplante Reduktion der Emissionen reicht allerdings nicht, um das Zwei-Grad-Ziel zu erreichen und der US-amerikanische Präsident Donald Trump verkündete kurz darauf bereits den Austritt aus dem Pariser Klimaab-kommen.*
- *Die Erderwärmung wird nicht als unmittelbare Gefahr wahrgenommen, wes-halb es schwer ist, Menschen zu überzeugen, ihr Verhalten zu ändern.*
- *Schlussfolgerung: Vergleichen Sie die Pro- und Contra-Seite und kommen Sie zu einem Ergebnis.*

When discussing climate change, two is the magic number. We need to stabilise global temperature within two degrees above pre-industrial levels, or else the extra input of greenhouse gases, for example those locked in the arctic ice, will wipe out most of the life on earth. In order to achieve that goal, we need to cut emis-sions by 80 % by 2050. This goal seems hard to achieve; one might even say it is impossible to achieve. Therefore, the question arises whether it makes any sense at all for individuals to act in a more environmentally friendly way if they are likely "to suffer chronic-ally due to someone else's bad habit" (l. 15).

introduction

People who think it does make sense may point out that no one, at least no doctor, would recommend a non-smoker who contracts lung cancer to start smoking because he will die anyway. Only deeply pessimistic and sarcastic people would do so. The same could be said to be true for global warming because we cannot bury our heads in the sand and do nothing just because the big players, for instance energy-intensive companies like Trimet, emit too much greenhouse gas.

main part: pros

On the contrary, the individual needs to set a good example to en-courage others to follow. Take an initiative such as 10:10. This initiative offers a website on which they bring together individual people and groups who want to make this world a cleaner, cleverer, low-carbon place. On the website one can find hundreds of examples of what individuals have already achieved to cut down emissions and thus get ideas for one's own projects.

On the other hand, there are good reasons that support the view that the individual is not powerful enough to stop global warming. Take Vanuatu as an example: the nation as a whole, and not just the individual inhabitants, led an exemplary life as far as the emis-sion of greenhouse gas is concerned. In spite of that fact, Cyclone Pam destroyed many people's houses. So their excellent behaviour did not save them from suffering the consequences of global warming.

transition – cons

The USA and China, who together are responsible for 40 % of our global greenhouse gas emissions, finally signed the climate change agreement in 2016. Whereas China seems to be quite serious about tackling climate change, the USA under Donald Trump even pulled out of the agreement again. In any case it will be almost impossible to stay within the 2-degree limit because efforts started too late and too half-heartedly.

The basic problem is that we are evolutionarily equipped to deal with immediate threats. Global warming, however, is not an immediate threat so we do not feel the need to react. Once people start to feel that threat, it will be too late.

Altogether, I truly believe that individuals alone are too ineffective **conclusion** to help with climate change. Of course, they can make some effort and set good examples, but if the big spenders do not change their behaviour radically, the 2-degree goal is unattainable. Then it might be wiser to enjoy the remaining years on our planet, without denying ourselves pleasures like weekend trips to Paris or Mallorca, because rough times are certainly ahead. *(532 words)*

3.2 *Wenn die Aufgabenstellung von Ihnen verlangt, die Thematik zu diskutieren („Discuss"), müssen Sie sich mit Pro und Contra auseinandersetzen. Ob Sie in der vorliegenden Aufgabenstellung in Ihrem Fazit der Bloggerin zustimmen, dass junge Menschen es heute so guthaben wie keine Generation zuvor, oder ob Sie ihre These ablehnen, bleibt Ihnen überlassen. Ihre Haltung muss begründet und nachvollziehbar sein.*

Eine besondere Herausforderung liegt für Sie darin, wie Sie das vorhandene Material in Ihre Lösung einarbeiten. Dabei sollen Sie die Bildquellen ausdrücklich <u>nicht</u> detailliert beschreiben. Das Material dient Ihnen als gedanklicher Anstoß zur Findung von Ideen und Argumenten oder zur Einbeziehung von relevanten Informationen. Folgender Aufbau ist möglich:

– *Hinführung zum Thema: Vergleich der Perspektive zwischen Jung und Alt*
– *Gedanken zum Hauptteil:*
   Möglichkeiten:
   • *Materielle Verhältnisse, Möglichkeiten der Mobilität und des Konsums*
   • *Lebenserwartung*
   • *Individuelle Freiheit und Entfaltung wie keine Generation zuvor*
   Probleme und Herausforderungen:
   • *Konfrontation mit existenziellen Herausforderungen wie Klimawandel*
   • *Leistungsdruck durch neue Job- und Medienwelt*
   • *Demokratie und Freiheit gefährdet durch antidemokratischen Populismus*
– *Abrundung des Textes mit Fazit, persönlicher Einschätzung, Ausblick o. Ä.: hilfreich, andere Perspektive einzunehmen*

A matter of perspective

While the young tend to see what is troublesome in their lives, the old tend to see what they didn't have when they were young. They feel the young have far more opportunities and better living conditions than they did in the past. Have the young really never had it so good?

Young people nowadays DO have opportunities they may not even be aware of.

No young generation as a whole has ever had more material possessions than this one. They have enough pocket money, go on vacations to remote places, and own expensive state-of-the-art electronic devices.

With a life expectancy of around 80 years, people born today may become older than any generation before, and enjoy what is possibly the best healthcare system ever.

The young enjoy political freedom and individual self-fulfilment to an unprecedented extent. They have a say in the way they dress, the school they attend, and the trade they want to learn. They experience a lot more respect and a lot less violence than previous generations. And they grow up in relative peace and democracy.

On the other hand, it is a fact that today's young generation are faced with huge environmental threats that literally endanger their existence. Because the majority of politicians, corporate leaders and voters refuse to take effective climate action and to live up to their responsibilities, the world is rather likely to become a place afflicted by heatwaves, floods, severe droughts and crop failures. Millions of climate refugees will need to be catered for. And in recent years it has become more and more obvious that the continuous loss of biodiversity is threatening our vital natural resources.

Another tough challenge the young are faced with is psychological distress. There are high expectations to excel at school, to have a successful career and to perform on social media platforms. There seems to be more competition than ever for attractive jobs, excellent grades and "likes" on Instagram, the digital currency that gains you social recognition. High expectations often result in pressure which affects a person's health and quality of life.

Last but not least, Brexit and the rise of populist movements in numerous European countries suggest that a society based on stable democratic values can no longer be taken for granted.

Alarmingly large numbers of juveniles have mental-health problems or express they are not happy at all with the stress levels in their lives. This has to be taken seriously.

But we should also see the great opportunities for today's youth, of course. A different perspective might help us gain a little peace of mind. conclusion

(436 words)

Prüfungsteil 2: Sprachmittlung

Das Besondere bei der vorliegenden Aufgabe ist, dass Sie Informationen aus zwei Texten zusammenfassen müssen. Damit Ihre Lösung einer klaren Struktur folgt, müssen Sie zunächst die wesentlichen Aspekte in beiden Texten markieren und diese dann einander zuordnen, also in Ihrer Lösung Vorzüge oder Nachteile aus beiden Texten in einem Abschnitt zusammenfassen.

– Vorzüge eines allgemeinen Tempolimits
- *Sicherere Autobahnen, weniger Unfälle mit tödlichem Ausgang*
- *Geringerer CO$_2$-Ausstoß*
- *Weniger Staus*

– Argumente dagegen sowie mögliche Alternativen
- *CO$_2$-Einsparungen nur sehr gering*
- *Kaum Effekt auf die Staubildung*
- *Stattdessen: Verkehrsbeeinflussungsanlagen zum Geschwindigkeitsmanagement*

– Vorwurf des VCD: Regierung macht bewusst keine Studien zum Thema, um Autoindustrie zu schonen

Dear Colleagues, greeting

In out last meeting we talked about the discussion around a general speed limit on German highways. In the following I sum up the arguments mentioned in the articles "Sind Autobahnen mit Tempolimit sicherer?" by Simon Haas published in the *Schwäbische Zeitung* and "Sind Autobahnen mit Tempolimit sicherer?" from the website of the science magazine "nano". introduction: reference to article

The benefits of a general speed limit on German motorways are as follows: It will make motorways safer if people drive more sensibly. According to statistical data, a speed limit of this kind might lead to a drop in the number of road deaths and persons who are seriously injured. It would reduce CO$_2$ emissions by approximately three million tons – a nine per cent decline. Moreover, it reduces the large differences in the speeds of vehicles on highways, which means less congestion. main part: pro arguments

Automobile associations object to it, countering that CO$_2$ savings would only be very small. They claim that a general speed limit would have no noticeable effect with regard to congestion on motorways. Instead, they prefer traffic management facilities which make it possible to set flexible speed limits according to weather conditions, traffic flow and traffic density. contra arguments

The environmental lobby group VCD accuses the Federal Government of deliberately retaining from funding studies on road safety and speed limits to the advantage of the automobile industry. accusations of the VCD

Thank you,
Nils closing *(227 words)* name

---

* We have decided to capitalize "Black" and "White" to signal that they are not natural categories but social ones (for more background information on this topic see e.g. https://www.theatlantic.com/ideas/archive/2020/06/time-to-capitalize-blackand-white/613159/).

**Schwarz wird in unseren neueren Publikationen großgeschrieben (und *weiß* wird durch die Schriftlage, also kursiv oder normal, gekennzeichnet), um deutlich zu machen, dass es sich nicht um Farbbezeichnungen handelt, sondern um Begriffe, die beschreiben, ob Menschen von Rassismuserfahrungen betroffen sind oder nicht.

Prüfungsteil 1: Leseverstehen und Schreiben   (70 %)

Der Prüfungsteil 1 besteht aus zwei Aufgabenstellungen, von denen Sie eine zur Bearbeitung auswählen.

Aufgabenstellung 1.1 – Tasks

Themenschwerpunkte: *Ethnic and cultural diversity, Aims and ambitions*

1 Outline the information about the narrator's old school and her new school.   (30 %)

2 Analyze the way in which the narrator's state of mind is reflected in her use of language.   (30 %)

3 Choose <u>one</u> of the following tasks:

3.1 "[T]he teachers here just assume that the guys and girls standing around me have the world at their fingertips." (ll. 9–11)
Using the quotation and the excerpt as a starting point, assess to what extent one's aims and ambitions are shaped by one's background.   (40 %)

OR

3.2 Write an article for an online teen travel magazine, discussing the pros and cons of voluntourism, a common form of travelling which combines voluntary work and exploring a developing country.   (40 %)

Text (excerpt from the novel)

When Michael Met Mina
by Randa Abdel-Fattah

Note: *Mina, a refugee from Afghanistan, used to attend Auburn Grove Girls High in Australia. After receiving a scholarship in Year 11, she now attends Victoria College.*

1 We file into the school hall for a special assembly. The entire campus of Auburn Grove Girls High would fit inside this hall. Ms Ham […] announces that the year tens have put on a Global Citizen Photography Reflections Exhibition following their two-week trip to Ghana. […]

5 'I am so proud of our year ten students who have demonstrated a real commitment to understanding the responsibilities that come with their privileges. You are all this country's future leaders and that is both an immense privilege and a burden.'

As I listen to Ms Ham drone on and on about how Victoria College graduates will run the country one day, two thoughts dawn on me. The first is that all the teachers

10 here just assume that the guys and girls standing around me have the world at their fingertips. And the second is that despite wearing the same uniform as everybody else, I feel like an imposter. Like I'm in the wrong manufacturing plant, only seconds away from a tap on the shoulder and a gentle but firm, You belong in the people-who-will-be-led production line, not this one.

15 At Auburn Grove Girls High, when teachers stood up to address us in assembly, it was to urge us to study hard, stay focused, remain resilient, set goals, seek support. If there was a 'leader', she was the exception, not the norm.

Listening to Ms Ham, I wonder if things would be different if we spent thirteen years being told that we were born to lead, and that the only thing that would ever hold

20 us back would be a limited imagination.

I'm starting to realise that being born into this social world is a little like being born into clean air. You take it in as soon as you breathe, and pretty soon you don't even realise that while you can walk around with clear lungs, other people are wearing oxygen masks just to survive.

25 Mr Morello decides to hold our Society and Culture class in the Middle School Atrium so we can see the year ten photography exhibition.

The photos have been blown up and mounted on canvas. There are shots of Victoria College students posing with young children. Photos of Ghanaian kids staring into the camera lens. Or just sitting. Or standing.

30 Zoe and Clara are standing near us and I hear them gushing to each other about how beautiful the children are. 'Oh my God they're just gorgeous!'

Something about the whole exhibition unsettles me, but I'm struggling to put it into words, even to myself.

I stand in front of a photograph of a young Ghanaian kid. Barefoot, in a singlet and

35 faded oversized jeans, he has a solemn expression on his face. There's something almost rehearsed in his pose and demeanour. A year ten girl named Sandra is crouched down on her knees, one arm around him, grinning at the camera. The whole photograph feels staged, as if he's just playing out a role for her benefit, like some kind of third-

world mascot helping people from the first world find themselves. I don't know why
40 it disturbs me, because it's a good thing that they're helping these kids, isn't it? But
still, there's a queasy feeling in the pit of my stomach.

'These photos are so much better than the ones we took when we went to Botswana
for our trip,' Paula says, as we stop and look at a photo of a group of the year ten
students digging a veggie patch.
45 'It's all a bit too National Geographic for me,' I say.
'What do you mean?'
'Hard to explain,' I murmur.

There are some things so deeply sedimented that the slightest excavation and the
walls will start to fall in on themselves.
50 'Do all the year tens go on these trips?' I ask Paula.
'Yeah, pretty much most of them.'
'How much does it cost?'
'Hmm, several grand I think. I'm not sure exactly.'
We keep moving, and then there's Michael, standing in our path.
55 'They're good photos, hey?' he says cheerfully.
'Mina doesn't think so,' Paula says with a smile and shrug.
'Have you gone on one of these trips?' I ask him.
'Yeah, with Paula too, in year ten. We went to Botswana. It was amazing. We
trekked through the Kalahari Desert –'
60 'I liked it when we tracked rhinos in Khama Rhino Sanctuary,' Paula says excitedly.
'Yeah, that was brilliant. We fixed up rundown buildings and built a sports pitch
at an orphanage, too.'
'That's nice,' I tell them.
Michael gives me a quizzical look. 'What's wrong?'
65 I shrug. 'The world's one big wide adventure playground for some people, I guess.'
Paula and Michael both look at me but choose not to reply. […]   *(789 words)*

Abdel-Fattah, Randa. When Michael Met Mina. *Sydney: Pan Macmillan Australia, 2016, 109–112.*

Annotations
l. 45 National Geographic – official magazine of the National Geographic Society, one of the
       largest non-profit scientific and educational organizations in the world
l. 53 grand – $ 1000

Aufgabenstellung 1.2 – Tasks

Themenschwerpunkte: *Saving the planet, Aims and ambitions*

1   Outline students' activities aimed at doing something about climate
    change as described in the article.   (30 %)

2   Analyze how the article attracts the reader's attention. Focus on the
    devices the author uses and the picture published with the text.   (30 %)

3   Choose <u>one</u> of the following tasks:

3.1 "Today's kids […] are change makers. They are fearless public speakers.
    They are real-life Harry Potter heroes." (ll. 8–10)

    Discuss whether this statement is a realistic description of your
    generation.

OR

3.2 After speaking at Grattan Elementary School, Kristen Tam gives a
    speech at a demonstration supporting environmental legislation. Write
    her speech, using the Grattan Elementary School children's example as a
    starting point and commenting on actions students could take to put
    pressure on lawmakers.   (40 %)

Text (article)

Today's kids are working to save the planet
by Robyn Purchia

FloridaStock. Shutterstock

Concepts like climate change are not too complex or scary for children to understand.

1 Room 205 b at Grattan Elementary School in Ashbury Heights looks like the classrooms I sat in as a kid. The walls are painted a bright, happy blue and filled with drawings and posters. There's a respectable stack of Nancy Drew books in the back. Squirmy fourth and fifth graders sit on the carpet around a teacher who asks them what
5 actions they can take to be respectful and responsible.

"Stop buying from destructive companies like Amazon," one of the students shouts.

Today's kids are not like the kids I remember from my school days. They are change makers. They are fearless public speakers. They are real-life Harry Potter he-
10 roes. In San Francisco, and around the world, young people are organizing mass demonstrations, pushing ambitious legislation, like the Green New Deal, forward and urging candidates to make climate change a priority.

Simply put, today's kids are already shaping their future on this planet.

At Grattan, fourth and fifth graders helped create an Ecology and Climate Action
15 Resolution calling for community action on ecological health and climate change. The resolution was finalized during Grattan's first, schoolwide Eco Action Conference last week.

The events showcased student presentations on environmental topics, such as on plastic pollution, climate change, water issues, biodiversity and electric cars. The kids

20 talked about changes they should make, including avoiding yummy Nutella snacks because the product contains palm oil.

"Kids do their own research," Meredith Charpantier, a teacher at Grattan and one of the event organizers, told me. "This is a great opportunity for them to dig deep."

Students Cassady Allen, Lise Arnaud and Katelyn Evans received special praise
25 for their environmental efforts. After an overnight field trip at Marin Headlands NatureBridge Environmental Science program, the fifth-graders decided to launch a campaign to reduce waste at school. Their target is plastic "sporks," or a spoon-shaped utensil with tines at the tip, packaged in light-weight plastic baggies.

Allen, Arnaud and Evans raised $400 for new, reusable cutlery by selling smoo-
30 thies. Unfortunately, they haven't raised enough for the school to buy a new dishwasher. But the students are hopeful they can reach a solution with the school that will allow future students at Grattan to reduce plastic waste.

"If you work hard enough and aren't lazy then you can make a change," the soon-to-be middle school students told me. "Most kids don't think they can make a change
35 and then they grow up and think that as a grown up. We're only three and we're changing the whole school!"

Kristen Tam, a graduating senior at Lowell High School, spoke at the conference and encouraged more elementary students to become activists. Along with participating in climate change demonstrations, Tam also led the effort to institute a trial "Green
40 Menu" program at San Francisco's public middle and high schools next year. The program will highlight sustainable products and educate students about the environmental impact of their diets.

"If you're persistent and continue to talk to people and push for things they will get done," Tam advised the elementary school students. "The more kids go into middle
45 school already knowing about this the better."

Leaders around the world should pay attention to young people like Tam and the elementary students at Grattan. Companies must become more sustainable if they want consumers to buy their products in the future. Politicians must prioritize environmental policies if they want to stay in power. Last week, young people in Europe voted mem-
50 bers of the Green party into power in what is being dubbed, a "Green Wave."

Parents and educators should also take note. Children aren't too young to understand concepts like climate change, plastic pollution and dramatic drops in biodiversity. They aren't too scared and the problems aren't too complex. In fact, as the students at Grattan demonstrate, sometimes children understand the need to act more than
55 adults.

"They know now and they are wise now," Serena Unger, a parent of a kindergartener at Grattan and one of the organizers of the conference, told me. "Children use the planet just as adults use the planet and we need to include them in what we do."

(686 words)

Source: Purchia, Robyn. "Today's kids are working to save the planet."
San Francisco Examiner. June 4, 2019. Accessed Sept. 27, 2019.
https://www.sfexaminer.com/news-columnists/todays-kids-are-working-to-save-the- planet/.

Annotations

l. 1   Ashbury Heights – neighborhood in San Francisco
l. 3   Nancy Drew books – long-running popular series of detective stories
l. 11   Green New Deal – proposed US law that aims to address climate change and economic inequality, e. g. by promoting renewable energies and resource efficiency
l. 49   last week – reference to the May 2019 European Parliament election

Der Prüfungsteil 2 besteht aus zwei Aufgabenstellungen, von denen Sie eine zur Bearbeitung auswählen.

Aufgabenstellung 2.1 – Task

Themenschwerpunkte: *Aims and ambitions, Saving the planet*

Your Irish friend is considering a gap year and wants to know what Germans think about this issue.
Based on the article, write him/her an email, outlining the expectations and reservations involved.

Text (Auszug aus dem Artikel)

Mut zur Lücke!
Von Deike Uthenwoldt

1 *Ferne Länder sehen, bedrohte Tiere retten, Sprachen lernen: Ein Gap Year zwischen Abitur und Studium ist beliebt und oft nützlich für den weiteren Lebensweg. Manche Angebote allerdings sind völlig überteuert oder wenig sinnvoll für die Karriere.*

Die Lücke zwischen Abi und Studium, in der Familie Brößling ist sie Pflichtpro-
5 gramm. „Die Kinder kommen durch das G8-Abi sehr jung aus der Schule und haben angesichts des steigenden Rentenalters noch genug Zeit, etwas anderes zu machen, als gleich zum Studium zu rennen", erklärt Mutter Katja Brößling, warum ihre Kinder nach der Schule einen Freiwilligendienst antreten sollen. Die Betriebswirtin zeigt sich offen für die Zukunftspläne der Kinder, ob Ausbildung oder Studium. Was genau es
10 werden soll, dürfen sie selbst bestimmen – solange sie vorher ein Jahr lang bewiesen haben, dass sie auf eigenen Beinen stehen können. „Ich finde dieses Jahr unglaublich praktisch für die jungen Leute", sagt sie. „Sie können sich ausprobieren. Ohne den Druck, gleich wieder im ersten Semester eine Leistung abliefern zu müssen."
Brößlings Sohn ist gerade 18 geworden und wird ab September einen Bundesfrei-
15 willigendienst in der Seehundauffangstation in Norden-Norddeich absolvieren. Die Tochter hat noch ein Jahr bis zum Abi, sie will sich politisch engagieren, am liebsten in Frankreich, und fragt gerade bei Parteiorganisationen im Nachbarland an. Zwischen-durch hatte die 16-Jährige auch mal mit einer Auszeit in Neuseeland geliebäugelt, aber ihre Eltern hatten ziemlich schnell deutlich gemacht, dass das Jahr selbst finanziert
20 werden muss – und möglichst gesellschaftlich sinnvoll sein soll […].
Seehunde retten, abgeschieden mit anderen Freiwilligen zusammenwohnen oder möglichst viel von der Welt entdecken und sie hier und da ein wenig besser machen – für die unterschiedlichen Zielvorstellungen junger Schulabgänger gibt es inzwischen einen Begriff: das „Gap Year", ein Lückenjahr also. Aber mit Pause und Nichtstun hat

25 es wenig zu tun: „Es geht um die Phase zwischen zwei Lebensabschnitten, die eine
neue Erfahrung mit sich bringt, über eine längere Zeit andauert und häufig mit einem
Auslandsaufenthalt junger Menschen in Verbindung gebracht wird", sagt die Geogra-
phin Manuela Bauer. Die Wissenschaftlerin schließt gerade ihre Promotion über „Gap-
Year-Reisen" ab und hat typische „Gappers" befragt, wie sie sagt. Auszubildende nach
30 der Lehre, Studierende zwischen Bachelor- und Masterabschluss, Abiturienten.

„Die Schulabgänger sind die zahlenmäßig größte Gruppe", sagt Bauer. Schon die
Altersverteilung ihrer Erhebung macht es deutlich: 18,9 Jahre alt waren die Probanden
im Schnitt, als sie ihre Reise antraten. Um diese jungen Erwachsenen ohne Berufser-
fahrung oder Studienabschluss für sich zu gewinnen, sie mit Papieren wie Arbeitsvi-
35 sum und Krankenversicherung zu versorgen oder sie vor Ort zu betreuen, sei ein „Gap-
Year-Markt" entstanden, der regelrecht mit der Auszeit nach dem Schulabschluss
wirbt, so Bauer. […]

Aber gerade die Volunteer Tourismus-Angebote sind umstritten: „Es ist überhaupt
nicht hilfreich, wenn junge Menschen für drei Wochen nach Nepal gehen, um dort mal
40 eben ein wenig Entwicklungshilfe zu leisten", sagt die Berufsberaterin Birte Biebuyck.
Das gelte finanziell – von 1000 Euro, die ein Freiwilliger für seinen Auslandseinsatz
zahlt, kämen gerade mal 17 vor Ort an –, aber auch menschlich: „Kinderprojekte sind
beliebt, aber ständig wechselnde Bezugspersonen und zu wenig vorbereitete Freiwilli-
ge schaden", so die studierte Theologin. […]   *(498 Wörter)*

Aufgabenstellung 2.2 – Task

Themenschwerpunkte: *Saving the planet, Aims and ambitions*

You are taking part in an international school project on environmental protection.
In a blog entry for the project website, sum up the positions on how to tackle the plastic
problem as presented in the two opinion pieces.

Brauchen wir eine Plastiksteuer?

Text 1 (Auszug aus dem Artikel)

Sinnvoll regulierend
Von Friedhard Teuffel, „Der Tagesspiegel", Berlin

1 Im Kreislauf der Natur hat sich längst auch der Abfall seinen Platz gesichert. Eben
noch Verpackung oder Bestandteil von Textilien oder Kosmetik, landet Plastik in
mikroskopisch kleinen Teilchen über das Meer zurück auf dem Teller, zum Beispiel
im Edelsalz Fleur de Sel oder in Muscheln. Eine Plastiksteuer durch die Europäische
5 Union könnte da weit mehr sein als Klientelpolitik für Gourmets. Sie könnte sinnvoll
regulierend wirken.
  Große Probleme erfordern gemeinschaftliche Lösungen. Deshalb ist Plastik auf der
Ebene der EU richtig aufgehoben. Es geht dabei nicht darum, dem Plastik komplett
den Garaus zu machen, so lange es zu wenig Alternativen gibt, um zum Beispiel
10 Lebensmittel länger frisch zu halten, und der ökologische Fußabdruck besser ausfällt
als bei anderen Verpackungsmaterialien. Mit einer Plastiksteuer könnte die EU vielmehr den schlechtesten Plastikarten den Kampf ansagen, indem sie beispielsweise
Rohbenzin besteuert.
  Es gibt auch viele sinnlose Plastikverpackungen, zu viele, die leicht ersetzt werden
15 könnten. Auch die sollten erfasst werden von einer europaweiten Besteuerung. Eine
solche Plastiksteuer wird komplex sein. Sie wird Mühen kosten und Zeit, um sie wirklich detailliert auszuarbeiten. Sie wird das übliche EU-Regulierungs-Abwehrbollwerk
provozieren. Doch all der Plastikmüll, der an Land und im Wasser anfällt, ruft dazu
auf, jede mögliche Gegenmaßnahme einzusetzen. Also auch die einer Besteuerung. Sie
20 muss jedoch Bestandteil einer ganzen Plastikstrategie sein, die zugleich Anreize zur
Vermeidung setzt, der Verpackungsindustrie mehr Vorschriften macht und Forschung
für Alternativen fördert. So wird ein gut abbaubares Paket daraus. *(234 Wörter)*

*Quelle: Teuffel, F. (2018, 6. August). Sinnvoll regulierend. Das Parlament. Nr. 32–33. Zugriff am
7.12.2019 von http://www.das-parlament.de/2018/32_33/menschen_und_meinungen/565756-565756.*

Text 2 (Auszug aus dem Artikel)

Untaugliches Mittel
Von Martin Ferber, „Augsburger Allgemeine"

1 „Mit Steuern steuern!" In der politischen Debatte ist es ein beliebtes Argument, neue Steuern einzuführen oder bestehende Steuern zu erhöhen, um so die Bürger zu einer Änderung ihres Verhaltens zu zwingen. Der Staat als Erzieher der Nation nach dem Motto: Ist es nur teuer genug, lassen die Menschen es sein. Nun soll – so der Vorschlag
5 – eine Plastiksteuer die Meere retten und eine weitere Verschmutzung verhindern.

So ehrenwert das Ziel ist, so untauglich ist das Mittel. Schon der Grüne Punkt, den die Verbraucher für die stoffliche Wiederverwertung der Verpackungen zu bezahlen haben, hat nicht zu einer Verringerung des Müllaufkommens beigetragen. Im Gegenteil. Gerade erst hat das Umweltbundesamt von einer neuen Rekordmenge berichtet –
10 220,5 Kilo pro Kopf im Jahr, ein trauriger Europarekord. Auch eine Plastiksteuer wird daran nichts ändern. Die einzelne Verpackung wird nur um einige Cent teurer, das spürt der Verbraucher kaum. Das Geld wiederum landet im Säckel des Finanzministers, der sich über die Einnahme freut, aber kaum bereit ist, es für die Säuberung der Weltmeere zur Verfügung zu stellen. So wie die 1902 eingeführte Sektsteuer schon
15 lange nicht mehr der Finanzierung der kaiserlichen Kriegsflotte dient, aber noch immer eine verlässliche Einnahmequelle darstellt. Schlimmer noch, die Plastiksteuer könnte sogar kontraproduktiv wirken, weil die Verbraucher glauben, mit der Steuer etwas Gutes für die Umwelt getan zu haben.

Nein, die Plastiksteuer hilft nicht weiter. Nötig ist vielmehr ein Umdenken bei der
20 Industrie wie bei den Verbrauchern. Der beste Müll ist immer noch der, der erst gar nicht anfällt. Ganz ohne Steuer. *(252 Wörter)*

Quelle: Ferber, M. (2018, 6. August). Untaugliches Mittel. Das Parlament. Nr. 32–33. Zugriff am 7.12. 2019 von http://www.das-parlament.de/2018/32_33/menschen_und_meinungen/565752-565752.

Lösungsvorschläge

Aufgabenstellung 1.1

1   *Der Textausschnitt informiert über einige deutliche Unterschiede zwischen den beiden Schulen, welche die Erzählerin, Mina, besucht hat. Auffallend ist zunächst der Größenunterschied, das Victoria College ist riesig verglichen mit Minas alter Schule. Außerdem sind das neue College und die Eltern der Schülerinnen und Schüler finanziell gut aufgestellt. Die Kosten einer zweiwöchigen Freiwilligenarbeit in einem Entwicklungsland sowie eine aufwändige Dokumentation darüber können problemlos getragen werden. Weiterhin informiert der Ausschnitt über unterschiedliche Lehrmethoden und Lehrziele, die vom sozialen Hintergrund der Lernenden bestimmt werden. In Minas alter Schule ging es um den sozialen Aufstieg, der, wie die Lehrenden mahnten, nur über Arbeit, Fleiß und Konzentration erreicht werden kann. Ganz anders am Victoria College. Die Schülerinnen und Schüler gehören zur sozialen Oberschicht. Daher steht ihnen die Welt offen, und es versteht sich von selbst, dass sie für die Besetzung führender Positionen vorherbestimmt sind. Die Lehrenden bestärken die Schülerinnen und Schüler in diesem Selbstverständnis und Selbstbewusstsein.*

The excerpt informs the reader about the different sizes of the two schools. The narrator's new school, Victoria College, is much larger than her old one, Auburn Grove Girls High.

In addition, at Victoria College school and students are financially privileged. Every year the Year 10 students go on a trip to work as volunteers in the community of a developing country. After the stay they put together an exhibition of the pictures taken during the two weeks of their stay. The fact that the photos are put up on large canvas proves that the new school – and the parents – have enough money to afford this sort of display in addition to the cost of the trip.

Furthermore, the teaching methods and objectives are different. At Auburn Grove, school teachers put pressure on pupils to ensure their future success in society. At Victoria College, teachers assure students of their privileged position and destined future success. There is no need to urge the boys and girls to work hard, because they are bound to lead the country in the future.

2   *Die Ausstellung der Fotos, die den diesjährigen Freiwilligeneinsatz der Lernenden des Victoria College in einem Entwicklungsland dokumentieren, wecken in der Erzählerin Mina unterschiedliche Gefühle. Zum einen ist sie völlig verunsichert, weil ihr hier in diesem Ambiente bewusst wird, dass sie aus einer ganz anderen Welt kommt als ihre Mitschülerinnen und -schüler und eigentlich gar nicht hierher gehört. Zwar hat sie aufgrund ihrer guten Leistungen ein Stipendium für das reiche Victoria College erhalten, dennoch fühlt sie sich hier wie eine Hochstaplerin, die befürchten muss,*

sogleich entdeckt und des Platzes verwiesen zu werden. Zum anderen verdeutlichen ihr die Art der Aufnahmen und Kommentare ihrer Mitschülerinnen und -schüler zu den Fotos die Diskrepanz, die zwischen ihrer Weltsicht und der der Mitlernenden besteht. Zur Darstellung der eigenen Verunsicherung und der Unbedarftheit ihrer Mitschülerinnen und Mitschüler nutzt sie Vergleiche. Mina weiß, dass die Hilfe gut gemeint ist, doch ihr ist unwohl, weil alles nur inszeniert, gekünstelt und voyeuristisch wirkt. Mit der Wirklichkeit, der Not und dem Elend in der Dritten Welt haben die Bilder nichts zu tun. Die Äußerungen der Schüler*innen sind völlig oberflächlich und beweisen, dass ihr Einsatz ihnen keine neuen Erkenntnisse gebracht hat. Die ganze Aktion macht den Eindruck einer Vergnügungsfahrt, verbunden mit einem gelegentlichen Abenteuer. Minas Verunsicherung und ihre innere Abneigung gegen diese Art von Hilfe für Entwicklungsländer spiegelt sich in ihren sehr einsilbigen und allgemeinen Äußerungen wider. Sie weiß nicht, wie sie ihre zwiespältigen Gefühle in Worte fassen soll. Zudem möchte sie aus Höflichkeit ihre Kritik nicht direkt äußern. Erst am Schluss gibt sie preis, was sie über den jährlich wiederkehrenden Einsatz denkt. Sie greift die Gruppe aber nicht direkt an, sondern verweist lediglich auf andere – „some people".

The narrator, Mina, feels uneasy and insecure among her privileged fellow students at Victoria College. Coming from a different background, which is poorer, she compares herself to a trickster ("I feel like an imposter", l. 12) who has somehow managed to get there, but will soon be found out. The seemingly endless boring speech of Ms Ham, who keeps praising the students and reminding them of the brilliant future which lies ahead of them ("I listen to Ms Ham drone on and on", l. 8), adds to her feeling of estrangement. Mina becomes aware that students here live in a different world, taking their privileges for granted, while the most people in the world are confronted with the realities of life. She uses another comparison here, describing how students are unaware of their own privilege: "being born into this social world is a little like being born into clean air. You take it in as soon as you breathe, and pretty soon you don't even realise that while you can walk around with clear lungs, other people are wearing oxygen masks just to survive" (ll. 21–24).

The superficial and trivial comments of the students on the airbrushed and staged photos ("Oh my God they're just gorgeous!" l. 31) further prove the discrepancy between their view of the world and hers. While her schoolmates talk about the cuteness of the children and the quality of the photos on display, Mina is more concerned with the reality, poverty and misery of the children in the pictures. Still, despite the feeling of uneasiness, Mina cannot criticise the students' volunteering directly, as is mirrored in the rhetorical question "it's a good thing that they're helping these kids, isn't it?" (l. 40). She only voices her disapproval indirectly. In the dialogue she stays friendly and calm, although "there's a queasy feeling in the pit of [her] stomach" (l. 41), and she merely hints at what she is really thinking ("I murmur", l. 47). She expresses her objection ("a bit too National Geographic for me", l. 45) in a way that is too discrete for her classmates to understand. Similarly, she comments on the students' pride in their work as volunteers – and the "amazing" (l. 58) adventures in the desert – with the dry remark, "That's nice" (l. 63). Her only criticism that is expressed more openly comes at the end of the excerpt, with the still rather subtle sarcastic statement, "The world's one big wide adventure playground for some people, I guess," (l. 65), by which she insinuates that the students are going on this annual trip more for their own entertainment than out of real concern for the poor.

3.1 *In der Aufgabe geht es um die Frage, inwiefern die soziale Herkunft die Bestrebungen und Hoffnungen eines Menschen beeinflusst beziehungsweise formt. Stellen Sie zunächst, ausgehend vom in der Aufgabenstellung angegebenen Zitat und dem Textausschnitt, die Problematik dar. Die Schülerinnen und Schüler am Victoria College gehören aufgrund ihrer Herkunft und des Wohlstands ihrer Eltern automatisch zur Oberschicht und damit zu einer Elite, die einmal eine führende Rolle im Land spielen wird. Allgemein gesagt, gelten Herkunft, Wohlstand und Bildung als prägende Indikatoren für die gesellschaftliche Stellung beziehungsweise den gesellschaftlichen Erfolg. Die Lehrenden am College gehen davon aus, dass die Jugendlichen zur Oberschicht gehören und ohne weiteres Zutun in eine erfolgreiche Zukunft blicken können. Anders ist es für Mina, die Tochter einer afghanischen Flüchtlingsfamilie. Sie ist aufgrund ihrer bescheidenen Herkunft nicht von vornherein mit Privilegien ausgestattet. Um sich zu verbessern und ihre Lebensziele zu erreichen, muss sie sich sehr anstrengen. Der Ausschnitt zeigt auch, dass die soziale Herkunft die Sicht auf die Welt bestimmt. Die Freiwilligen des Victoria College kennen die Realität eines Entwicklungslands nur oberflächlich als Touristen und Touristinnen, während Mina aufgrund eigener Erfahrung einen wesentlich tieferen Einblick hat. Nachdem Sie die privilegierte Situation der Lernenden aus dem Textausschnitt dargestellt haben, können Sie in einem zweiten Schritt anführen, mit welchen Schwierigkeiten Kinder aus weniger betuchten Familien zu kämpfen haben, um ihre Situation zu verbessern und in der Gesellschaft aufzusteigen, damit sie eigene Wünsche erfüllen und Ziele erreichen können. Sozialer Aufstieg ist nicht selbstverständlich, und nicht in allen Ländern steht Menschen aus ärmeren Verhältnissen die Welt offen. Runden Sie Ihre Bewertung des Zitats durch einen geeigneten Schluss ab. Möglich wäre beispielsweise eine Forderung an die Politik und Gesellschaft, deren Aufgabe es ist, die soziale Mobilität zu fördern.*

The characters in the excerpt from the novel *When Michael Met Mina* belong to two different social classes. The students at Victoria College come from rich families, whereas Mina, the daughter of migrant parents, grew up in poorer circumstances. These two different backgrounds shape the characters' identity and their aims and ambitions. As children of well-off parents and equipped with a good education, the Victoria College students have all the necessary means to succeed in life. The teachers keep reminding them constantly that they belong to the ruling class, that they will occupy leading positions in business and politics and that they "have the world at their fingertips" (ll. 11/12). The students are not yet really aware that they are an elite group with their future laid out for them. They take their advantages for granted.

Mina is the daughter of immigrants parents and therefore less privileged. People from poorer backgrounds have much greater difficulty in accomplishing their aims. She was not born "with a silver spoon in her mouth" and to climb socially she had to show effort and initiative. She only won a scholarship to Victoria College because she was intelligent, and exerted herself. The fact that she seems to be the only student from her old high school proves that Mina is the exception, and she feels like an outsider, even an impostor, who does not really belong to this class of society. Mina knows she will not be independent or able to choose freely in life, as she is not one of the leaders but one of "the people-who-will-be-led" (ll. 13/14).

For children from richer homes, the world is their oyster, and they are free to take advantage of all the opportunities on offer to fulfil their aims and ambitions in life. Children from poorer families find themselves in a different position when they think about their future lives. They have to overcome numerous obstacles before they can achieve what they hope for. To start with, their parents might not be able to afford proper schooling for their offspring. Many children have to work to help feed the family. As a consequence, lack of education will limit their chances of advancement, which means they will have difficulties entering training and finding work. Sociologists and psychologists confirm that children's early formative years and primary school education provide a foundation for the rest of their lives. Although there are examples of celebrities who have improved themselves and climbed socially, such as Oprah Winfrey, Demi Moore and Arnold Schwarzenegger, they do not represent the majority. Young people from humble backgrounds have to try harder. Many are pushed by their parents, who know how important a good education is for future success. They urge their children to "work twice as hard" in order to have a good start for realising their ambitions.

People's social circumstances play a crucial role in influencing their hopes and aspirations. To achieve equal opportunities for all, the gap between rich and poor needs to be bridged. Children from disadvantaged groups, such as immigrants, refugees or ethnic minorities, must particularly have the chance to progress according to their abilities. To this end, governments must provide a decent living standard and access to education for children from all backgrounds. Social mobility and equality are fundamental prerequisites for an open society. If the rift between the haves and the have-nots keeps widening and people are denied equal opportunities, social tensions are bound to erupt.

3.2 *Bei dieser Aufgabe sollen Sie die Vor- und Nachteile des sogenannten „Voluntourismus", d. h., der Kombination von Freiwilligendienst* (volunteering) *mit einer Reise* (tourism) *darstellen. Bei einem Artikel bietet sich an, Ihre Lösung wie einen Aufsatz (Einleitung – Hauptteil – Schluss) zu strukturieren und eine Überschrift zu ergänzen.In einer kurzen Einleitung könnten Sie den Bezug zu Ihren Adressaten* (teens) *herstellen, indem Sie auf die Situation von Schulabgängerinnen und -abgängern hinweisen, die zuweilen nicht recht wissen, was sie jetzt anfangen sollen (Studium, Lehre, freiwilliges ökologisches Jahr o. Ä.). Den Hauptteil sollten Sie nach Vor- und Nachteilen für die Reisenden und für das Land gliedern. Es mag zunächst so aussehen, als ob ein freiwilliger Einsatz in einem Entwicklungsland völlig unproblematisch und begrüßenswert sei, doch zeigen sich bei näherer Betrachtung auch einige Nachteile sowohl für die Person, die den Freiwilligendienst antreten möchte, als auch das Land, in das die Reise geht. Hier könnten Sie Fragen nachgehen, wie z. B.: Was bringt den Reisenden der Einsatz (neue Erfahrungen, Arbeiten im Team) und was bringt er dem Entwicklungsland (Unterstützung im Gesundheitswesen, Verbesserung der Lebensverhältnisse, Kampf gegen Armut und Hunger)? Ist ein Kurzeinsatz wirklich eine Hilfe? Stören die Reisenden die Situation, etwa den Arbeitsmarkt im Land? Ist Hilfe willkommen? Da Sie für ein Reisemagazin für junge Leute schreiben, könnten Sie ab und zu auch die direkte Anrede der Leserschaft („you") wählen.*

Not much of a help

Every year school-leavers often don't really know what they would like to do after school: study at university, start an apprenticeship or look for a work placement. For those who want to take a break from learning and travel the world, 'voluntourism' (volunteering in the countries you visit while travelling) would seem the ideal alternative, as you can help people in poorer countries and experience a different culture at the same time. However, voluntourism is not as perfect as it seems, and has its pros and cons.

Voluntourism offers several personal rewards. When you travel to a developing country and work there, you are confronted with a different society and culture. This experience might help you to learn about the world and broaden your horizons. In addition, when you work together with others, you can improve your teamwork skills and perhaps gain professional orientation, which means you could find out what you want to do or learn after you have finished volunteering.

Voluntourism also has positive effects on developing countries. Volunteers who work as nurses, for example, may improve medical treatment and help raise standards of hygiene in poorer countries. While volunteers work without pay, they still provide the manpower to build houses, work on fields or build clean water wells. In this way, they contribute to fighting poverty and improving poorer people's standard of living.

On the other hand, there are negative sides to voluntourism. On a personal level, it can be costly because you have to pay for your airfare, lodging and other expenses. In addition, volunteers are often inexperienced and do not have enough knowledge to be of much help. Furthermore, locals may complain that volunteers take away jobs from people in the country and thus increase unemployment. Another negative point is that developing countries may become too dependent on volunteers for skills and might rely on help from outside instead of training and empowering their own workforce. The most recent criticism concerns the fact that volunteers only provide help temporarily. This can be especially dangerous and detrimental when helpers in orphanages form a close relationship with children and leave them again after only a short time, for example. This disruption can create problems in children's emotional and psychological development.

In a nutshell, voluntourism is not as unproblematic as it seems at first sight. Although the motive of volunteers, especially young people, to help others in need is certainly unselfish, critics argue that it might be better and more helpful if people donated the money they intended to spend on their volunteering trip. Even more importantly, assistance for developing countries should not be relegated to private initiatives. Instead, governments of richer countries should allocate more funds to provide assistance, such as sending more doctors and skilled workers into deprived areas, for instance.

Aufgabenstellung 1.2

1 *Da in der Aufgabenstellung nicht präzise gesagt wird, ob nur die Aktivitäten der Schülerinnen und Schüler an der Grattan Elementary School und an der Lowell High School zusammengefasst werden sollen oder ob alle im Text erwähnten Initiativen von Schülerinnen und Schülern gemeint sind, ist es ratsam, alle im Text genannten Aktivitäten einzubeziehen. Der Operator „Outline" erfordert, dass nur die wichtigsten Aspekte erwähnt werden; man kann diese z. B. in „politische Aktivitäten", „Information und Aufklärung" und „konkrete Veränderungen" gruppieren.*

The students described in the article were active in various ways to help the environment. First of all, they tried to change something on a political level by organising demonstrations, pushing legislation or motivating their political candidates to focus their attention on climate change, for example. At Grattan Elementary School they created a resolution calling for community action and organised a schoolwide Eco Action Conference. Here, political activism was accompanied by a campaign to raise awareness about environmental issues with presentations about various environmental topics that also included specific advice for students to avoid palm oil products or to become activists too, for example. One senior student initiated a trial programme called "Green Menu", which informs students at public middle and high schools in San Francisco about the environmental impact of their diet. Some students effected practical changes by raising money to buy reusable cutlery to replace the disposable plastic products at their school.

2 *Hier muss einerseits der Artikel nach rhetorischen und stilistischen Mitteln abgesucht werden, die die Aufmerksamkeit der Leser*innen wecken, andererseits das Bild analysiert werden. In diesem Artikel findet man Beispiele, einen Vergleich, einen Gegensatz, eine Klimax sowie Zitate und Anaphern. Wichtig ist neben der Auflistung der rhetorischen Mittel jeweils ihre konkrete Funktion im Text zu erklären.*
Bei der Bildanalyse ist relativ offenkundig, dass die Eisbären auf den Eisschollen den Klimawandel symbolisieren. Inwiefern aber ist das Bild mit seiner Bildunterschrift und der Hauptaussage des Textes (siehe Überschrift) verknüpft? Dies gilt es zu erklären.

In the picture you can see ice floes floating on the sea with two polar bears on one of them. The cub is following its mother. The caption says that "climate change is not too complex or scary for children". The picture symbolises climate change and invites the reader to draw a comparison between the little polar bear, which has to find its way in a changing environment, and children, who also have to find their own way through life. Just as the cub has no protection against global warming, the children cannot avoid the topic of climate change either, which is why the author suggests that it is not too complex for them because it is the reality that they live in.

The author uses comparison and contrast to show that even though the interior of an elementary classroom has not changed much in the last decades ("Room 205 b […] looks like the classrooms I sat in as a kid," ll. 1/2), the students have ("Today's kids are not like the kids I remember from my school days," l. 8). Using the words "They are" (ll. 8/9) as an anaphoric structure, the author highlights how these children are different from children back then. She characterises them with a climax and calls them "change makers", "fearless public speakers" and "real-life […] heroes" (ll. 9/10). She provides the reader with specific examples, mentions names (cf. ll. 24 and 37) and gives details of the various initiatives started by young people to protect the environment to illustrate the fact that children can make a difference. Additionally, she includes powerful quotes from children (cf. ll. 34–36, 43/44) and teachers (cf. ll. 56, 57/58) that suggest that children can indeed shape their environment and initiate real change.

3.1 *Der Operator „discuss" bedeutet, dass sowohl Argumente präsentiert werden müssen, die die These untermauern, als auch Gegenargumente. Am Ende soll eine Schlussfolgerung gezogen werden. Im Kern geht es um drei Aspekte. Bringt die heutige Generation Veränderungen hervor? Sind die jungen Menschen von heute angstfreie Redner und Rednerinnen? Und sind sie echte Heldinnen und Helden?*

It sounds very flattering when Robyn Purchia describes my generation as "change makers", "fearless public speakers" and "real-life Harry Potter heroes". Is this a correct assessment of today's youth or is the author's admiration for our generation maybe exaggerated? In the following, I will review whether these labels are justified and fit my generation or not.

In my opinion, young people are always change makers compared to their parents. Adults have settled and they are often afraid of change because they think their life could deteriorate instead of improve. Teenagers, however, are life's change agents. Their role is to question and challenge their parents' and grandparents' beliefs and convictions. It is not surprising that parents and grandparents often vote for established parties, whereas teenagers would vote for political renewal and change. So the question is not whether young generations are change makers but whether this generation is more of a change maker than our parents' generation was when they were our age. In the '90s, young people had better prospects for the future and felt safer. In contrast to that, my generation is under threat. In the last few years we have experienced a global pandemic that was quite unexpected. While my parents' generation could still ignore environmental issues, it has now become quite obvious that we need really drastic measures to turn the tide. So I think Robyn Purchia is right that this generation is more of a change maker – not because it is more audacious but because it has to be.

Are the teenagers of my generation fearless public speakers as well? My first impulse would be to doubt that. In every classroom you can find shy people and people that love to be seen and heard. The latter are usually the ones that speak up. However, even though we might not all be fearless public speakers, we are probably more used to having an audience. While our parents consumed modern media by watching TV, playing computer games and reading online blogs, my generation is producing content, be it on YouTube, Instagram or Snapchat, to name just a few of the apps that are based on people presenting themselves in front of others. We grew up with an audience, which is why we are probably actually less afraid of the public than our parents. Does that make us "real-life Harry Potter heroes"? When you elevate the teenagers of a whole generation to "heroes", you are most certainly misinterpreting reality. Generalisations of that kind are rarely true. We might, however, conclude that our generation has to fight climate change because our parents' generation has not succeeded yet. This, then, can be compared to Harry Potter, who has to fight evil because Lord Voldemort is still there and no one has yet been able to defeat him.

3.2 *Bei der Rede schlüpfen Sie in die Rolle von Kristen Tam. Im Artikel wird berichtet, dass sie Demonstrationen beigewohnt und auf einer Konferenz gesprochen hat und die Grundschülerinnen und Grundschüler davon überzeugt hat, selbst aktiv zu werden. Auch bei der Einführung eines Modellversuchs für ein „Green Menu" war sie federführend beteiligt. Sie sprechen also aus der Perspektive einer Umweltaktivistin auf einer Demonstration. Dabei sollen Sie ausgehend von den Aktivitäten der Grundschülerinnen und Grundschüler Vorschläge machen, wie Schüler*innen auf Politiker und die Gesetzgebung Einfluss nehmen können.*

Dear Students,

I am glad to see so many of you on the streets today fighting for environmental legislation. When I see all of you out here, it is not hard for me to believe that we can make a difference. Sometimes it seems as if what one person does has little impact on our environment, but together we can change the world. One drop of water can hardly cool off the streets on a summer's day but a heavy rain can make that difference and change the temperature. Let's be that rain.

I realized that last week at Grattan Elementary School, where I was invited to their schoolwide Eco Action Conference. Young children not only gathered information on complicated topics like plastic pollution, climate change, water issues, biodiversity and electric cars by themselves, they also gained knowledge they could use in practice about palm oil and which products to avoid. The additional aim of the conference was to create an Ecology and Climate Action Resolution calling for community action on ecological health and climate change. These kids gathered information. These kids figured out what to change about their personal shopping habits. These kids found a way to put pressure on lawmakers with their resolution.

In the same way that these kids managed to make a difference, you can too.

You can influence your lawmakers too. But how can you proceed when you want to initiate change not only in your family and your school but on a wider scale as well?

First of all: get media coverage. Lawmakers keep a close eye on what catches the media's attention. If you get coverage of your initiative in the newspapers or online and maybe get mentioned on the radio, you can be sure that sooner or later lawmakers will also hear about you.

Contact your congressman or congresswoman. Write e-mails and letters describing your initiative. The more e-mails they get about a certain topic, the more likely it is that they or their staff will listen to you.

Get other people involved as well. If your school starts an initiative to help the environment, it doesn't have to be limited to the school. Collect signatures for your initiative so that politicians realize that the topic is widely supported.

If you then still feel like politicians don't listen to what young people say, go on strike. The Fridays for Future movement has shown that if children show civil disobedience, politicians suddenly start to listen. If you refuse to go to school and protest instead, you will get media coverage and attention from lawmakers. Tell them what needs to be done and spread your message for the environment.

Thank you for your attention!

Prüfungsteil 2: Sprachmittlung

Aufgabenstellung 2.1

In einer E-Mail an eine Freundin oder einen Freund fassen Sie die wichtigsten Aspekte des Textes zusammen. Führen Sie in einer kurzen Einleitung zum Thema hin, indem Sie auf die in der Aufgabenstellung dargestellte Situation eingehen. Im Hauptteil sollten Sie auf die Erwartungen (Reisen, Sprachen lernen, gut für Lebenslauf, eigenständig werden, Nutzen für die Allgemeinheit, Orientierung) und mögliche problematische Aspekte (Kosten, nicht immer hilfreich für Lebenslauf, fehlender Nutzen bzw. Probleme für das Zielland) eingehen.

Hi Dave,

Thanks a lot for your last email. You wrote that you were thinking of taking a gap year and I think that's a brilliant idea. I've just read an interesting article on that topic called "Mut zur Lücke" (courage to have a gap).

A gap year abroad can be very important for young people because they can gain new experience, try out new things, travel the world and become more independent because they have to stand on their own two feet. It can also provide an orientation for their future career and help them learn new languages.

As a volunteer you can work in development aid projects, support environmental organisations or work for political causes. You can really make a difference.

But you will also need a work permit, health insurance and a visa. There are lots of associations that organise gap years, but you have to be careful because some of them just want to make a profit. In some cases it's just kind of tourism, because for every € 1,000 paid by the volunteers, on average only 17 reach the country they visit. Other projects are quite controversial, like working with children, for example, which is quite popular with volunteers. Children need long-term attachment figures and when volunteers leave after a relatively short period of time, it's more likely to cause damage to the children than to help them.

I hope you find this information useful.
Let me know what you decide.

I'm looking forward to your reply,
Sahra

Aufgabenstellung 2.2

Suchen Sie für Ihren Blogeintrag eine passende Überschrift, die auf die Problematik „Plastiksteuer – Ja oder Nein" hinweist und möglichst zum weiteren Lesen motiviert. Nach einer kurzen Einleitung stellen Sie dann in zwei Abschnitten die Argumente der Verfasser für bzw. gegen eine derartige Steuer dar. Eine eigene Stellungnahme ist nicht erforderlich. Mögliche Titel wären z. B. "Do we need a tax on plastic?", "Will a tax free us from plastic pollution?" oder "To tax or not to tax – the solution to plastic pollution?"

Do we need a tax on plastic?

The amount of plastic being produced is constantly rising. To stem the plastic deluge the introduction of a special tax on plastic has been suggested. However, opinions are divided on the effectiveness of such a measure.

Supporters of a plastic tax argue that the only way to reduce the amount of plastic is by making it more expensive. Plastic was first used for packaging or producing textiles and cosmetics, but microplastics have now entered our food chain. The problem has achieved such a dimension that only a common effort by all EU member countries will help to tackle the issue. What is needed is a tax on plastic. The tax should primarily be levied on the worst type of plastic but also on unnecessary plastic packaging. This tax will, of course, be met with the usual opposition, but it is absolutely essential to reduce plastic waste on land and in the sea. As part of a new strategy, taxing plastic will create an incentive to avoid using plastic packaging altogether and encourage the research into biodegradable materials.

Opponents of a plastic tax maintain that the introduction of such a tax would be a completely unsuitable measure for stemming the plastic deluge. You cannot change people's behaviour with a tax. There are enough examples which prove that taxation does not solve a problem. The German system *Grüner Punkt*, for example, which was meant to help reduce waste and encourage recycling, was a failure. Consumers just do not care if the price of a product goes up by merely a few cents. In addition, there is no guarantee that the money raised through taxation will be used to eliminate marine plastic pollution. Instead of making plastic more expensive, producers must develop more biodegradable products and consumers must change their habits to reduce the amount of waste altogether.

Prüfungsteil 1: Leseverstehen und Schreiben (70 %)

Der Prüfungsteil 1 besteht aus zwei Aufgabenstellungen, von denen Sie eine zur Bearbeitung auswählen.

Aufgabenstellung 1.1 – Tasks

Themenschwerpunkte: *Aims and ambitions; Ethnic and cultural diversity*

1 Outline the biographical information given on the author and his parents. (30 %)

2 Analyze how Choudhury's attitude towards the traditional view of American immigration is conveyed. (30 %)

3 Choose <u>one</u> of the following tasks:

3.1 Assess to what extent the cartoon reflects what Choudhury and his family have experienced in the US. (40 %)

" THE TROUBLE WITH A MELTING POT IS THAT SOMEBODY ALWAYS GETS BURNED. "

Dan Rosandich/cartoonstock

OR

3.2 You are participating in an international school project on identity. Write an article for the project website in which you discuss the importance of place in shaping one's identity. (40 %)

Text (excerpt from the novel)

The Epic City
by Kushanava Choudhury

Note: *This is an excerpt from the introductory chapter of 'The Epic City', Choudhury's literary portrait of Calcutta, the city of his birth, from where his family moved to the United States of America.*

1 Of all the people who came to Ellis Island in the first decades of the twentieth century, more than half went back. They never told us that on our seventh-grade class trip.

The American immigrant myth says that migration is a reset button. The New World offers deliverance from the past, liberation from the Old World's limited hori-
5 zons. The myth states: 'The past is gone. The future awaits. Start over.'

It never really works like that. That was the story no one ever told about America. The past is never left behind. It haunts every world you live in. Sometimes it drags you back.

By the time I visited Ellis Island on that class trip, I had already migrated halfway
10 around the world four times, flipping back and forth between continents like a dual-voltage appliance. My parents were Indian scientists, torn between nation and voca-tion. Twice they moved to America, twice they moved back. They were unwilling to leave their country and they were unable to stay. When he was around forty, my father quit his cushy job at a government research institute in Calcutta. He wanted one more
15 chance, he said […].

So, when I was almost twelve, my parents and I moved to Highland Park, New Jersey.

Our move carried no Emma Lazarus cadences. We certainly had not arrived tem-pest-tossed, beating at the golden door. Our coming was equivocal, always tied to re-
20 turn. Living in New Jersey, we hardly saw ourselves as immigrants. My parents expec-ted to go back to India, like many of their Bengali friends, someday, eventually. On Saturday nights, they gathered at each other's homes, ate fourteen-course meals brim-ming with various types of fish and meat, and derailed each other's sentences in loco-motive Bengali, their conversations full of memories of Calcutta. Return, the duty of
25 return and the dream of return, were spoken of endlessly while eating platefuls of goat curry and hilsa fish. Few, of course, actually went back. There were too many good reasons not to. Nationalism and nostalgia did not pay the bills, raise children or ad-vance careers. And yet that dream of a return to the great metropolis cocooned them like a protective blanket from the alien world all around.

30 As for me – my friends, my neighbourhood, my Calcutta life was gone. In New Jersey, I was in seventh grade in a public school that had almost no Indian students. Cocooning was not an option. I had to fit in fast. I wasn't assimilating as much as passing. So much of what went on inside my head was from another place. I had happy childhood memories of mid-morning cricket matches during summer vacations, of
35 games played in gullies, rooftops, courtyards and streets. When I moved, it was the streets of the city as much as my childhood that I left behind.

We had not had an easy few years in America. The man who had offered the job to my father had made promises he did not keep, and so my father was forced to find other work, work he grew to despise. From time to time, there would be talk of another move, to Georgia, to Colorado, and I would pull down the posters in my room and prepare. We stayed put, the three of us adrift in the treacherous shoals of the lower middle classes, a world of chronic car trouble and clothes from K-Mart. In the fall of my senior year, a piece of good news finally came to our two-bedroom apartment. I had been accepted early to Princeton University.

Every immigrant who has lugged worthless foreign degrees through customs knows that where you go to college [...] determines your lot in life. When the acceptance letter from Princeton arrived, my parents acted as if someone had come to our door with balloons and a giant cardboard cheque. It was their happiest day in America. But it wasn't mine.

It is probably universally true that education drives a wedge between us and our hometowns, our families, our earlier selves. But for the immigrant the gap is greater, that divergence in mentality more extreme. My trajectory was taking me farther afield, to Princeton, while a part of me was elsewhere, in another country, in another city. Through all my sojourns I had carried memories on my back like Huien Tsang's chair, until at seventeen, I felt hunched over nostalgia like a middle-aged man. When the Princeton letter arrived, I had what my friend Ben called a 'premature midlife crisis'.

At night, I couldn't sleep. By day I sleepwalked through classes. Each evening, while my friends assembled at Dunkin' Donuts, complained about how there was nothing to do in our little town and roared together into the night on long aimless drives, while they enjoyed the languor of spring and that sweet American affliction called senioritis, I stayed home and stewed. In my mind, I hatched a plan. I would go back.

India lives in its villages, Mahatma Gandhi had said. So, even though I was a city boy who had never spent a night in an Indian village, I wrote letters back home to arrange to teach in a village school. Instead of Princeton, I would take a year off and head to rural Bengal, I told my parents. But in our two-bedroom apartment full of shared immigrant striving, such a detour was out of the question.

Instead I just drove. The black night, the shimmering yellow lines on inviting ribbons of asphalt, the radio jammed loud. Enveloped by night and noise, the mind gave way to a deeper calling. Just drive. It was the mantra of our Jersey youth, an exhortation, a command, an ideology, something hardwired in us as teenage boys. Night after night I took my parents' Toyota and just drove, without destination, without purpose, to escape. [...]

After graduating from college, while friends set up their apartments in New York, Boston, and Los Angeles, I headed to Calcutta, to join the *Statesman*. [...] *(997 words)*

Source: Choudhury, Kushanava. "The Epic City. The World on the Streets of Calcutta." London: Bloomsbury, 2017, xi–xvi.

Annotations

l. 18   Emma Lazarus – 1849–1887, author of "The New Colossus", a poem engraved on the base of the Statue of Liberty, which ends with the following verses:
        Send these, the homeless, tempest-tossed to me:
        I lift my lamp beside the golden door.

l. 42   K-Mart – inexpensive department store chain in the USA

l. 44   Princeton University – prestigious university in New Jersey, USA

l. 52   trajectory – *here:* career path

l. 54   Huien Tsang – Chinese Buddhist monk and scholar, travelled throughout India in ancient times

l. 61   senioritis – *colloquial:* decreased motivation to study displayed by students during their last year at school

l. 73   college – *here:* Princeton University

l. 74   *The Statesman* – an influential Indian English-language daily newspaper founded in 1875

Aufgabenstellung 1.2 – Tasks

Themenschwerpunkte: *Saving the planet; The impact of the media on society; Aims and ambitions*

1   Outline Damon Gameau's reasons for making the film *2040*.   (30 %)

2   Analyze the means used in the article (Text A) and the film poster *2040* (Text B) to present the film's central ideas.   (30 %)

3   Choose <u>one</u> of the following tasks:

3.1   "It is hard not to look at the inspirational Greta Thunberg and all the student climate strikers today [...] and not feel that we're in the middle of another historical moment." (Text A, ll. 60–63)

    Using the quote as a starting point, comment on the role young people play in the environmental movement.   (40 %)

OR

3.2   Write a speech for an international youth conference called *Sustainable Future*. In your speech, assess how film projects like *2040* help face ecological challenges.   (40 %)

LK 2021-4

Text A (excerpt from the article)

A vision of 2040: everything we need for a sustainable world already exists
by Damon Gameau

1 [...] When my daughter was two years old, I found myself struggling to finish any article relating to the dire state of our environment. I would get halfway through the piece, then disengage and move on to something else. I assumed I wasn't the only parent to feel this way.

5 Curious to understand why I seemed incapable of persisting, I reached out to the environmental psychologist Renee Lertzman. She explained that when we receive information charged with fear, dread or anxiety, the limbic system in our brain can be activated, which can override the prefrontal cortex, an area of the brain associated with creative thinking and problem solving. These days our news feeds are filled with
10 images and stories of a bleak future. This is what we bombard our consciousness with, the images we expose our children to and they may also be why many of us feel paralysed when it comes to taking action on solutions to save our planet.

The diagnosis and acceptance of our problems is crucial but – much like when visiting a doctor – along with wanting a clear, detailed diagnosis, we also want to know
15 what we can do to improve or even cure our condition. This is what I wanted to offer up to my now five-year-old daughter. A story that focuses on the solutions to our environmental dilemmas and reveals a different version of the future. Because as the neurologist Viktor Frankl explained in his Auschwitz memoir, *Man's Search for Meaning*, if hope or faith in a better future becomes absent, the human spirit rapidly
20 deteriorates.

Over the last three years I've been making a film called *2040*. It's a visual letter to my daughter showing her what the world could look like that year if we put into practice some of the best solutions that exist today. I call it an exercise in "fact-based dreaming", as everything I show her in the future has to already exist today.

25 In three years of research and interviews, what emerged were solutions that improve health, income inequality, security and communities with the bonus of drastically reducing emissions and regenerating ecosystems. These solutions include decentralised solar micro-grids in remote villages that allow the buying and selling of energy between homes and keep money in the local economy. They include regene-
30 rative agriculture practices which take carbon from the atmosphere and return it to the soil with the cascading benefits of water retention and nutrient-dense food. And also the turbocharged sequestering power of seaweed, which can grow up to half a metre a day while restoring marine habitats and providing communities with food, fibre, fertilisers and biofuels.

35 But perhaps the most poignant solution I came across was the wide-reaching impact the education and empowerment of girls and women would have.

It is clear we have everything we need right now to create a better 2040.
[...]

A friend rang me on the morning the UN released its global assessment report
40 which found that 1 million species now face extinction due to our activities. His 12-

year-old son was in tears at the breakfast table, asking what could be done – and my
friend wanted to know what to say to him.

My first response was to tell his son that it is OK to feel very upset and important
to express those feelings – perhaps not enough of us do. But it was also important to
45 let him know that there are millions, likely billions, of people who care deeply about
his future and are becoming galvanised to invent, share and implement the solutions to
this crisis.

They are the "hope in the dark" that Rebecca Solnit writes about in her book of the
same title. The flurry of inspirational activity that is taking place right now in the
50 shadows, largely unreported. The world is facing its shadow in a variety of ways – and
we can remind ourselves, and our children, that a shadow cannot exist without a source
of light always being present.

The Canadian philosopher Marshall McLuhan described the way we move forward
in society as being like driving a motor car using only the rearview mirror. We use our
55 past experiences to inform us. It is here that we can also find legitimate hope for future
generations.

Just decades before the abolitionists achieved their goal, they were labelled "utopian" and mocked for imagining the economy could survive without slaves. The suffragettes were repeatedly derided for taking to the streets: "Sensible and responsible
60 women do not want to vote," said the former US president Grover Cleveland. It is hard
not to look at the inspirational Greta Thunberg and all the student climate strikers
today, plus the impacts of Extinction Rebellion in the UK, and not feel that we're in
the middle of another historical moment.

I made this film for my daughter and for her generation. I made it for parents and
65 for anyone feeling overwhelmed or losing hope. It offers up a reframing of our ecological predicament as an opportunity to draw on our ingenuity and to rise to the challenge with creativity and empathy. It is a call to all to share our visions and dreams of
a better world. If we don't, we are likely to become a part of someone else's vision.

(874 words)

*Gameau, Damon. "A vision of 2040: everything we need for a sustainable world already
exists." The Guardian. May 20, 2019. Accessed Jan. 7, 2020.
https://www.theguardian.com/environment/2019/may/21/determination-and-passion-how-these-
renewable-energy-resources-can-save-our-planet,*
Copyright Guardian News & Media Ltd 2021

Annotations
l. 32   to sequester – *here:* to absorb / bind carbon dioxide
l. 46   to galvanise – *here:* to stimulate, to activate
l. 57   abolitionist – person who wants to stop / abolish slavery
ll. 58 / 59 suffragette – woman who fights for women's right to vote
l. 62   Extinction Rebellion – global environmental movement

Text B (Film Poster)

Der Prüfungsteil 2 besteht aus zwei Aufgabenstellungen, von denen Sie eine zur Bearbeitung auswählen.

Aufgabenstellung 2.1 – Task

Themenschwerpunkte: *Aims and ambitions*

As an intern at the Society for Computer Science you have been asked to contribute a blog entry to the society's website.

Write a blog entry in which you sum up the information on Richard Socher's career and his assessment of Europe's technological competitiveness in the field of artificial intelligence (AI).

Text (Auszug aus dem Interview)

Die Uhr tickt
Von Steffan Heuer

1   *brand eins: Herr Socher, Sie arbeiten als Chefwissenschaftler für den Unternehmens-*
    software-Anbieter Salesforce im Silicon Valley. Ihr Weg von Leipzig über Saarbrücken
    nach Kalifornien ist ein Beispiel für die Abwanderung von Talenten. Warum gab es
    für einen Hoffnungsträger auf dem Gebiet der künstlichen Intelligenz (KI) wie Sie kei-
5   *nen Platz in Deutschland?*
    Richard Socher: Das liegt an meinen Forschungsinteressen. Ich habe mir die besten
    Informatik-Studiengänge der Welt angesehen und verglichen, wo die meistzitierten
    Aufsätze zum Thema Sprachverarbeitung entstanden sind. Leider waren die klügsten
    Köpfe mit wenigen Ausnahmen in den USA, an den Universitäten Stanford, MIT, Car-
10 negie-Mellon oder Berkeley. Ich wollte meinen Doktortitel dort erwerben, wo sich
    Neues und Großes tut. Nach dem Studium kontaktierten mich Risikokapitalgeber, die
    mir für die Vermarktung meiner Arbeit Geld geben wollten. Eine solche Gelegenheit
    lässt man sich nicht entgehen. […]
    Mit einem Doktortitel von der Universität Stanford in der Tasche – hätten Sie Ihre
15 *Firma nicht auch in Europa gründen können?*
    Leider nicht. Ohne einen Business-Plan hätte mir niemand ein paar Millionen Dollar
    gegeben, selbst wenn ich an demselben Thema geforscht hätte. Das ist das größte Pro-
    blem: Doktoranden und Professoren sind in Europa nicht eng genug verbunden mit der
    Start-up-Szene und Geldgebern.
20 *Kürzlich haben Experten unter Leitung der Universität Stanford zum zweiten Mal den*
    „AI Index Report" veröffentlicht, eine jährliche Bilanz zum Thema künstliche Intelli-
    genz. Das Fazit: KI-Forschung und ihre Kommerzialisierung nehmen weltweit zu. Ist
    das ein echter Boom oder nur ein Hype?

Wir machen in der Tat auf breiter Front Fortschritte. Systeme können Beachtliches
25 beim Deep Learning leisten und damit die Handlungen von Software-Agenten steuern.
Sogar bei der Verarbeitung von Bildern sind sie in den vergangenen Monaten sehr viel
besser geworden. Die KI-Forschung läuft seit mehr als 50 Jahren, aber jetzt haben wir
eine Schwelle überschritten, weil es nicht mehr nur spannende, aber eigentlich nutzlose
Forschungsprojekte gibt, sondern immer mehr praktische Anwendungen […].

30 *Ist noch Zeit, um Europa für diesen Wettbewerb fit zu machen?*
Die Uhr tickt. Wachstum hängt davon ab, ob ich meine Volkswirtschaft effizienter
machen kann. Und künstliche Intelligenz wird der entscheidende Faktor dafür sein. Ihr
wirtschaftliches Potenzial ist noch viel größer als das des Internets oder von Smartphones. Die Fertigung ist traditionell eine von Deutschlands Stärken, doch auch da
35 lässt sich mit KI viel bewerkstelligen. Insofern ist es ermutigend, dass Deutschland,
Frankreich und Großbritannien strategische Visionen für künstliche Intelligenz formuliert haben.

Wie kann man verhindern, dass weiterhin kluge Köpfe in die USA auswandern?
Als Professor in Deutschland ist mein Einkommen ziemlich gedeckelt, sodass etwa die
40 Ankündigung, 100 neue Lehrstellen für KI zu schaffen, schnell auf die Realitäten des
globalen Talent-Wettbewerbs prallt. Wenn ich eine Koryphäe bin, kann ich in anderen
Ländern ein Wahnsinnsgeld verdienen. Das soll nicht heißen, dass ich in Europa oder
Deutschland keine gute Forschung betreiben und ein tolles Forschungslabor aufbauen
kann, aber wenn ich dieselbe Arbeit woanders verrichte und das Zehn- oder Fünfzig-
45 fache verdienen kann, ist das natürlich sehr verlockend.

Wie könnte man Gründer, die auf KI setzen, gezielt fördern?
Man sollte sich einmal die Geschichte des Silicon Valley genauer ansehen. Einiges ist
organisch gewachsen, und diesen Erfolg kann man schlecht durch Regulierungen her-
beizaubern. Aber man sollte Gründern das Leben leichter machen – angefangen bei
50 den Vorschriften in Sachen Personal. Wenn ich noch in der Phase bin, in der ich mein
Geschäftsmodell entwickle und justiere, muss ich in der Lage sein, meine Belegschaft
flexibel anzupassen.
Was man auch nicht vergessen sollte, sind die Standortvorteile, die Deutschland in
Sachen KI hat. Das Land verfügt über ein sehr gutes Gesundheitswesen. Warum kann
55 man nicht eine landesweite, anonymisierte Datenbank anlegen, in die zum Beispiel alle
Gehirn-Computertomografien eingespeist werden. Das wäre ein enorm wertvoller Da-
tensatz, um Systeme für maschinelles Lernen zu trainieren und zu verbessern. Damit
wären diese Daten eine Art öffentliches Gut, mit deren Hilfe die Bundesrepublik zu
einem Weltmarktführer für Medizin-KI werden könnte, weil sich anhand dieser Daten-
60 sätze hervorragende Algorithmen entwickeln lassen. Das könnte die Basis für ein ganzes Ökosystem von Start-ups werden.   *(647 Wörter)*

brand eins, Ausgabe 03/2019

Annotationen
Z. 2   Leipzig und Saarbrücken: Studienorte Sochers
Z. 25 Deep Learning: ein KI-Verfahren, das menschliches Lernen nachahmt und sich dabei an der
       Funktionsweise des menschlichen Gehirns orientiert
Z. 25 Software-Agenten: Computerprogramme, die zu autonomem Handeln fähig sind

Themenschwerpunkte: *Saving the planet; Aims and ambitions*

Your British friend is doing a school project on different aspects of mobility in Europe and asks you for information about the situation in Germany.
Write an email to him/her summarizing the information given in the article on the development of private transport in German cities and on the Domagkpark project.

Text (Auszug aus dem Artikel)

Freiheit und Status
Von Niclas Seydack

1 […] Über Carsharing-Apps wie BMWs Drive Now oder Car2go von Daimler lassen sich Amalia, Benni oder Thilo orten – Leihautos, die wie gute Freunde heißen und mitten in den Straßen warten. Thilo, ein BMW X1, steht an diesem Morgen nur 300 Meter entfernt, reserviert und entriegelt per Smartphone. […]

5 Zwei Millionen Deutsche nutzen regelmäßig Carsharing. Nicht für ein paar Tage im Urlaub, sondern für zwanzigminütige Fahrten zum Restaurant oder ins Kino. Intensivnutzer sind laut einer Studie von Nordlight Research unter 35 und leben in großstädtischen Regionen. In Berlin, Hamburg oder München. Viele haben nie ein eigenes Auto gehabt. Es gibt Experten, die glauben: Die Millennials leben vor, was bald Alltag

10 sein könnte: Autos wandeln sich von einem Ding, das man besitzt, zu einem Service, den man nutzt.

Was passiert da gerade mit der Liebe der Deutschen zum eigenen Auto? Ist Carsharing nur ein Hype der Großstädte, oder schon Verkehrswende?

Nimmt man in Schwabing die Abfahrt vom Mittleren Ring, sagt Thilo bald: Sie

15 haben Ihr Ziel erreicht. Den Domagkpark. Nach 40 Minuten statt 20, für den doppelten Fahrpreis. Thilo will nach Minuten bezahlt werden, nicht nach Strecke.

Im Domagkpark durch die Straßen zu rollen, ist, als wäre man in das Set eines Science-Fiction-Films geraten. Die Häuser mit Laubengängen und bodentiefen Fenstern sind schneeweiß. Eine Frau saugt Staub von ihrer Terrasse, schaut zum Spielplatz,

20 zur meterhohen Rutsche, verchromt wie eine Raumstation.

Die Stadtplanerin Maria Knorre trägt gerne sehr bunte Kleider und eine rote Brille, sie experimentiert im Domagkpark, wie Mobilität in deutschen Großstädten eines Tages aussehen könnte. Im Auftrag der EU forscht sie gewissermaßen am lebenden Objekt: Hier wohnen viertausend Menschen, die seit dem Bau des Viertels im Jahr 2012

25 hergezogen sind, sie inklusive. Maria Knorre also zeigt ihr „Legoland“.

Erster Halt: die Mobilitätsstation, eine Flotte Leihroller und -fahrräder, Ladesäulen für Elektroautos, eigens reservierte Carsharing-Parkstreifen. Oberbürgermeister Dieter Reiter, sagt Knorre, kam Anfang Juli, um persönlich die Station zu eröffnen.

Anschließend führt sie auf ein Hausdach. Zwischen Gräsern und Farnen zeichnet

30 sie die Straßen mit dem Zeigefinger nach: „Kein einziges parkendes Auto.“ Mit Ausnahme der Carsharing-Wagen, die sind erlaubt. Den Anwohnern haben sie verboten,

ihre eigenen Autos auf die Straßen zu stellen, sie parken in Tiefgaragen. In der Zukunft, die sich Maria Knorre vorstellt, sind private Autos unsichtbar. Das löst keine Probleme, aber es soll ein Signal sein: Die Straße gehört wieder den Menschen. […]

35 Eine Chance, sagt Knorre, sind die Jungen. Die Millennials in den Großstädten, für die ein Selbstfindungstrip nach Indien oder das neue iPhone Status symbolisiert, aber kein eigener BMW. Millennials haben befristete Jobs, befristete Mietverträge, serielle Kurzzeitbeziehungen mit wechselnden Partnern. Warum nicht auch mit wechselnden Autos?

40 Doch was sie chic finden, ist für die Carsharing-Anbieter teuer. Weder die Daimler Tochter Car2Go noch BMWs Drive Now verdienen Geld. Darum geht es auch nicht. Viel wichtiger für die Firmen ist, vorn dabei zu sein, wenn sie Geld mit etwas anderem verdienen müssen als dem Verkauf von Autos. […]

Im Mai dieses Jahres haben Daimler und BMW angekündigt, ihre Carsharing-Ab-
45 leger zu fusionieren. Neben seinen 4 000 Autos in Deutschland bringt Daimler den Taxivermittler Mytaxi mit, BMW Suchmaschinen für Parkplatz und Aufladestationen für Elektroautos und 3 400 Autos. Aus Autobauern werden „Mobilitätsdienstleister mit voll vernetzter Fahrzeugflotte,“ sagt auch VW-Markenchef Jürgen Stackmann. […]

Maria Knorre, die Stadtplanerin, träumt von einer App, die den schnellsten Weg
50 vom Startpunkt zum Ziel ermittelt. Und zwar mit allen Verkehrsarten: Carsharing, öffentlicher Nahverkehr, eigene und geliehene Fahrräder und Elektroroller. Flexibel und mit einem Klick bezahlbar. Nutzer könnten sogar kleine Auszeichnungen erspielen. Wenn sie viel Rad fahren, würde Knorre die Meldung schicken: „Glückwunsch, du gehörst zu den Top-100-Stickoxid-Vermeidern Münchens.“

55 Technisch wäre das alles möglich. Nur hat so eine App kaum eine Chance, sagt Knorre. Die Autobauer (oder, wie es so schön heißt: Mobilitätsdienstleister) entziehen sich die Geschäftsgrundlage, die sie gerade aufbauen, wären sie bei einer App dabei, die dann eben auch mal vorschlägt: Verzichte auf unser Carsharing und nimm öfter dein Fahrrad. *(646 Wörter)*

„Freiheit und Status“, Niclas Seydack, SZ.de vom 16.12.2018

Annotation
Z. 15 Domagkpark: Areal in München mit Wohnungen, Geschäften, Restaurants, Wohnheimen und Schulen

Aufgabenstellung 1.1

1 *Bei dieser Zusammenfassung sollen Sie sich auf die biografischen Informationen, die der Text zu Kushanava Choudhury und seinen Eltern enthält, konzentrieren. Bei der Vorgehensweise ist es sinnvoll, alle Informationen im Text zu markieren und diese anschließend aufgeteilt nach Choudhurys Eltern und ihm selbst aufzulisten. Auch für die ausformulierte Lösung bietet sich diese Zweiteilung an, um eine klare Struktur zu erhalten.*

Kushanava Choudhury's parents were Indian scientists who moved to America twice and back to their home country twice. At about 40 years of age, his father gave up a well-paid government job at a research centre in Calcutta to take up a new opportunity in New Jersey. His parents did not feel like immigrants, however, always considering the option of returning to India, especially after it turned out that the promise of work which had been made to his father was not kept and he had to take other work, which he began to despise. Life in the US continued to be financially insecure and his family led a lower middle-class existence, with constant problems with the car and cheap clothes, always ready to move back to their home country. Memories of India were cultivated together with their many Bengali friends and they dreamed of returning. Choudhury himself remembers happy days as a child in India, and when he moved with his parents to the US it felt like he was leaving his childhood behind as well. He went to a state school in grade seven where there were almost no other Indian students and felt forced to fit in quickly. It came as a pleasant surprise to his family in their restricted circumstances that he was accepted to the prestigious university of Princeton. While they were very happy about this, he did not share their feelings and secretly nurtured his plan to go back to India. However, his parents would not accept his arrangement to teach at a Bengali village school. He spent some restless years at college, alienated from his friends and driving aimlessly, and instead of living in a big American city after graduation like they did, he went back to Calcutta to work for the traditional English-language daily newspaper, *The Statesman*.

2 *In Ihrer Analyse sollen Sie darstellen, wie Choudhurys Meinung zur traditionellen Sichtweise auf Immigration in Amerika (Stichwort: „melting pot") im Text dargestellt wird. Grundsätzlich glaubt Choudhury nicht, dass es möglich ist, seine Vergangenheit komplett zurückzulassen. Dies belegt er anhand von statistischen Informationen dazu, wie viele Menschen in ihre Heimatländer zurückkehren. Zudem zeigt er an seiner persönlichen Erfahrung, dass viele Familien sich nicht komplett assimilieren und mit der amerikanischen Kultur „verschmelzen", sondern, dass sie wie seine eigene Familie parallele Strukturen aufbauen. Auch er selbst ist nach Indien zurückgekehrt, da er*

sich nie komplett integriert gefühlt hat. Sprachlich nutzt er unter anderem Vernei-
nungen, Sprachbilder und Wiederholungen, um seine Sichtweise zu verdeutlichen.

The author had already visited Ellis Island, the US official port of immigration as a teenager, during a class trip, but he claims that nobody told him that the American myth, believed to function like a "reset button" (l. 3), did not always work. At least in the case of his parents it did not liberate them "from the Old World's limited horizons" (ll. 4/5). They are frequently disappointed. They cling to their Bengali culture and friends and share their desire to eventually move back to India (cf. ll. 25, 28) and thus reverse immigration, although this might not be possible for many of them because "[n]ationalism and nostalgia did not pay the bills, raise children or advance careers" (ll. 27/28). They are torn between the necessity of survival and the duty and dream of return (cf. l. 24), which in many cases, as with his parents, served as a protection from an alien world. Choudhury relies on statistics when he relates that more than half of the immigrants (cf. l. 2) went back to their country of origin and that the promise of the myth that one will forget the past and create a new future is not guaranteed.

He talks about his own family to prove his point. His parents are described as "Indian scientists" (l. 11) and he is apparently not happy with the constant prospect of moving from one place to another and back again: "I had already migrated halfway around the world four times" (ll. 9/10). Drawing on further personal experience – as another stylistic device – he informs his readers that his family did not have "an easy few years in America" (l. 37).

A frequent stylistic device employed in his text is the usage of negative language. His perception of the American myth is dominated by phrases like, "It never really works like that" (l. 6), "the story no one ever told" (l. 6) or "[t]he past is never left behind" (l. 7). His experience of school was that he "wasn't assimilating" (l. 32) and his family did not have an easy time in America (cf. l. 37). Allusion is another stylistic choice to underline the fact that his family's move to America was not as is suggested in Emma Lazarus's famous poem promising hope for the homeless, which is engraved on the base of the Statue of Liberty right next to Ellis Island. All of these language traits are instrumental in contrasting myth with (Choudhury's) actual experience.

The text also uses imagery. To characterise his parents' financial position, he sees his family "adrift in the treacherous shoals of the lower middle classes" (ll. 41/42) To describe his own psychological state he uses a simile when he finds himself "hunched over with nostalgia like a middle-aged man" (l. 55). Words with negative connotations reinforce and intensify the powerful impact of immigration on his life. For instance, he talks about a past that "haunts every world you live in. Sometimes it drags you back" (ll. 7/8) and, in an antithesis, describes his parents as people "unwilling to leave their country and […] unable to stay" (ll. 12/13). Several times, he emphasises the wish to go back to India by using repetitions like "dream of return" (l. 25), "dream of a return" (l. 28) and "nostalgia" (ll. 27, 55).

As a result, the author describes his attitude of doubt if not criticism towards American values, promises and the American Dream in general, which he characterises as a myth that is not compatible with his life experiences, and presents himself as torn between two worlds, eventually gravitating to his native country when he is able to fulfil his own dream of returning to Calcutta and working there as a journalist.

3.1 *Hier müssen Sie einen Bezug zwischen dem Cartoon und Choudhurys Familie herstellen und darlegen, inwiefern der Cartoon die Erfahrungen der Familie widerspiegelt. Dies ist nicht ganz eindeutig zu lösen. Der Cartoon selbst enthält nur wenige Informationen. Lediglich auffällig ist es, dass die Aussage von zwei Männern getätigt wird, die selbst scheinbar keinen Migrationshintergrund haben.*
Choudhurys Familie ist nur bedingt Teil des „melting pot". Sie umgeben sich mit indischen Familien und Choudhurys Eltern haben immer vor, nach Indien zurückzukehren. Choudhury selbst hat zunächst versucht sich zu integrieren, fühlte sich jedoch immer anders als seine Mitschüler*innen. Sein Abschluss an einer amerikanischen Eliteuniversität würde ihm viele Türen öffnen und entspricht dem Werdegang des American Dream. Schlussendlich hat jedoch auch er den Entschluss gefasst, nach Indien zurückzukehren und diesen in die Tat umgesetzt.

The picture in the cartoon shows two middle-aged White men talking about a newspaper headline that says, "America: Melting Pot". The caption of the cartoon carries its message in a nutshell: America being a melting pot – something which is praised globally – comes with a disadvantage, as somebody will always lose what is at stake, whether that is their language, their culture or their identity; in other words, they will suffer badly. This concept seems to give American immigrants only one choice and that is to assimilate.

The cartoon uses plain imagery, showing two men from different sections of American society and high-rise buildings in the background. One of the men is in a baseball cap and casual clothes, and the other is wearing a fancy hat, shirt, tie and trench coat, but they both share the same facial expression of surprise. They seem to be disparaging about the newspaper headline, thus underlining the cartoon's message, which questions how beneficial the concept of a multicultural society really is.

Choudhury's parents, who do not feel rooted either in America or in their home country and always nurture the idea of going back to India at some stage, clearly do not warm to the melting pot concept of assimilation and surround themselves with other Indian immigrants instead. At weekends, they eat their traditional food together at each other's homes, cherish memories of their home country and are pulled by their duty and dream of returning. The author, on the other hand, initially adapts to his new home and school and is even successful in applying to a prestigious American university, but never loses his feelings of nostalgia and develops a strong desire to return as well.

The downside of the "melting pot" might be that this concept does not recognise individuality or culture, and forces people to be part of a process that destroys their traditions and values. This might result in a feeling of not belonging and, as in the case of the Indian family, a strong desire to return to their country of origin. It might also entail a sense of disappointment, as a society where someone from a different culture gets burned is the opposite of a welcome culture where everyone is free to develop their own skills and realise their own desires. Assimilation might be the key to success, but it comes at a cost.

There are, however, experiences that are not reflected in the cartoon. Choudhury's success in obtaining a place at Princeton would seem to embody the achievement of the American Dream, for his parents, at least, who, we are told, "acted as if someone had come to [their] door with balloons and a giant cardboard cheque. It was their happiest day in America" (ll. 47/48). At the same time, however, Choudhury lets us know that it was not his happiest day in that country. Even as a teenager he felt like an outsider at his school, with few classmates from his ethnic group, and although he tried to assimilate, he never really felt at home in his new surroundings and could not forget his old memories of India.

In conclusion, although one of the building blocks of the American Dream seems to be assimilation and the readiness to overcome past experiences and open oneself up to new ideas, that does not always work for everyone, especially for ethnic groups with strong ties to their old traditions like Choudhury's family. The term "melting pot" was coined by the historian James T. Adams in his book "The Epic of America" from 1931 and describes America as a land in which life should be better and richer and fuller for everyone, with opportunity for each according to ability or achievement, notwithstanding their origins, religion or conviction. Later, the idea of the salad bowl was developed, which symbolises the fact that immigrants can integrate into society but keep their own culture. This concept allows immigrants to remain who they are and does not force them to conform to mainstream society. In this way, individual ethnicities should be recognised and not subdued, thus leaving room for the main reason why people immigrate, which is to live in peace and freedom and leave old restrictions and suppression behind – in accordance with the promise expressed in the poem by Emma Lazarus, which is engraved on of the Statue of Liberty: "Send these, the homeless, tempest-tossed to me: I lift my lamp beside the golden door!"

3.2 *Für einen gelungen Artikel sollten Sie sich an eine klare Struktur halten. Beginnen Sie mit einer Überschrift, die zu Ihrem Artikel hinführt. Um Ihre Argumentation im Hauptteil interessant zu gestalten, können Sie wissenschaftliche Erkenntnisse, Zitate oder spannende Fakten zum Thema einarbeiten.*

Where you live is who you are – or is it?

Although they try hard to integrate, young immigrants in the US often fail to succeed there. They feel rejected and develop a longing for the place they came from. Recent research has shown that the influence of their former environment or place of origin is often more important for shaping their identity than mainstream society.

The importance of place in shaping one's identity has particularly been observed in second- or third-generation immigrants to the UK or the US in that young people often revert to the traditions of their parents and their religious or cultural heritage. In his autobiography *The Epic City*, for instance, Kushanava Choudhury describes how, as a young immigrant from India, he was willing to live his American Dream and attend a prestigious university in New Jersey, but then decided to leave the US again after graduation to work as a journalist in his native country. His parents, scientists from Calcutta, had originally supported his university career in the US and even hindered him from taking up a teaching job in rural India. However, his happy childhood memories of cricket matches in the summer vacation and of games played outdoors in the city made him feel so nostalgic and detached from his environment that he used to stay at home brooding instead of going out with his friends, so that he eventually went back to Calcutta to work as a journalist.

His case, like many others, shows that people's relationship to place can be very emotional and have a long-term impact on their lives. With young people especially, their environment shapes who they are. The surroundings in which we spend our daily lives feels familiar and gives us a feeling of belonging. Environmental psychology tells us that there is a landscape of memory in the interaction between place and society that works on a practical level as much as on an emotional one.

However, in a global world dominated by the Internet we also have to take arguments into account that speak against the importance of place. Today, people are used to international travel from a young age, participating in school exchanges all over the world and spending gap years abroad after leaving school. People who often move around have a different relation to place. We spend a lot of time on the Internet where we communicate with people from all over the world. There is now even the saying "home is where my friends are", which results in place losing meaning or taking on a new one.

In conclusion, it can be said that place still contributes to shaping identity in certain situations, especially when migration is not voluntary but a result of poverty, suppression or war atrocities. In these cases, there is a strong feeling of loss and loneliness. Overall, however, in a globalised world where large parts of our lives take place online, place is starting to lose its importance.

Aufgabenstellung 1.2

1 *'Outline' bedeutet zunächst, dass Sie auf den Einleitungssatz (Texttyp, Autor, Erscheinungsdatum etc.) verzichten können. Da Sie nur Gameaus Gründe zusammenfassen müssen, bietet es sich an, diese im Text zu unterstreichen und dann Stück für Stück zu übertragen.*

In general, Gameau wants to send a positive message to his daughter and her generation and to many other people that we have the power to make a change in our fight for the environment.

He has found out that without hope and faith in the future people would restrain from taking action, so he wants to focus on how to tackle problems and to have a better vision of the future. Gameau's research into the issue came up with a lot of people who do care strongly about our earth and rather look ahead than back to help it. One crucial point is the education of girls and the empowerment of women, whose potentials have been neglected for a long time.

In the end he appeals to everyone to become part of this change by joining organisations or initiatives to make a lasting difference.

2 *Bei der Bearbeitung der Aufgabe bietet es sich an, zunächst die zentrale Intention des Films zu nennen. Im Anschluss lässt sich dann gut erst der Text und dann das Poster dementsprechend analysieren und vergleichen. In der Prüfung lag das Bild in Farbe vor.*

Gameau's film *2040* focuses on solutions to environmental problems. It gives hope to people and motivates them to tackle these issues. He is looking to a bright future involving all generations by showing them what is already possible.

The article from *The Guardian* mirrors this intention. It starts off with Gameau's personal story indicating that he is on the same level with the readers and they all have similar concerns.

He compares the state of our environment to a disease when he says that it's "much like […] visiting a doctor" (ll. 13/14) where we get a "diagnosis" (ll. 13, 14) when we get to know the truth. After that we want to "improve or even cure our condition" (l. 15).

Gameau switches between a colloquial style and scientific talk. The background information given comes from experts like the psychologist Renee Lertzman and Rebecca Solnit. This shows Gameau's careful research into the topic and his consideration for others.

His choice of words is really positive. The sub-headline already states that "everything we need […] already exists" (subheading). There are also positively connoted words like "improve" (l. 15), "care deeply" (l. 45) and a neologism "fact-based dreaming" (ll. 23/24), which supports the idea of succeeding at the goals set. Similar to that we can find a common saying turned around to make it sound more positive: "a shadow cannot exist without a source of light" (ll. 51/52), which stresses the light rather than the shadow. He also sees "hope in the dark" (l. 48), a strong metaphor that speaks in favour of his utopian vision. Lots of examples from successful movements in history like the suffragettes and abolitionists finally round up the overall picture created in the text.

The film poster does the same. It features a father and his daughter, i. e. two generations, in the centre. They are planting a tree, an action that is highly emotional and rather symbolic when we think of the future. Trees would also help fight climate change, so they stand for leaving a long-lasting positive impact on the environment. In the foreground a pavement gradually turns into a green field, and behind the two we can see a green metropolis with the skyscrapers' facades overgrown by plants. There are magnetic rails that stand for modern, CO_2 free transport. Even the title of the film *2040* is halfway overgrown by green tendrils. The whole poster is designed with green as the main colour, which is very different to most dystopian films, where red and black dominate. Next to the title the appeal "Join the REGENERATION" catches the readers' eyes because they recognize the wordplay regenerate – generation.

To sum up, text and poster mirror the positive and progressive approach to the topic of sustainability.

3.1 *Die Aufgabe ist sehr dankbar, da man sofort an* Fridays For Future *denkt. Im Folgen-*
den wird versucht, pro und contra zu erörtern. Vor allem die Contra-Seite ist hier
nicht leicht darzustellen.
Zwei Herangehensweisen wären denkbar: festzustellen, dass es die eine Jugend nicht
gibt oder dass es den Jugendlichen mitunter sehr schwer gemacht wird, sich so in den
politischen Prozess einzubringen, wie sie es auch wollen.

Greta Thunberg. Only a few years ago, this was just the name of a single protester against climate change.

Now, it's the name behind a worldwide movement to save the Earth. Greta's '*Skol-strejk för klimatet*' has unleashed a great power all around the globe and has opened eyes and minds to the fact that we need to take action. Thanks to her, it is now 'hip' to be green. Now, young people can no longer be ignored. This surely is a movement that will go down in history. For a long time, politicians have been talking about tackling environmental problems, conventions have been held, protocols signed, but hardly anything has changed. Now, with so many young people taking part in the Fridays for Future protest marches, even long-established parties of 'old, white men' like the CSU in Germany fly the flag for sustainability. Due to the power of social media younger generations have a lot more influence on the government's policies. Ideas spread easily and teenagers today are willing to break a habit of owning status symbols like cars, for example. They ride their bikes, share cars and know how environmentally friendly their food and their clothes are. They have taken the lead and set the course for a better world.

Yet there is also the other side of the coin. The Fridays for Future protesters come from rather educated levels of society. Unfortunately, there are also quite a lot of young people who don't really care. The number of voters among 18-24-year-olds is declining. Still too many seem to be leaving it to the older generations to take care of their future. Mass consumption of clothes, mobile phones, etc. is still an issue and too many people still travel the world on long-distance-flights for a two-week holiday. These people are also often the ones who mock vegetarians or vegans for their lifestyle.

Additionally, young people who do want to make a change are sometimes threatened by older generations when they tell them that taking part in protest marches will be considered truancy and, thus, affect their marks and their career chances. They may feel barred from the legislative process, too, with the big parties nominating candidates who are from the 50+ generation.

All in all, there hasn't been a more political youth since the protests in the 1960s. But they need to reach out to the older generation, too, and the latter have to accept that young people can take responsibility as well. In working together, we can succeed in making the world a better place.

3.2 *Nur mit Hilfe der Informationen aus dem Prüfungstext ist es nicht so einfach, die Vorteile solcher Dokumentationen hervorzuheben. Die Aufgabenstellung erlaubt jedoch das Einbinden anderer Filme. Während* 2040 *tatsächlich Lösungen aufzeigt, zeichnen die meisten Dokumentarfilme ein eher negatives Bild der Zukunft (siehe zum Beispiel: Al Gore:* Still an Inconvenient Truth; *Ali Tabrizi:* Seaspiracy; *Kip Andersen und Keegan Kuhn:* Cowspiracy; *Markus Imhof:* More than Honey *…). Auch diese können jedoch die Zukunft positiv beeinflussen, indem sie aufrütteln und Menschen dazu bewegen, ihr eigenes Verhalten zu hinterfragen und zu verändern.*
Die folgende Lösung zeigt, wie man die Aufgabe nur anhand von 2040 *als Beispiel lösen kann.*

Dear fellow members of my generation,

Most of us are now at the precipice of our future: Within a decade we will train for jobs, maybe start a family and a career. But there is one thing that is different to generations before. We are more concerned than ever about it being sustainable.

Since the 1980s, scientists have warned against climate change seen in a rise in the Earth's temperature, melting polar caps and weather extremes. But it is our generation that will be remembered for standing up, protesting and demanding action. We are ready to fight for our rights for a future on a habitable planet for all generations now and yet to come.

But sometimes it can be quite unnerving, frustrating and demotivating to continue fighting when other people do not seem to understand or agree or slow down the legislative process necessary to save our world. We often hear that this technology still needs to be developed, that a certain idea is hardly more than a plan, etc. This attitude ultimately causes fear and negligence, as psychologists have found out. What we need to keep on fighting is hope. Interestingly, there are a number of film projects that take this hopeful approach to saving the planet. Let me tell you about one. It is a documentary called *2040* and features a father who created a visual letter to his daughter to show her that everything we need for a sustainable world already exists. That's what I call good news! A utopian rather than the usual dystopian approach or an inconvenient truth about the ecological challenges we have to cope with!

Damon Gameau underwent three years of research and interviews and found out that we could start right from where we are now to rescue our world. So why shouldn't we? Let us spread the message of the film by showing it in every classroom around the globe. Let us show it to the politicians and lobbyists who still put money and procrastination before action. It would open eyes and plant a vision of hope in the hearts and minds of all people.

Gameau says that his film not only addresses future generations but everyone on this planet. His story appeals to our emotions and we can fully identify with his ideas. Maybe this way more people will feel the urge to take action. Visual impressions can often say more than words.

Let me finish by saying that no matter what, our Mother Earth needs us to change. We are the cause of her ailment and that is why we have the responsibility to cure her.

I hope our conference can contribute to this great goal.

Thank you.

Aufgabenstellung 2.1

Hier sind Sie dazu aufgefordert, einen Blogeintrag für die Internetseite der „Society for Computer Science" zu schreiben, in dem Sie die Informationen über Richard Sochers Karriere und seine Beurteilung von Europas Stand im Bereich der künstlichen Intelligenz zusammenfassen. Sie schreiben aus der Perspektive eines Praktikanten.

Europe's Artificial Intelligence (AI) – a Brain Drain to be Avoided

In an interview published in a German business magazine in March 2019, the chief scientist of a Silicon Valley technology firm talks about his reasons for abandoning his German university career and about the challenges facing European computer start-ups, and warns of a European brain drain in the light of the lack of opportunities and connections between the world of science and the economy.

Richard Socher received his training as a computer scientist at two German universities before he decided to obtain his PhD at Stanford, which is renowned for its high scientific standard. He continued his work at Silicon Valley, because he was contacted by investors offering to finance his particular research interests. In Europe, he would not have been able to find risk venture capitalists to finance his work without a business-plan, which, from his point of view, highlights the missing link between science, investors and start-ups in this part of the world.

According to Socher, the AI potential is even greater than that of the Internet or smartphones and will play a major role in industrial production, which is already a traditional German asset.

However, in order to avoid a further brain drain from Europe, research and working conditions need to be improved so that international competitiveness does not fall short due to the lack of financial incentives. Good research and great laboratories are still possible in Europe or Germany, yet scientists will be very tempted to leave if they can earn ten or fifty times the amount for the same work elsewhere.

The history of Silicon Valley is something to be learned from. Much of it has grown organically and success of this kind cannot be fostered by regulations. Start-ups in Europe, however, could be supported more by making their lives easier, starting with lending them more flexibility in hiring staff whilst they are developing and adjusting their business model.

Nonetheless, Socher is hopeful, as Germany, France and Great Britain have developed common strategic visions for their AI systems. Additionally, Germany's advantages as a location should be taken into account: our health system could be used to create a data base of brain scans to train and improve AI systems for machine learning, for example.

As a consequence, these data could thus be transformed into a public good, enabling German medical AI to become a global market leader and hence forming the basis for a complete system of sustainable start-ups.

Aufgabenstellung 2.2

Die E-Mail ist an einen Freund oder eine Freundin gerichtet, darf also auch ein wenig informell sein. Denken Sie daran, eine Begrüßung zu schreiben und ein wenig „Smalltalk zu machen". Im Hauptteil gilt es nur, die Fakten des Artikels zusammenzufassen,

Hi Julie,

How are you doing? I hope you are fine. When I read your email, I was quite surprised to find out that we are dealing with the same topics in geography. We also had a project week on the future of mobility in our country. That is why I know a lot about this topic now. ☺ Lucky you!

Most of the info I'm giving you is from a German quality paper called *Süddeutsche Zeitung*.

In general, private transport in Germany is undergoing major changes, experts say. It's those under 35, the millennials, who often don't own cars any longer. They are speeding this development up because they often only have temporary work contracts, move a lot and live in big city regions like Berlin or Munich, etc. They understand cars as a service, not a status symbol. They prefer sharing to buying a vehicle. As an example, the article reports about a project in Munich. A re-erected quarter of 40,000 inhabitants called *Domagkpark* is where they are doing a kind of experiment on mobility in urban regions. The European Union supports it financially too. The architects have focused on the *people* owning the street and not the other way round as in most European cities now. There is bike and scooter sharing, charging stations for electric cars and an underground car park where the few privately owned vehicles have to be "hidden", since they would not be allowed in the parking lots in the streets, which are only open to car sharing vehicles.

Sounds like a cool concept, doesn't it? The city planner who has realised this project dreams of an app that is supposed to combine all the means of transport, bikes, scooters, cars, etc., to help you find the shortest way to travel. The thing is that the car manufacturers are not very happy with all this. They are trying to concentrate on new business ideas since the number of vehicles sold is rapidly declining and car sharing does not generate profits. Let's hope that they will find a compromise. Have you got anything similar to Domagk-park in your region? I'd love to hear about it. Let me know how your school project is going.

Take care
Antonia

Prüfungsteil 1: Leseverstehen und Schreiben (70 %)

Der Prüfungsteil 1 besteht aus zwei Aufgabenstellungen, von denen Sie eine zur Bearbeitung auswählen.

Aufgabenstellung 1.1 – Tasks

Themenschwerpunkte: *Aims and ambitions; Ethnic and cultural diversity*

1 Outline the information on the protagonists. (30 %)

2 Analyze how New York and its people are portrayed. Refer to narrative perspective and use of language. (30 %)

3 Choose one of the following tasks:

3.1 In the extract Neni observes: "Even in New York City, even in a place of many nations and cultures, men and women, young and old, rich and poor, preferred their kind when it came to those they kept closest. And why shouldn't they?" (ll. 18–20)
Taking Neni's attitude as a starting point, discuss the benefits and challenges of integrating into a new and diverse community. (40 %)

OR

3.2 *Integrating Cities,* an international organization focusing on migration and integration, is looking for best practice examples of campaigns promoting integration. Someone has posted the illustration below on the organization's blog.
Write a blog entry assessing its effectiveness. (40 %)

*NYC Mayor's Office of Immigrant Affairs (2017).
Immigrant Heritage Week 2017. Retrieved May 18, 2020
from https://www1.nyc.gov/assets/immigrants/downloads/
pdf/immigrant-heritage-week-2017-calendar.pdf*

Text (excerpt from the novel)

Behold the dreamers
by Imbolo Mbue

Jende and Neni Jonga emigrated from Cameroon to the United States, where they are currently seeking legal status. In this excerpt, the couple is in midtown Manhattan, where Jende's cousin Winston has been celebrating his birthday.

1 Though he loved New York City, every winter he told himself he was going to leave it for another American city as soon as he got his papers. The city was great, but why spend four months of the year shivering like a wet chicken? […] If Bubakar hadn't cautioned him that it was best he remained in the city (it might complicate matters if
5 they tried to move his case to another jurisdiction, the lawyer had said), Jende would have been long gone, because there was no reason why a man should willfully spend so many days of his life in a cold, costly, congested place. […]

"Let's go sit at Columbus Circle for a little bit," Jende said, and [Neni] quickly agreed […]. Jende began talking about how great a time he'd had talking to one of
10 Winston's friends, but she was barely listening. She was noticing something for the first time: She was realizing that most people on the street were walking with someone who looked like them. On both sides of the street, going east and west, she saw people walking with their kind: a white man holding hands with a white woman; a black teen-ager giggling with other black (or Latino) teenagers; a white mother pushing a stroller
15 alongside another white mother; a black woman chatting with a black woman. She saw a quartet of Asian men in tuxedos, and a group of friends who had different skin colors but were dressed in similar elegant chic styles. Most people were sticking to their own kind. Even in New York City, even in a place of many nations and cultures, men and women, young and old, rich and poor, preferred their kind when it came to those they
20 kept closest. And why shouldn't they? It was far easier to do so than to spend one's limited energy trying to blend into a world one was never meant to be a part of. That was what made New York so wonderful: It had a world for everyone. She had her world in Harlem and never again would she try to wriggle her way into a world in midtown, not even for just one hour.
25 When they got to Columbus Circle, […] they sat beneath the statue of Christopher Columbus, side by side, hand in hand, surrounded by skateboarders and young lovers and homeless people, looking north as cars came around the circle and went up Central Park West. The spring air was crisper than she would have wished, but not crisp enough to send her rushing into the subway. And even if it had been, she would have stayed in
30 the circle, because it wasn't every night she got a chance to enjoy the sounds of the city and its millions of lights blinking around her, reminding her that she was still living in her dream. Bubakar had assured them that they could be in the country for many years, which meant they could be in the city for many years. A massive smile involuntarily appeared on her face at the thought, and she moved closer to Jende and leaned
35 against him.

"This is the best place in the whole city," he said to her. She did not ask why he thought so, because she knew why.

In his first days in America, it was here he came every night to take in the city. It was here he often sat to call her when he got so lonely and homesick that the only balm
40 that worked was the sound of her voice. During those calls, he would ask her how Liomi was doing, what she was wearing, what her plans for the weekend were, and she would tell him everything, leaving him even more wistful for the beauty of her smile, the hearth in his mother's kitchen, the light breeze at Down Beach, the tightness of Liomi's hugs, the coarse jokes and laughter of his friends as they drank Guinness at a
45 drinking spot; leaving him craving everything he wished he hadn't left behind. During those times, he told her, he often wondered if leaving home in search of something as fleeting as fortune was ever worthwhile.

"You know what I'm realizing now?" he said to her.

"What?" she asked, looking at him adoringly.

50 "We are sitting in the center of the world."

She laughed. "You're so funny."

"No, think about it," he said. "Columbus Circle is the center of Manhattan. Manhattan is the center of New York. New York is the center of America, and America is the center of the world. So we are sitting in the center of the world, right?" *(775 words)*

Mbue, Imbolo. Behold the Dreamers. London: 4th Estate, 2016, 81, 94–96.

Annotations

Title Imbolo Mbue: a female American author born in Cameroon, Africa
l. 3 Bubakar: the immigration lawyer handling the Jongas' case
l. 5 jurisdiction: the city or state which has the legal authority to make decisions and judgments
l. 41 Liomi: Jende and Neni's son

Themenschwerpunkte: *Ethnic and cultural diversity; Saving the planet; Aims and ambitions*

1   Sum up the information about Kate Milman and her organisation "Wild Things".   (30 %)

2   Analyze how the author's view on the project "Wild Things" is conveyed in the article, also taking into consideration the photos published with it.   (30 %)

3   Choose <u>one</u> of the following tasks:

3.1   "Often children can feel at home in the woods in a way they find more difficult in the community they have landed in […]." (ll. 44/45)
Using the quote as a starting point, assess how projects like "Wild Things" can help refugee children with their integration into new social surroundings.   (40 %)

OR

3.2   For the magazine "Youth", write an article commenting on the importance of offering children opportunities to encounter nature.   (40 %)

Text (excerpt from the article)

'I feel I've come home': can forest schools help heal refugee children?
by Patrick Barkham

Setting off on a tracking hunt.
Photograph: Wild Things

1 When Kate Milman was 21, she paused her English degree at the University of East
Anglia to join protests against the Newbury bypass. It was 1996, and the road was
being carved out through idyllic wooded countryside in Berkshire. She took up residence in a treehouse, in the path of the bulldozers, and lived there for months. It was a
5 revelation. She lived intimately with the catkins, the calling birds, the slow-slow-fast
change in the seasons. Despite being in a precarious position as a protester, she felt
completely safe and her brain was calmed. [...]

Finally, however, she was evicted from her forest heartland. The men and their
machines arrived beneath her tree. Kate was arrested under a newly created "aggravat-
10 ed trespass" law and barred from joining the protests again. The wood was ripped apart.

"That level of grief – it felt like losing somebody," Kate says now. It was a highly
complex woodland and she had come to know it intimately. "I knew how beautiful it
was at dawn and at full moon, and then it was bulldozed. When you watch that amount
of stupidity, when you have that much grief and impotence, what can you do with it?"

15 The idea for Wild Things, a workers' cooperative set up to provide children with
experience of the natural world, was born. For three days each week, she and her fellow
co-op members, Kath, Kat and Nick (her partner), provide half-day sessions for groups
of nine pupils from various city schools.

I've come to a Wild Things day at Bestwood Country Park, a hilltop woodland on
20 the edge of Nottingham. The wind runs through the canopy in waves, worrying the
leaves, but it is calm and snug in the green, brambly understorey. The slender trunks
of silver birches shine in the low sunlight. [...]

The children we're with today are mostly 10-year-olds, members of an "English as
a second language" group from Forest Fields primary and nursery school. The school's
25 bucolic name belies its location in central Nottingham. Its 620 children speak 52 languages. Everyone in today's group arrived in Britain in the last two years. Several
started school only two months ago. They are from Pakistan, Afghanistan, Romania
and Syria, and some came from refugee camps. "You don't know what they've seen,"
says their teaching assistant, Yasmin Khaliq, who speaks five languages. She has been

30 bringing groups to Wild Things for nine years. "It's a godsend," she says. "It's all
outdoors, they are seeing things with their own eyes, there's no language barrier." […]
Wild Things has worked with many migrant children who grew up in rural areas.
Meanwhile British-born city children belong to a country called Indoors: they ask
Kate, "What's mud?" or, "Why are there so many trees here?" It is often only in Britain
35 that rural children from overseas are confined to city-centre flats. Their questions –
"Are there elephants?" or, "Are there deadly snakes here?" – are rooted in experience
of their countries of origin. For many, Kate says, the woods awaken lost memories and
a yearning for home. "As soon as we light a fire, they say, 'Ah, I know this' or they
point to a plant and get really animated. They are in their element."
40 One group last spring included a partially sighted girl. "Walking up into the woods,
she stopped and said, 'Listen to that sound!'" remembers Kate. "It was the buzzing of
the insects." It reminded the girl of her former country. At the end of her six weeks, she
said, "I feel like I've come home." The Wild Things staff frequently hear similar decla-
rations. "Often children can feel at home in the woods in a way they find more difficult
45 in the community they have landed in, where technology is everything, money is everything, they are at the bottom of the pecking order and there are massive tensions in the
area. In the woods they are on a level playing field. They can just be kids again." […]
Even so, forest school teachers are acutely aware that they offer only a tiny taste
of magic in childhoods where more time is spent indoors than in any preceding gener-
50 ation. "We help a child to fall in love with nature and we don't know if they'll ever be
able to access it again," Kate says. She thinks for a moment. At least the children now
know the woods are there. The place may call to them at any point in the future. "It's
better to know there's a bit missing. It might be something you can use in your later
life," she says. "To know that the woods can make you feel better." […]   *(773 words)*

Sharing treasures back at camp.
Photograph: Wild Things

Barkham, Patrick. "'I feel I've come home': can forest schools help heal refugee children?" The Guardian.
9 May 2020. Accessed 12 Sept. 2020 from https://www.theguardian.com/education/ 2020/may/09/i-feel-ive-come-
home-can-forest-schools-help-heal-refugee-children, Copyright Guardian News & Media Ltd 2022.

Annotations

l. 5   catkins: small flowers hanging like pieces of string from the branches of trees
ll. 9/10 aggravated trespass: unlawfully being on private property
l. 25   bucolic: rural, rustic
l. 46   pecking order: *here:* status, a social hierarchy

Der Prüfungsteil 2 besteht aus zwei Aufgabenstellungen, von denen Sie eine zur Bearbeitung auswählen.

Aufgabenstellung 2.1 – Task

Themenschwerpunkte: *The impact of the media on society; Aims and ambitions; Saving the planet*

For a school project, a Scottish friend of yours needs information about recent trends in social media. Write him/her an email in which you sum up the information in Julia Rathcke's article about opinion influencers and their impact on consumers.

Text (Auszug aus dem Artikel)

Fraglicher Instagram-Trend: Wenn aus dem Influencer ein „Sinnfluencer" wird
Von Julia Rathcke

1 […] Es gibt Models, die um den halben Erdball fliegen, um dort eine Stunde lang den Strand aufzuräumen und die Bikinibilder dann auf Instagram hochzuladen. Es gibt Veganer, die Fleischprodukte anprangern, dann aber Avocado- und Tofugerichte präsentieren, deren Zutaten alles andere als umweltfreundlich produziert und importiert wer-
5 den. Und es gibt Menschen, die Biobaumwollshirts für 4 Euro bei Primark kaufen.
Julia-Maria Blesin aus Hannover kämpft gegen diese Widersprüche. Sie betreibt einen Blog, einen Instagram-Account und verfolgt ein Motto: Green, Fair & Fun. Die 30-Jährige gibt Tipps für Plastikvermeidung, bewirbt Naturkosmetik, recycelte Rucksäcke und vor allem fair produzierte Mode. Julia-Maria Blesin ist mit ihrem Blog
10 „nicetohavemag" Teil eines Phänomens, das aktuell die sozialen Netzwerke aufzuwerten versucht: die sogenannten Sinnfluencer.
Immer öfter wollen Werber, sogenannte Influencer, nicht mehr nur Marketingmotor für ein beliebiges Produkt sein, sondern auch für eine Idee, die dahintersteht. Noch bewegen sich die Sinnfluencer damit in einer Nische, doch ihre Bedeutung wächst.
15 […]
Vor allem junge Menschen wollen wissen, woher ihr Pullover kommt und was in ihrer Gesichtscreme steckt. Es gibt längst zahlreiche Handy-Apps, mit denen Kunden im Laden Produkte scannen, um das vor dem Kauf zu überprüfen. Die Geiz-ist-geil-Mentalität scheint einer Art Achtsamkeitsmantra zu weichen: Passen wir auf uns auf,
20 dann passen wir auch auf unseren Planeten auf. […]
Green Travel, Fair Fashion, Lesswaste-Lifestyle – mit Schlagworten wie diesen ist der Ökotrend längst sprachlich im Internet verortet. Doch wie ist das mit den Sinnfluencern? Dient ihr Nachhaltigkeitswerben wie so oft auf Instagram nur dem Selbstzweck oder dem Greenwashing des Gewissens?

25   Sind Sinnfluencer Aktivisten oder letztlich doch nur Werbeträger? Und was war eigentlich zuerst da? Die Ökozahnbürste aus Holz im Drogeriemarktregal? Der Influencer, der dafür werben will? Oder der Kunde, der danach verlangt?

    Johanna Gollnhofer, Professorin für Marketing an der Universität im schweizerischen St. Gallen, forscht zu nachhaltigen und digitalen Transformationsprozessen in
30 der Wirtschaft. Ihrer Meinung nach beeinflusst sich alles gegenseitig: die Nachfrage das Angebot, das Angebot die Vermarkter, die Vermarkter die Verbraucher.

    Was zuerst da war, lässt sich nicht sagen. „Aber die Bedeutung der Influencer wird immer größer", sagt Gollnhofer. „Soziale Medien ermöglichen eine Interaktion mit den Konsumenten, sie bauen eine parasoziale Beziehung zum Influencer auf, Nutzer
35 nehmen ihn als Experten für das wahr, wofür er wirbt."

    Untersuchungen zeigen immer wieder, dass Konsumenten bei Kaufempfehlungen mittlerweile sogar eher auf Influencer vertrauen als auf enge Freunde. Dieses Prinzip funktioniert selbstverständlich auch beim Thema Nachhaltigkeit. „Influencer sind Marketinggold", sagt Expertin Gollnhofer.
40   In der Branche gilt: Je mehr Menschen einem Influencer auf Instagram folgen, desto mehr Geld bezahlen Firmen ihm für Kooperationen. Wie viel, darüber schweigt die Branche. Von ein paar Hundert Euro bis hin zu mehreren Zehntausend Euro für ein Posting mit einem bestimmten Produkt sind allerdings durchaus üblich.

    Sinnfluencer sind also größtmögliche Multiplikatoren für Produkte, mit denen
45 Kunden zugleich ein gutes Gewissen erwerben […].

    Blesin fing an zu recherchieren, unter welchen Bedingungen ihre Jeans und T-Shirts hergestellt werden. Mit der Reichweite ihres Blogs schließlich wuchs auch ihr Verantwortungsbewusstsein: „Zu welchem Kauf bewegen wir Menschen?" Diese Frage stellte sich Blesin immer wieder.
50   Mittlerweile empfiehlt die Bloggerin nur noch fair produzierte Mode und inhabergeführte Läden mit Produkten, die unter nachweislich guten Bedingungen hergestellt werden und denen oft das Geld für Werbung fehlt. „Wenn man die Preise der einfachen Ketten sieht, ist das schon schwer, Ökomode zu vermitteln", sagt die 30-Jährige. […]

(542 Wörter)

*Quelle: Rathcke, Julia. „Fraglicher Instagram-Trend: Wenn aus dem Influencer ein ‚Sinnfluencer'
wird". MAZ online. 8. Juni 2019. RND RedaktionsNetzwerk Deutschland*

Annotation
Z. 34 parasozial: nicht interaktiv, sondern einseitig kommunizierend

Themenschwerpunkte: *Aims and ambitions; The impact of the media on society*

You are taking part in an online workshop with a social studies class at your American partner school. Together you are examining trends in the usage of digital media in different countries.

Write an email to the workshop group, outlining the situation in Germany and individual attempts to reduce digital consumption as described in the article.

Text (Auszug aus dem Artikel)

Wie das Leben leichter wird
Von Elke Hartmann-Wolf

Wie Smartphone und Internet bewusst und sinnvoll nutzen? Digitaler Minimalismus verschafft uns mehr Zeit und Gelassenheit. Eine Anleitung.

1   Es sind zwölf Wörter, die sein Leben verändern. Bedächtig tippt Jan Rein sie in seine Tastatur: „Ab sofort bin ich nur noch telefonisch oder per Post zu erreichen." Er zögert noch einmal, dann drückt er auf Return und klappt den Laptop zu. Ein ganzes Jahr lang wird der Ernährungswissenschaftler und Buchautor nicht mehr im Internet aktiv sein,
5   nicht mehr bloggen, posten, teilen, twittern und auch keine selbst gefilmten Kochvideos auf seinen YouTube-Kanal hochladen. Ein kalter Entzug beginnt.

[…] In seiner sich selbst auferlegten Abstinenz wähnte sich Rein anfangs allein, wie ein Außenseiter. Er ist es aber nicht. Die Zahl jener, die genug davon haben, im freien Fall durch die unendlichen Weiten des Datenraums zu taumeln, sie wächst. Im-
10 mer mehr Menschen wollen es nicht mehr länger raffinierten Algorithmen überlassen, was sie vor dem Bildschirm treiben, sondern lieber selbst durch ihr Leben navigieren. Sie sehnen sich nach einer Balance zwischen Echtwelt und Pixelwelt.

Emanzipierte Nutzer des Netzes entwickeln konkrete Methoden, die sich an ihren eigenen Bedürfnissen und Wünschen orientieren. Sie hinterfragen den Wert jeder Ak-
15 tivität, jeder App und jedes Angebots. Wofür verwende ich meine Zeit und worauf Aufmerksamkeit, wo verschwende ich sie nur? Lediglich jene Bildschirmaktivitäten, die sinnvoll sind und Lebensqualität erhöhen, haben Platz. Alles Übrige kann weg. Take the best, forget the rest.

Mit einem Masterplan kehrt Jan Rein aus seinem einjährigen Screen-Sabbatical
20 zurück. Für YouTube dreht er keine Videos mehr, sondern verlinkt nur noch seinen Blog. E-Mails checkt er nur noch einmal täglich. Maximal eine Stunde verwendet er darauf, auch wenn die Inbox noch nicht geleert ist. Die sozialen Netzwerke nutzt er privat nur noch, um mit seinen Verwandten in Brasilien zu kommunizieren. Ansonsten lanciert er dort am späten Nachmittag eine gute Stunde lang seine Food-Themen.
25 Seitdem hat Rein genügend Zeit, Sport zu treiben, spazieren zu gehen oder seine Freunde zu treffen. Er wolle, so sagt der Gießener, kein „Internet-Bashing" betreiben. Die neuen Technologien brächten viele Vorteile, erforderten aber von jedem Einzelnen

einen reflektierten Umgang. „Meinen Weg habe ich gefunden, ich bin ausgeglichener und fühle mich frei." […]

30 Noch sind freilich viele von uns verstrickt in den Fängen des Netzes, verheddert im digitalen Gespinst. Durchschnittlich 196 Minuten täglich klebte jeder Deutsche im Jahr 2018 am Bildschirm seiner digitalen Begleiter – eine Verdreifachung innerhalb der letzten zehn Jahre. Rund 80-mal greifen wir pro Tag zum Smartphone. Einer Studie der Technischen Universität München zufolge haben 85 Prozent der Bundesbürger ihr
35 Smartphone immer griffbereit, 25 Prozent haben es rund um die Uhr bei sich.

Die Studie „Freizeit Monitor 2018" bestätigt, dass das digitale Leben einen immer größeren Stellenwert einnimmt. Es dominiert die Liste der Aktivitäten, die sich in den letzten fünf Jahren größerer Beliebtheit erfreuen. Ganz oben rangiert als Zeitfresser das Smartphone mit einem Zuwachs von rund 80 Prozent, gefolgt von Internet-An-
40 wendungen und sozialen Netzwerken.

Studien belegen, wir verbringen heute rund ein Drittel weniger Zeit mit Freunden, um gemeinsam einem Hobby nachzugehen, als vor Beginn der Digital-Ära. Auch feiern die Deutschen seltener Feste, selbst mit den Kindern wird weniger gespielt. Dabei schätzen wir uns und unser Zeitbudget selbst häufig völlig falsch ein. Wahrnehmungs-
45 psychologen sprechen in einem solchen Fall von einem „blinden Fleck". […]

Unklar ist, welche Auswirkungen die dramatische Zunahme von Digitalzeit auf unsere Gesundheit hat, ob sie womöglich die Fälle von Depressionen oder Einsamkeit ansteigen lässt. […] *(540 Wörter)*

Quelle: Hartmann-Wolff, Elke. „Wie das Leben leichter wird". FOCUS Magazin. 22. Sept. 2019. Zugriff am 07. Jan. 2020 von https://www.focus.de/digital/internet/wissen-wie-das-leben-leichter-wird_id_11139724.html. (Zwischenüberschriften des Originaltextes wurden weggelassen. Ein sprachlicher Fehler in der Textvorlage wurde entsprechend der geltenden Norm korrigiert.)

Aufgabenstellung 1.1

1 *In this task, you have to concentrate on the information given on Jende and Neni. This includes information on their family, their life before the situation portrayed in the text, their life now and their plans for the future.*
   Family
   – *Jende and Neni have a son.*
   – *Jende has a cousin in New York.*
   – *They still have family in Cameroon.*
   Life before
   – *Jende came to New York first (in order to escape poverty); he felt alone and home-sick; they talked on the phone often.*
   – *Neni and their son joined him later.*
   Life now
   – *The family lives in Harlem, New York.*
   – *They have a lawyer and hope to get legal status soon.*
   Plans for the future
   – *They both love New York.*
   – *Neni wants to stay there.*
   – *Jende wants to move away because of the cold winters.*

Jende and Neni Jonga are a married couple who immigrated from Cameroon. They live in Harlem while waiting for their immigration status to be approved. Though they have family in NYC and Neni likes living there, Jende wonders if they should move to a warmer climate. Jende moved to the USA first and was often homesick before his wife Neni and their young son, who both had stayed with their family in Cameroon, joined him. They have hired an immigration lawyer who recommends they not leave the area during the legal process.

While on a night out in Manhattan, they go to Columbus Circle, where Jende used to go alone to call his wife in Cameroon. Though he often doubts whether they should have made the trip to a new country, he realises that Columbus Circle is in fact at the centre of the world.

(145 words)

living in Harlem

plans for the future

what happened before

feelings about Manhattan and NY

2   *Here, you have to look at the narrative perspective and the use of language.*

Narrative perspective
- *omniscient narrator*
- *describes Jende's and Neni's feelings towards New York and how they see its people:*
  - *Jende thinks: "[t]he city [is] great" (l. 2).*
  - *Neni likes the diversity of New York: "That was what made New York so wonderful: It had a world for everyone." (ll. 21/22)*
  - *According to Jende the city is "cold, costly, congested" (l. 7). → Alliteration*
  - *To Neni, New York is the city of her dreams. (cf. l. 32)*

Use of language	*Effect/function*
– *alliteration: e. g. "cold, costly, congested" (l. 7)*	– *increases negative impression*
– *antonyms: e. g. "men and women, young and old, rich and poor" (ll. 18/19)*	– *express diversity of NYC*
– *repetition: e. g. "a black woman chatting with a black woman" (l. 15)*	– *stress how people stick to their own kind/uniqueness of the city*
– *rhetorical question: "And why shouldn't they?" (l. 20)*	– *insight into Neni's feelings*

The story is told by an omniscient narrator, that is, the readers are not only aware of the actions of the protagonists but also learn about their thoughts and feelings, and their perception of NYC. The readers are thus more likely to identify with the protagonists. Jende disapproves of the climate in New York, but is also fascinated by it: "The city was great, but why spend four months of the year shivering like a wet chicken?" (ll. 2/3). The author uses alliteration to increase the negative impression of the city, calling it "cold, costly, congested" (l. 7).

omniscient narrator shows NYC from protagonists' perspective

Jende's perspective

alliteration

Neni, who is much more enthusiastic about NYC, noticed that "[m]ost people were sticking to their own kind" (ll. 17/18) and that "[t]hat was what made New York so wonderful: It had a world for everyone" (ll. 21/22). By the use of antonyms like "men and women, young and old, rich and poor" (ll. 18/19), New York is presented as a diverse place with many contrasts. Neni's sensual perception of the city is revealed when she gets "a chance to enjoy the sounds of the city and its millions of lights blinking around her," (ll. 30/31).

Neni's perspective

antonyms

contrast

Repetition is used in the text to describe how people stick to their kind, "a black woman chatting with a black woman" (l. 15), for example. It is also used at the end of the text, when Jende says, "center of Manhattan […] center of New York […] center of

repetition

America […] center of the world" (ll. 52–54), which emphasises the uniqueness of the city.

A rhetorical question is used to give insight into Neni's thoughts and feelings about people sticking to their own kind: "And why shouldn't they?" (l. 20).

rhetorical question

(291 words)

3.1 *In this task you have to discuss the topic, so you have to find arguments for both sides. The wording of the task is not very clear. Are you supposed to concentrate on the benefits and challenges of a diverse community or are you supposed to discuss different degrees of integration (and assimilation)? Try not to get lost in your argumentation. To what conclusion do you want to come at end of your argument? Find suitable arguments, explanations and examples and leave out aspects that would belong to the topic in general but lead too far away from what you want to say. Start by explaining Neni's attitude in your introduction.*

- *Benefits of integrating into a new and diverse community:*
  - *Integration instead of assimilation is an enrichment for society.*
  - *A diverse society makes it easier for immigrants to settle in.*
- *Challenges of integrating into a new and diverse community:*
  - *Subcultures and different attitudes and religions can cause conflict.*
  - *Certain aspects, like a common language, are key for integration.*

Neni approves of the fact that, even in a multicultural society like New York City, people tend to socialise with their own kind. She believes there is a place for everyone in New York and one does not necessarily need to adapt or assimilate to succeed.

introduction
Neni's attitude

According to the concept of the melting pot, or assimilation, immigrants have to adapt to their new environment completely. This means they have to give up their own culture and sometimes even their own religion. However, why should they forget about their roots? Integration, according to the concept of the salad bowl, means immigrants are not expected to deny their past. Immigration can also be considered an enrichment to society regarding lifestyle, food, music and the arts.

main part
advantages

different cultures and religions are an enrichment for society

If you come to a society that is already very diverse, it is easier to find your place in the community. You will find other people who are like you and not feel alone or alienated. According to Neni, anyone can find someone who is "their kind" in New York City and thus avoid confrontation.

in a diverse culture it is easier to settle in

However, while it can be an enrichment and make it easier to build a life in a diverse society, you still have to adapt partly in order to integrate into society. When immigrants first arrive in the new country, they can feel homesick, and thus seek out their own people and form a subculture instead of adapting to their new environment. If the immigrant's culture is very different from that of

challenges

subcultures and different ways of living can lead to conflict and prejudice

the new neighbours, this can cause conflict. In recent years, prejudice has increased. After 9/11, for instance, tolerance towards Islam almost vanished in the USA. Furthermore, the native population might feel threatened by additional competitors for jobs as well as living space.

natives fear competition

The most important aspect of integration is language skills, without which one cannot find a qualified job. Thus, learning the language is vital to succeed in any new society. Moreover, a lack of language skills will prevent you from socialising and making new friends outside your own bubble.

language is a key factor in integration

While diversity can have a positive effect on society and make it easier for new immigrants to settle in, certain core values and a common language are necessary for a society to avoid conflict and make it possible for different people to live together in harmony.

conclusion

(386 words)

3.2 *As the task is to write a blog entry you can stick to a more colloquial style. Your blog entry should contain a heading, a short introduction, a main part and a conclusion. You can either first describe the picture, interpret it and then assess its effectiveness in a second step or combine the description, interpretation and evaluation.*

Description
- *picture shows five people from different ethnic and cultural backgrounds: young woman with a headscarf, three men with different hairstyles, beards and skin colours, one elderly person of Asian origin*
- *all look happy, peaceful and self-confident*
- *caption: "Immigrants are NY: Upholding our Values"*
- *in the lower section of the picture there is a mirrored version of the New York skyline*

Analysis
- *two ways of interpreting the caption: immigrants are part of New York as they are holding up American values, or immigration is an important part of America, therefore immigrants should be valued*
- *people depicted show ideal immigrants (happy and peaceful)*
- *skyline as a reflection of immigrants symbolises the message that immigrants are an important part of NYC*

Assessment of effectiveness
- *the image leaves out possible negative effects or conflict*
- *as a campaign for immigration, the picture is supposed to illustrate an ideal version of a multicultural society, so it is very effective*

Campaigning diversity

heading

I've just seen the illustration that says "Immigrants are NY: Upholding our Values" and I find it very effective, as it shows the diversity in the city.

introduction

The upper section of the illustration depicts five people who are from different ethnic and religious backgrounds and of differing ages and genders. The young woman pictured is wearing a headscarf, while three young men have different hairstyles, beards and skin colours. The elderly person of Asian origin looks peaceful. In fact, they all look happy and self-confident, which is the goal of integration.

main part
description of upper section

analysis

The caption "Upholding our Values" fits the current situation in the USA very well. Lots of people fear that immigrants might undermine American values, when the opposite is often the case. Most of them came to the USA to pursue the American Dream: freedom of speech, religious freedom, freedom of movement and freedom to realise their goals.

caption

analysis

At the bottom of the illustration, you can see the New York skyline, which looks like a reflection on the water, because it is upside-down. The skyline symbolises the message that immigrants are an essential part of New York.

description of lower section

analysis

You could argue that this illustration is slightly naive, because it shows an idealised picture that does not consider existing problems and conflict. However, a campaign is supposed to show the goal of immigration, which is to live together in peace and self-determination.

assessment

(232 words)

Aufgabenstellung 1.2

1   – *As a student, Kate Milman paused her studies to protest the building of a road.*
    – *She lived in a treehouse for months and formed an intimate relationship with nature.*
    – *When the forest was cut down, she decided to found an organisation that would offer children the opportunity to learn about and experience nature.*
    – *Three days a week she and other members of Wild Things offer half-day sessions for groups from different city schools.*
    – *Many of the children are refugees, who are reminded of home by the forest. There is no language barrier.*
    – *For British-born children it is often their first time being in a forest, as they have spent most of their lives indoors.*

Kate Milman interrupted her studies to take part in a protest action to prevent a forest from being cut down to build a road. She lived in a treehouse for months to stop the bulldozers and during that time became aware of the nature surrounding her. Despite the fact that the protest was not successful and she was arrested, the experience changed Kate's outlook. She then started the non-profit organisation "Wild Things" with her friends. It is a forest school run by four educators who bring refugee and inner-city children

Milman as a protester

founded "Wild Things"

back to nature. Kate and her colleagues see the impact nature has
on these children. Many refugees lived close to nature in their own
countries and immediately feel at home in the forest. It is also a
non-verbal experience for them that is more comfortable than integrating into their new environment. For city children who do not
have much contact with nature, they learn that everyone is equal.
In this programme, they can be children again without any pressure to fit in.   *(172 words)*

refugee children

city children

2 – *In general, the author paints a positive image of the initiative.*
   – *He uses quotes from staff and children to show the necessity for and importance of*
     the project.
   – *He gives background information on the founder to show why the organisation was*
     founded.
   – *He gives background information on the children to stress why the project is im-*
     portant.
   – *The heading contains a question and a quote which offers an answer to the ques-*
     tion.
   – *The pictures give an insight into the activities at the camp.*
   – *The author talks about his own positive experiences at the camp (report).*
   – *He also uses poetic language, alliteration and enumeration.*

The author, Patrick Barkham, definitely approves of the project
and its impact.

introduction

To arouse the reader's interest, he uses a catchy headline and photos. The headline contains the quote "I feel I've come home" and
the question "can forest schools help heal refugee children?" to
make the readers curious about the issue. Although the quote
comes before the question, it offers a possible answer and implies
that forest schools can indeed help children heal. Later in the text,
quotes from staff support this impression when they say, "In the
woods they are on a level playing field. They can just be kids
again," (l. 47). The first photo shows children discovering the
forest together, "[s]etting off on a tracking hunt", and the second
picture shows them "[s]haring treasures back at the camp". Both
pictures show an activity at the camp, which combines fun and
getting to know the forest better. As the girl in the first picture is
wearing a headscarf, the picture shows the multicultural aspect of
the camp.

main part
headline and
photos
quotes

In the first part of the text, Barkham conveys Kate Milman's background (cf. ll. 1–18), so the reader can understand why she founded
the forest school. To describe the calming effect of the forest on
Milman, the author uses the alliteration "precarious position as a
protester" (l. 6). Milman's inspiring experience in the forest, her

background infor-
mation on the
founder

alliteration

adventurous fight for nature and her disappointment when the road is built result in a positive climax when the initiative is formed: "The idea for Wild Things, a workers' cooperative set up to provide children with experience of the natural world, was born," (ll. 15/16).

The author reveals his personal experience, reporting: "I've come to a Wild Things day" (l. 19). To convey the beauty of nature in the park, Barkham uses poetic language: "The wind runs through the canopy in waves, worrying the leaves, but it is calm and snug in the green, brambly understorey. The slender trunks of silver birches shine in the low sunlight," (ll. 20–22).

personal experience

poetic language

The author also quotes staff member Yasmin Khaliq directly, when she says, "[y]ou don't know what they've seen," (l. 28) to express the dire situation some of the children have come from, and enthuses "[i]t's a godsend" (l. 30) to emphasise the effect of the project. To point out the large variety of countries the children come from, the author uses enumeration, writing: "Pakistan, Afghanistan, Romania and Syria, and some came from refugee camps," (ll. 27/28).

direct quotes from staff

enumeration

The author goes on to point out that there are also British children in the project who have never experienced nature. In this way he criticises the upbringing of inner-city children, bemoaning the fact that "[m]eanwhile British-born city children belong to a country called Indoors" (l. 33).

information on children

Finally, the author stresses the importance of the project by showing the children's naiveté when they ask questions like: "What's mud?" and "Why are there so many trees here?" (l. 34).

quotes from children

By the use of all of these devices, the author successfully convinces the reader of the project's importance.   *(509 words)*

conclusion

3.1 *Refer to the quote in your introduction. A good way to include it is to explain its meaning in your own words and then lead over to the question you are supposed to answer. When you "assess" something, you have to decide on the value or the state of something and give reasons for your decision. Here you have to decide if you think that projects like "Wild Things" can help refugee children. As the text suggests that it does, it is far easier to follow this line of argument. The text also contains possible arguments and proof to support these. You could include the following aspects:*
- *project gives children self-confidence*
- *no language or cultural barriers*
- *can help improve language skills instead and help make new friends in different groups*

According to the quote, the forest school offers the children refuge and a protected environment, where they can feel relaxed and safe. Integration in an environment like this is much easier than trying

introduction
reference to quote

to fit into a new society where they have to cope with various problems and challenges.

Projects like Wild Things can give children the power and self-confidence to deal with the everyday challenges they face. Issues like the language barrier, difference in appearance, behaviour and culture and other social divisions do not matter in the forest. Everybody is accepted as they are and the task of learning about nature is feasible. The experience can be very empowering.

main part
first argument

The most important step in adapting to a new society is acquiring communication skills. The project can help with this as the children learn new terminology and how to communicate in small, supervised peer groups. They meet other children, learn about their lives and interests and make new friends.

second argument

Social projects for children like Wild Things offer an initial step towards the smooth and successful integration into society. However, follow-up projects are needed to reinforce these positive effects. Projects at schools are vital to improve language skills and to overcome prejudice. For both refugee and inner-city children, programmes like these can be a key to further achievements in life.

conclusion
what's next

(219 words)

3.2 *Start your article with a convincing headline. You are writing for a young audience, so your style should not be too formal. As you are supposed to write a comment, you have to find convincing arguments which explain why it is important that children encounter nature. You could refer to the following aspects:*
 – problems if children spend most of their life indoors:
 • *unhealthy, lack physical activity*
 • *do not learn important skills like swimming or riding a bike properly*
 • *lack social contact with peers, do not develop important social skills*
 • *pace and reward system of video gaming reduces frustration tolerance*
 – value of projects that offer children opportunities to encounter nature:
 • *children learn about nature*
 • *they interact with other children in supervised groups*
 • *become more self-confident*
 • *physical exercise (health)*

Mother Nature and her Children

heading

Many children today spend most of their time indoors looking at a screen. Because they hardly go out, they are becoming increasingly unhealthy, anti-social and uninterested in the world around them. Parents have all but given up trying to convince their children to put their phone down and go play outside. The number of children who can't swim or ride a bike has increased rapidly and obesity is on the rise. Fewer and fewer young people do sports

problems if children spend most of their life indoors

regularly, which also contributes to an unhealthy lifestyle. Additionally, the pace and reward system of video gaming reduces children's frustration tolerance. This is why they give up very soon when there's a real-world problem. Some of them are in danger of losing touch with reality.

They haven't developed certain social skills because they don't meet their friends very often and lack personal contact. They don't know how to deal with others if there's an argument, for example, and even dating will become more difficult for them later in life.

These issues often can't be solved within the family or at school. However, they can be mitigated by regular trips into nature. Many children have little experience with nature and know even less about the plant and animal kingdom. Most of what they see to do with nature is in fact on a screen. That's why forest-school projects like Wild Things are so vital. They bring pupils into the forest and teach them about nature. The children take part in lots of exciting activities which offer an alternative to the virtual world, and interacting with other children in a supervised group improves their social skills. Being away from the temptations of electronic media opens their eyes to the real world. They will become more self-confident when they are successful in a team, and this will increase their frustration tolerance. Not only that, the physical exercise that comes with walking through the woods improves their health. Another benefit is that it's a place of equality. It is free and anyone can go there, regardless of their parents' social status. Therefore, nature schools will help equip them for the future.   *(360 words)*

value of projects that offer children opportunities to encounter nature

Prüfungsteil 2: Sprachmittlung

Aufgabenstellung 2.1

You are to sum up the information in an email to a friend. Your style should not be too formal. Include the following aspects in your solution:
- *The most recent generation of influencers is trying to combine an idea with marketing products.*
- *They support ecological and social issues like:*
  - *reducing plastic waste,*
  - *natural cosmetics,*
  - *recycling and*
  - *fair trade.*
- *The importance of these kinds of influencers is rising as young people especially care about these things.*

- *People trust influencers more than close friends.*
- *Influencers receive money for their posts.*

Subject: Recent trends in social media

Hi Dave,

I've just read an interesting article about recent trends in social media, called "Sinnfluencers". That's a play on words, because "Sinn" means "sense" or "meaning" in German. They're influencers who are trying to make the world a better place by what they're doing. They promote environmentally-friendly products that have a low carbon footprint and are produced under fair trade conditions. For example, 30-year old Julia-Maria Blesin from Hanover runs a blog and an Instagram account under the motto "Green, fair and fun". Instead of promoting the unsustainable products of big companies, she gives advice on how to avoid plastic and advertises natural cosmetics, recycled rucksacks and fairly-produced "slow" fashion. She wants to use her influence in a positive way and call attention to some of the world's injustices as well as our impact as consumers.

According to current research, influencers' opinions are more impor- tant to consumers than those of their closest friends, so they're a gold mine for companies, who sometimes pay them tens of thousands of euros to promote a product. Whereas ordinary influencers contribute to the excessive consumption of unnecessary items, "Sinnfluencers" try to increase environmental and social awareness with their recommendations.

I'm really excited about this recent trend. It's moving in the right direc- tion, I think.

Love,

Dareema *(219 words)*

Aufgabenstellung 2.2

In this task you are to give an outline of the current situation. Avoid getting into too much detail. You should include the following aspects:
- *people in Germany spend more and more time on the internet (mobile phones, surfing on the internet, social media)*
- *cutback in spare time for social activities and recreation*
- *not known whether digital consumption might impact our mental health (causing loneliness or depression)*
- *Jan Rein took a year off from being online and changed his user habits when he got online again*

Subject: Doing without social media

Dear members of the workshop group,

I'd like to tell you about a fascinating article I read called "How life gets easier" by Jan Rein.

The author went without the internet for a whole year and was only available by telephone or mail. At first he felt like an outsider, but after a while he realized he had a lot more free time to do sports, take a walk, and meet friends. Since his one year "screen sabbatical", he now uses social media in a totally different way. He only checks his emails once a day for one hour, no matter how many emails he's received. And he only uses social networks to communicate privately with his relatives.

In 2018, the average German spent more than 196 minutes a day in front of a screen, which is triple what it was 10 years before. Germans use their smartphones about 80 times a day and spend one-third less time with friends or pursuing hobbies than before the digital era. They don't have as many parties or play as much with their children as they used to. Most people have a "blind spot" when it comes to judging how much time they spend online. Studies confirm that digital life dominates people's activities. The effects on people's health is still under investigation, but they suspect it contributes to increasing cases of depression and loneliness.

I hope my information on Germany helps with the group's research.

Best regards,

Dennis

(250 words)

Prüfungsteil 1: Leseverstehen und Schreiben (70 %)

Der Prüfungsteil 1 besteht aus zwei Aufgabenstellungen, von denen Sie eine zur Bearbeitung auswählen.

Aufgabenstellung 1.1 – Tasks

Themenschwerpunkte: *Aims and ambitions; Ethnic and cultural diversity*

1 Outline the information on Amar and his family. (20 %)

2 Analyze the way Amar is characterized. (40 %)

3 Choose <u>one</u> of the following tasks:

3.1 Comment on Amar's decision to pursue his own ambitions instead of following his parents' advice. (40 %)

OR

3.2 You are invited to deliver a speech at the Generation Equality Youth Conference. You have come across a quotation about Vice President Kamala Harris' inauguration: "When she takes the oath of office, little girls and boys across the world will know that anything and everything is possible." *(American Senator Amy Klobuchar)*

Taking this quotation as a starting point, write your speech discussing the chances of achieving the American Dream today. (40 %)

Text (excerpt from the novel)

Asymmetry
by Lisa Halliday

Note: *Amar, the narrator, was born in the USA, where he grew up and lived after his parents had fled from Iraq with their older son, Sami, in the 1970s.*

1 […] According to Calvin Coolidge, economy is the only method by which we prepare today to afford the improvements of tomorrow. Whatever else you think about Coolidge, the statement does seem more or less correct, and when I came across it for the first time shortly after starting graduate school I thought: At last, I'm pursuing a pro-
5 fession befitting of my neuroses.

This is because my mind is always turning over this question of how I'm going to feel later, based on what I'm doing now. Later in the day. Later in the week. Later in a life starting to look like a series of activities designed to make me feel good later, but not now. Knowing I'll feel good later makes me feel good enough now. Calvin Coo-
10 lidge would approve, but according to my mother there is another term for such super-modulated living, and it translates roughly into not being able to live like a dog.

You would be happier, she has been heard to say, if you were more like your brother. Sami lives in the moment, like a dog.

For the record, my brother's name means *high, lofty,* or *elevated* – not traits you'd
15 readily associate with an animal that sniffs assholes and shits in plain sight. But I suppose my parents could not have predicted his canine spontaneity when they named him; nor could they have known that the one they named *making a home* would grow up to have nothing in his refrigerator but seven packets of soy sauce and an expired carton of eggs.

20 In December of 1988, on the flight to Baghdad from Amman, our parents forbade us from bringing up two subjects with our Iraqi interlocutors: Saddam Hussein and Sami's piano, never mind the ten years of music lessons he'd taken from our homosexual landlord downstairs. At any rate, what most of my aunts and uncles wanted to discuss around my grandmother's kitchen table was the exotic extent of my American-
25 ness: my Brooklyn accent, my Don Mattingly jersey, my pristine navy-blue passport and my embossed City of New York Certification of Birth. This last, of course, meant that I would be entitled to run for the American presidency one day, and while Sami and I practiced juggling oranges with our cousins in the back garden our elder relatives discussed this prospect with all the sobriety and momentousness of a G7 convention.
30 President Jaafari. President Amar Ala Jaafari. President Barack Hussein Obama. I suppose one does not sound so very much more unlikely than the other. And yet, at twelve years old, I knew perfectly well that my parents' truer hope was that I too would do as they had done, and as my brother looked all but certain to do, and that was to become a doctor. A doctor is respected. A doctor is never out of work. Being a doctor opens
35 doors. Economics my parents also consider respectable, but reliable? No. Ungraspable (my father's word). And even if one is more likely to ascend to the office of the presidency with a doctorate in economics than with a medical degree under his belt, my mother no longer mentions my eligibility these days, maybe because she thinks the position does not befit a man largely incapable of escaping, except infrequently and
40 accidentally, a consciousness trained on how every action undertaken is later going to make him feel. […]

I once heard a filmmaker say that in order to be truly creative a person must be in possession of four things: irony, melancholy, a sense of competition, and boredom.

Whatever my deficiencies in the first three areas, I enjoyed such an abundance of
45 the fourth that winter in Iraq that by the time we returned to New York I had eked out my first and only poetry cycle. What else did I do? Spent hours upon hours juggling, which is to say dropping and picking up oranges in the backyard until I could no longer see them for the dusk. With my father and Zaid I visited our relatives buried outside Najaf, and in the evenings sat at the kitchen table, doodling in the margins of my home-
50 work – an inordinate amount of homework, to make up for all the school I was missing

– while my grandfather sat beside me, slowly rotating the pages of *Al-Thawra*. One evening, he looked over to see me adding a few details to a sinking warship. If you're going to be president of Amrika, he said, you're going to have to do better than that. […]

55 Our grandmother's roof had a distant view of the Tigris, and as he stood beside me up there, smoking and squinting toward Karrada, my brother told me about how, on hot summer nights in the seventies, he and our parents would carry mattresses up to the roof in order to sleep in the relief of the river's breeze. It was not warm the night I heard this story; nor was there a mattress to hand […]. Still, in the moonlight, my
60 brother lay down, patted the space beside him, and as we stared up at the stars together Sami predicted it would not be long before Iraq was glorious again. Pothole-free roads, glittering suspension bridges, five-star hotels; the ruins of Babylon, Hatra, and the ste-lae of Nineveh all restored to their majesty and made visitable without the supervision of armed guards. Instead of Hawaii, honeymooners would fly to Basra.

[…]   *(912 words)*

Source: Halliday, Lisa. Asymmetry. London: Granta, 2018, 149–153.

Annotations

l. 1   Calvin Coolidge: 30th president of the United States (1923–1929)

l. 20   Amman: capital of Jordan

l. 21   Saddam Hussein: dictatorial Prime Minister and President of Iraq until 2003, sentenced to death in 2006

l. 25   Don Mattingly jersey: sweatshirt with the number of US baseball player Don Mattingly

l. 49   Najaf: city in central-south Iraq

l. 51   Al-Thawra: newspaper of the Arab Socialist Ba'ath Party, officially banned, but continuing to exist

l. 53   Amrika: Iraqi pronunciation of America

l. 56   Karrada: upper middle-class district of Baghdad, Iraq

Themenschwerpunkte: *Aims and ambitions; Ethnic and cultural diversity; The impact of the media on society; Saving the planet*

1 Sum up the challenges Barack Obama refers to in his speech and the advice he gives to H.B.C.U. graduates on how to deal with them. (30 %)

2 Analyze the way Barack Obama appeals to the 2020 graduates. (30 %)

3 Choose <u>one</u> of the following tasks:

3.1 "No generation has been better positioned to be warriors for justice and remake the world." (ll. 45/46)

Write a blog entry for the website of the "Conference of Youth", discussing Obama's attitude towards today's younger generation. (40 %)

OR

3.2 Assess the benefits and challenges of distance learning, using the message of the cartoon as a starting point. (40 %)

Source: Shiers, Frank. "Graduation at an online school". Federal Way Mirror. June 6, 2014. Accessed March 11, 2021 from https://www.federalwaymirror.com/opinion/graduation-at-an-online-school-cartoon/.

Text (Excerpt from a speech)

Excerpt from Obama's 2020 H.B.C.U. Commencement Speech
by Barack Obama

*On May 16, 2020, former President Barack Obama gave a virtual commencement speech
to the graduates of historically black colleges and universities (H.B.C.U.).*

1 […] Graduating from college is a big achievement under any circumstances. And so
many of you overcame a lot to get here. You navigated challenging classes, and challenges outside the classroom. Many of you had to stretch to afford tuition. And some
of you are the first in your families to reach this milestone.

5 So even if half this semester was spent at Zoom University, you've earned this
moment. You should be very proud. Everybody who supported you along the way is
proud of you […].

Now look, I know this isn't the commencement any of you really imagined.
Because while our H.B.C.U.s are mostly known for an education rooted in academic

10 rigor, community, higher purpose – they also know how to turn up. Nobody shines
quite like a senior on the yard in springtime. […] And I know that in normal times,
rivals like Grambling and Southern, Jackson State and Tennessee State, might raise
some eyebrows at sharing a graduation ceremony.

But these aren't normal times. You're being asked to find your way in a world in

15 the middle of a devastating pandemic and a terrible recession. The timing is not ideal.
And let's be honest – a disease like this just spotlights the underlying inequalities and
extra burdens that black communities have historically had to deal with in this country.
We see it in the disproportionate impact of Covid-19 on our communities, just as we
see it when a black man goes for a jog, and some folks feel like they can stop and

20 question and shoot him if he doesn't submit to their questioning.

Injustice like this isn't new. What is new is that so much of your generation has
woken up to the fact that the status quo needs fixing; that the old ways of doing things
don't work; and that it doesn't matter how much money you make if everyone around
you is hungry and sick; that our society and democracy only work when we think not

25 just about ourselves, but about each other.

More than anything, this pandemic has fully, finally torn back the curtain on the
idea that so many of the folks in charge know what they're doing. A lot of them aren't
even pretending to be in charge.

If the world's going to get better, it's going to be up to you. With everything sud-

30 denly feeling like it's up for grabs, this is your time to seize the initiative. Nobody can
tell you anymore that you should be waiting your turn. Nobody can tell you anymore
"this is how it's always been done." More than ever, this is your moment – your generation's world to shape.

In taking on this responsibility, I hope you are bold. I hope you have a vision that

35 isn't clouded by cynicism or fear. As young African Americans, you've been exposed,
earlier than some, to the world as it is. But as young H.B.C.U. grads, your education
has also shown you the world as it ought to be.

Many of you could have attended any school in this country. But you chose an H.B.C.U. – specifically because it would help you sow seeds of change. You chose to
40 follow in the fearless footsteps of people who shook the system to its core – civil rights icons like Thurgood Marshall and Dr King, storytellers like Toni Morrison and Spike Lee. […]

And I'm here to tell you, you made a great choice. Whether you realize it or not, you've got more road maps, more role models, more resources than the civil rights gen-
45 eration did. You've got more tools, technology, and talents than my generation did. No generation has been better positioned to be warriors for justice and remake the world.

Now, I'm not going to tell you what to do with all that power that's in your hands. Many of you are already using it so well to create change. But let me offer three pieces of advice as you continue on your journey.

50 First, make sure you ground yourself in actual communities with real people – working whenever you can at the grass-roots level. The fight for equality and justice begins with awareness, empathy, passion, even righteous anger. Don't just activate yourself online. Change requires strategy, action, organizing, marching, and voting in the real world like never before. No one is better positioned than this class of graduates
55 to take that activism to the next level. And from tackling health disparities to fighting for criminal justice and voting rights, so many of you are already doing this. Keep on going.

Second, you can't do it alone. Meaningful change requires allies in common cause. As African Americans, we are particularly attuned to injustice, inequality, and strug-
60 gle. But that also should make us more alive to the experiences of others who've been left out and discriminated against.

So rather than say, "What's in it for me?" or "What's in it for my community? And to heck with everyone else," stand up for and join up with everyone who's struggling – whether immigrants, refugees, the rural poor, the L.G.B.T. community, low-income
65 workers of every background, women who so often are subject to their own discrimi- nation and burdens and not getting equal pay for equal work; look out for folks whether they are white or black or Asian or Latino or Native American. As Fannie Lou Hamer once said, "nobody's free until everybody's free."

And on the big unfinished goals in this country, like economic and environmental
70 justice and health care for everybody, broad majorities agree on the ends. That's why folks with power will keep trying to divide you over the means. That's how nothing changes. You get a system that looks out for the rich and powerful and nobody else. So expand your moral imaginations, build bridges, and grow your allies in the process of bringing about a better world.

75 And finally, as H.B.C.U. graduates, you have to remember that you are inheritors of one of America's proudest traditions. Which means you're all role models now – whether you like it or not. Your participation in this democracy, your courage to stand up for what's right, your willingness to forge coalitions – these actions will speak volumes. […]   *(994 words)*

*Source: Obama, Barack. "Obama's H.B.C.U. Commencement Speech." The New York Times.
May 16, 2020. Accessed May 17, 2020 from https://www.nytimes.com/2020/05/16/us/obama-hbcu-
speech-transcript.html. (Minor grammatical mistake in the original corrected.)*

Annotations

l. 5   Zoom University: distance schooling taking place on the Zoom video conferencing platform

l. 12   Grambling and Southern: public, historically black universities in Louisiana

l. 12   Jackson State and Tennessee State: public, historically black universities in Mississippi and Tennessee

ll. 19/20   reference to the killing of Ahmaud Arbery, a 25-year-old black man shot while jogging by two white men in Georgia in 2020

l. 41   Thurgood Marshall: first African-American judge on the Supreme Court

l. 41   Toni Morrison: American novelist, essayist, Nobel Prize recipient, and college professor (1931–2019)

ll. 41/42   Spike Lee: American film director, screenwriter, actor, and professor (born in 1957)

l. 51   grass-roots level: ordinary people regarded as the main body of an organization's membership

l. 67   Fannie Lou Hamer: American voting and women's rights activist, community organizer, and leader in the civil rights movement (1917–1977)

Der Prüfungsteil 2 besteht aus zwei Aufgabenstellungen, von denen Sie eine zur Bearbeitung auswählen.

Aufgabenstellung 2.1 – Task

Themenschwerpunkte: *Saving the planet; Aims and ambitions; The impact of the media on society*

"Sustainable development", an online campaign by the European Youth Forum, was established to contribute to young people's understanding of the environment. It is interested in experiences that set an example for more and better environmental awareness.
Write a blog entry for the campaign's website in which you outline the information on the general idea of "Moral Games" and on their players as reported by Juliane Frisse.

Text (Auszug aus dem Artikel)

Das Spiel für eine bessere Welt
Von Juliane Frisse

1 Dies ist die Geschichte von drei Freunden, die mit einem Google-Doc und einem massiven Silberring die Welt retten wollen. Also, zumindest ihren Teil dazu beitragen wollen: weniger Fleisch essen, Flüge und Plastiktüten vermeiden, nur noch faire T-Shirts kaufen. Da die Freunde fanden, dass sie ihr Potenzial hier bisher nicht ausgeschöpft
5 hatten, beschlossen sie zu testen, ob es besser klappt, wenn sie ein Spiel daraus machen. Sie nennen es „Moral Games". […]
   Chris Starke, Cyril Brandt und Nils Köbis, alle Anfang 30, kennen sich seit Jugendtagen. Heute arbeiten sie als Wissenschaftler oder wissenschaftsnah, beschäftigen sich beruflich mit politischer Kommunikation, Verhaltensökonomie, Sozialpsycholo-
10 gie und Bildungsprojekten in Konfliktregionen. „Uns ist bewusst, dass das alles etwas schräg wirkt, wenn man von außen drauf schaut", sagt Chris.
   Die „Moral Games" spielen Chris, Cyril und Nils seit etwa vier Jahren. Sie begannen, weil sie ihr Konsumverhalten ändern wollten, im Alltag mehr im Einklang mit ihren Werten leben wollten. Es ging ihnen vor allem um Nachhaltigkeit und Umwelt-
15 schutz, aber auch um faire Produktionsbedingungen. „Wir haben uns zwar alle in antirassistischer Arbeit, für Menschenrechte, in der Flüchtlingshilfe oder in der Bildungsarbeit engagiert", sagt Cyril. „Doch bei den alltäglichen Entscheidungen haben wir gemerkt, dass wir keine signifikanten Fortschritte machten." […]
   Ihre „Moral Games" haben ein ausgefeiltes Regelwerk. Chris, Cyril und Nils haben
20 es gemeinsam entwickelt und immer wieder angepasst. Grob funktioniert das Ganze so: In fünf verschiedenen Kategorien sammelt jeder von ihnen Plus- und Minuspunkte. Kategorie 1 ist Fleisch essen, Kategorie 2 Fisch essen, 3 Plastikverbrauch, 4 Bio- und Fair-Trade-Produkte und 5 Lebensmittelverschwendung.

Jeder Spieler startet bei Null in eine neue Woche. Um Pluspunkte zu bekommen,
25 muss man in einer Kategorie eine perfekte Woche schaffen: Wer zum Beispiel sieben
fleischfreie Tage vorweisen kann, darf sich zehn Punkte gutschreiben. Für Nachhaltig-
keitsfails gibt es Abzüge: ein Fischstäbchen essen? Macht sechs Minuspunkte. Ein
Steak: zwölf. Für einen To-Go-Becher gibt es zwei Punkte Abzug. Wer sich ein nicht
fair produziertes Kleidungsstück kauft, muss sich zehn Prozent des Preises als Minus-
30 punkte aufschreiben.

Welches Verhalten wie bepunktet wird, entscheiden die Freunde zusammen. Dabei
orientieren sie sich an Fragen wie etwa: Wie schlimm sind die ökologischen Folgen
eines Verhaltens? Wäre es einfach möglich, anders zu handeln?

An jedem Montag wird abgerechnet. Dann tragen Cyril, Nils und Chris ihre Punkte
35 in ein gemeinsames Google-Doc ein. Sobald einer von ihnen 222 Punkte erreicht hat
– was bei einem gemäß den Spielregeln perfekten Lebensstil nach sechs Wochen möglich ist –, hat er die Runde gewonnen und ist der neue „Moral King". Alternativ wird
zum Sieger erklärt, wer nach zwölf Wochen die meisten Punkte gesammelt hat. Cyril
trage inzwischen den Spitznamen „Moral Two-Face", erzählen die Freunde: Einerseits
40 gewinne er oft, andererseits leiste er sich auch häufig moralische Totalaussetzer – Pha-
sen mit viel Fleisch, Plastikflaschen und To-Go-Müll.

Als Preis wird der „Moral King" von den anderen beiden zu einem gemeinsamen
Essen ins Restaurant eingeladen, und er darf den Ring tragen. Die Verlierer müssen
ihren Rückstand zum Sieger spenden – pro Punkt 1 Euro. Gespendet wird am Jahres-
45 ende, dann rechnen Chris, Cyril und Nils auch ihre Flüge ab: Wer geflogen ist, muss
ebenfalls Geld für einen guten Zweck geben. Die Organisationen, die sie unterstützen,
suchen sie gemeinsam aus. Bisher haben sie an die Amadeu Antonio Stiftung, Ärzte
ohne Grenzen, Reporter ohne Grenzen und Atmosfair gespendet. […]

Auch die Bilanz von Nils, Chris und Cyril fällt nach inzwischen siebzehn Runden
50 „Moral Games" positiv aus: Ihren Fleischkonsum haben sie, so schätzen sie, um etwa
80 Prozent reduziert. Sie berichten außerdem, dass sie weniger fliegen als früher, inzwischen immer einen Stoffbeutel und einen Mehrwegbecher dabeihaben und nur noch
Fair-Trade-Kaffee kaufen. […]

Für Nils, Chris und Cyril ist das Spiel auch ein Weg, ihre Fernfreundschaft zu pfle-
55 gen: Sie leben in Düsseldorf, Münster und Amsterdam. Durch die „Moral Games"
haben sie trotzdem fast jeden Tag Kontakt. Regelmäßig schicken sie Nachrichten hin
und her, wie etwas punktemäßig einzuordnen ist – und treffen sich, wenn sie den Run-
densieger zum gemeinsamen Essen einladen. […] *(644 Wörter)*

Frisse, Juliane. „Das Spiel für eine bessere Welt." ZEIT ONLINE 15. Dezember 2019. Zugriff am
23. August 2020 von https://www.zeit.de/die-antwort/2019-11/nachhaltigkeit-umweltschutz-alltag-
moral-games.

Annotationen

Z. 1   Google-Doc: Online-Textverarbeitungsprogramm, mit dem Dokumente erstellt und gemeinsam
            mit anderen bearbeitet werden können

Z. 26/27   Nachhaltigkeitsfail: Verstoß gegen Nachhaltigkeitsbemühung

Z. 47   Amadeu Antonio Stiftung: Stiftung, die sich gegen Rechtsextremismus, Rassismus und
            Antisemitismus wendet; benannt nach Amadeu Antonio Kiowa, der durch rechtsextreme
            Gewalt in Deutschland umgekommen ist

Z. 48   Atmosfair: gemeinnützige Klimaschutzorganisation mit dem Schwerpunkt Reisen

Aufgabenstellung 2.2 – Task

Themenschwerpunkte: *The impact of the media on society; Saving the planet*

Your Scottish friend is preparing a speech on "Digitalization and Climate Change" for the UN Youth Assembly 2022.
Write him/her an email summing up the information Elisabeth Schmidt's article provides on this topic.

Text (Auszug aus dem Artikel)

Klickscham statt Flugscham? – Internet produziert so viel CO_2 wie Flugverkehr
Von Elisabeth Schmidt

Die Internetnutzung in Deutschland produziert jedes Jahr so viel CO_2 wie der gesamte Flugverkehr. Und die Menge könnte sich in den nächsten zehn Jahren verdoppeln, warnen Forscher.

1 Noch vor dem Frühstück WhatsApp-Nachrichten verschicken, Fotos mit Freunden teilen, in der Straßenbahn ein YouTube-Video schauen, im Büro Dutzende E-Mails beantworten: Alltag. Wer denkt hier an CO_2-Ausstoß oder Umweltbelastung?

  Ralph Hintemann, Energieforscher am Borderstep-Institut für Innovation und
5 Nachhaltigkeit in Berlin, rechnet vor: Wir schreiben in Deutschland rund eine Milliarde E-Mails pro Tag. Dabei fallen 1 000 Tonnen Kohlenstoffdioxid an, ein Gramm pro E-Mail. Eine Stunde Video-Streaming produziert so viel CO_2 wie ein Kilometer Autofahren, so der Wissenschaftler. Auch bei Suchanfragen entsteht das Klimagas: Laut Google produziert eine Anfrage etwa 0,2 Gramm CO_2. Bedenkt man, dass jeden Tag
10 3,45 Milliarden Mal gegoogelt wird, kommt eine beträchtliche Menge zusammen. […]

  Natürlich: Nutze ich ein E-Paper statt einer Zeitung, schreibe ich eine E-Mail anstelle eines Briefes, schone ich Ressourcen wie Papier oder Wasser. Doch Digitalisierung ist nicht per se nachhaltiger und umweltschonender. Nachrichten, Fotos, Videos oder Akten verschwinden in einer Cloud. Der weltweite Datenaustausch ist nur mög-
15 lich, weil rund um den Globus Milliarden Server in teils gigantischen Rechenzentren permanent arbeiten. Die Server müssen gekühlt werden, die Rechner benötigen Strom. Weltweit produzieren IT-Geräte und -Anwendungen 800 Millionen Tonnen CO_2 pro Jahr – das entspricht in etwa den Gesamttreibhausgas-Emissionen Deutschlands.

  Wissenschaftler des Borderstep-Instituts arbeiten zurzeit an einer Studie zum Ener-
20 gieverbrauch deutscher Rechenzentren. Hintemann spricht von einem regelrechten „Boom" in den letzten Jahren: Viele neue Rechenzentren seien entstanden. „Das bedeutet aber auch, dass der Energiebedarf deutlich angestiegen ist. Die Rechenzentren brauchen heute 14 Milliarden Kilowattstunden in Deutschland. Das sind 40 Prozent mehr als im Jahr 2010." Setze sich diese Entwicklung fort, so der Forscher, würden
25 Rechenzentren in den nächsten Jahren doppelt so viel Energie benötigen wie heute. Von „Digitalscham" oder „Klickscham" ist bereits die Rede. Dabei kann jeder einzelne Nutzer etwas dazu beitragen, Energie und damit CO_2 einzusparen. Steffen Holzmann,

Green-IT-Experte bei der Deutschen Umwelthilfe, rät: alte E-Mails löschen. Sich von
nicht benötigten Newslettern abmelden. Fotos und Videos statt in einer Cloud auf Spei-
30 chermedien wie CDs, DVDs oder externen Festplatten speichern. „Das sind Technologien, die Bibliotheken einsetzen, um Dinge zu archivieren, und das braucht auch
wenig oder keine Energie – solange ich diese Dateien nicht benutze", erklärt Holzmann.

Ein weiteres Mittel sei die sogenannte Daten-Deduplizierung. Holzmann nennt da-
35 bei das folgende Beispiel: „Betriebsausflug. 50 Leute sind unterwegs. Am Ende macht
Herr Meier ein wunderschönes Foto, schickt es per E-Mail an alle 50 Leute. Das heißt:
Es liegt dann in seinem Postfach, es liegt in 50 weiteren Postfächern, überall liegen
fünf Megabyte für dieses Foto. Die Hälfte dieser Postfächer leitet das Foto automatisch
an eine private E-Mail-Adresse weiter oder an Oma Hilde oder sonst jemanden. Es
40 wird außerdem per WhatsApp geteilt. Es wird hinterher auch nochmal in der Cloud
synchronisiert, weil WhatsApp automatisch mit der Cloud synchronisiert wird. So werden aus fünf Megabyte Bild plötzlich bis zu einem Gigabyte Daten, das auf verschiedenen Serversystemen bereitgehalten werden muss.

Dieses exponentielle Wachstum bedeutet natürlich auch ein exponentielles Wachs-
45 tum im Energieverbrauch." Daten zu deduplizieren meint, Daten nicht mehr an so viele
Stellen zu verteilen, um damit Energie und CO_2 einzusparen.

„Der Großteil des Energieverbrauchs des Internets liegt in den Rechenzentren, in
den Netzen – und hier sind natürlich die Unternehmen gefragt, die diese Rechenzentren
betreiben", sagt Hintemann, der auch das Netzwerk energieeffiziente Rechenzentren
50 vertritt. Dass Energieeffizienz gelingen kann, zeigt das Rechenzentrum des TÜV Nord
in Hannover. Daten aus mehr als 70 Ländern werden hier verarbeitet. Vor vier Jahren
wurden die Serverräume umgebaut. Rund 750 Tonnen CO_2 spart der TÜV dadurch pro
Jahr ein und verbraucht nur noch halb so viel Energie wie vor dem Umbau. [...]

(610 Wörter)

*Schmidt, Elisabeth. „Klickscham statt Flugscham? – Internet produziert so viel CO_2 wie
Flugverkehr". ZDF heute Nachrichten. 28. November 2019. Zugriff am 20. Mai 2020 von
https://www.zdf.de/nachrichten/heute/klickscham-wie-viel-co2-e-mails-und-streaming-verusachen-
100.html.*

Annotationen

Titel Klickscham: schlechtes Gewissen angesichts der durch digitalen Konsum erzeugten CO_2-Emissio-
nen

Z. 28 Deutsche Umwelthilfe: Umwelt-, Natur- und Verbraucherschutzorganisation mit Sitz in Hannover

Z. 34 Daten-Deduplizierung: *Englisch:* data deduplication

Aufgabenstellung 1.1

1   *Outlining a text means showing its essential features without going into detail. You can concentrate on the two categories mentioned in the task, one being Amar, the other his family.*

Amar
- *of Iraqi ancestry*
- *born in the USA, "Americanized"*
- *studying economics*
- *worries a lot about what impact his current actions will have on his future*
- *writes poetry*
- *recalls family visits in the 1980s in Basra*

his family
- *parents: doctors, fled to the US in the 1970s, want their son to become a doctor too, disapprove of Amar's career plans*
- *older brother Sami: came to America as a child, studies medicine, easy-going (lives in the moment), proud to be Iraqi, tells Amar about Iraq's past and glorious future*
- *relatives: see Amar as future US president due to his place of birth, must not be told about the liberal ideas of Amar's parents (no politics mentioned when visiting them), rooted in old traditions*

Amar's parents fled to the USA from Iraq with his older brother Sami in the 1970s. As Amar himself was born and raised in America he speaks with an American accent and dresses in a Western style. Amar, who also writes poetry, worries a lot about how his current actions will influence his future, he even calls this a neurosis. | Amar's parents
Amar

His parents are not satisfied with him studying economics. His mum wants him to live in the moment, a behaviour typical of his brother, who is also very proud of his ancestry. His father has never accepted that Amar has no intentions of studying medicine to become a doctor like Sami and his parents. | his parents' opinion on him
Sami, his brother

His Iraqi relatives have to be treated with care as far as political issues are concerned, since they are quite traditional. But what they are dreaming of for Amar is a career as American president, for his US passport and his birth certificate entitle him to run for it. | his Iraqi relatives

(163 words)

2   *When characterizing the protagonist in a fictional text, you can refer to the following categories: narrative perspective, atmosphere and language.*

A first-person narrator, e. g., is quite subjective in what he/she tells us, whereas a third-person or an omniscient narrator can keep a certain distance from the character described and be more objective then.

A certain atmosphere in an excerpt may evoke a particular feeling in the reader, which in case of a first-person narrator also allows us to conclude that he/she is timid, stubborn, aggressive, etc.

What others say about the character or how he/she talks about him/herself or others also gives us a good insight into the person's soul.

The less we get to know directly about a protagonist, the more indirectly is he/she characterized. You have to quote from the text to prove your analysis.

Language	*Effect/function*
– *first-person narrator*	– *subjective view on events, family, etc., Amar can choose what he is going to tell us*
– *irony (cf. ll. 4/5, 9/10)*	– *ironic self-reflexion supports the idea that Amar is not very self-confident*
– *choice of words: negative connotations (cf. ll. 10/11, 35, 38)*	– *show gap between two cultures, Amar might feel torn between his ancestry and his Americanness*
– *comparison (cf. ll. 11, 33, 38)*	– *brother seems to be better, more accepted/loved by family*
– *incongruity (cf. ll. 14–18)*	– *paradoxical situation when it comes to the brothers' names and their meanings, irony behind it also proves Amar's insecurity*

Amar is mostly indirectly characterized by what he says and does and how his family sees him. He seems to be quite insecure, not very self-confident, doubtful, torn between two cultures and somehow struggling with his Iraqi heritage.   **thesis** / adjectives to describe him

The most dominant means employed is the first-person narrator. The reader gets an exclusive insight into Amar's feelings and thoughts. We get to know his family through his eyes. This is quite subjective, but helps us understand why he is feeling this or that way.   first-person narrator

The use of irony can be sensed quite easily. He has "at last found [out] that he [is] pursuing a profession befitting of [his] neurosis" (ll. 4/5) when he reads the Coolidge quote for the first time. He thinks that "Coolidge would approve" (ll. 9/10) of his lifestyle, but his own mother does not. The incongruity of the meaning in the brothers' names is also quite ironic. Amar's translates to *"making a home"* (l. 17), which he has no intention of doing, whereas Sami's means *"high, lofty, or elevated"* (l. 14), which Amar says   use of irony / incongruity does not fit with "an animal that sniffs assholes and shits in plain sight" (l. 15). The slang words seem to help him cope with his mother's reproach that he should be more able "to live like a dog" (l. 11), that means someone lives in the moment. When he describes how his aunts and uncles discuss his career prospects he states they are doing it "with all the sobriety [...] of a G7 convention" (l. 29), which is clearly an exaggeration used to express irony. His parents also constantly compare the two brothers much to Amar's disadvantage. His mum says he is "not [...] able to live like a dog" (l. 11), he leads a "supermodulat[ed]" life (ll. 10/11), and she "no longer mentions [his] eligibility" (l. 38). His father considers his studies "[u]ngraspable" (l. 35) and his relatives see an "exotic extent of his Americanness" (ll. 24/25) or tell him that he has "to do better than that" (l. 53) if he wants to run for president.

exaggeration to express irony

comparison

negatively connoted words

Amar seems to have grown a thick skin over the years. He does not appear to be unhappy, though. His ironic self-reflection rather suggests that he can understand his parents and all the other family members and therefore has learnt to cope with their criticism since he has obviously ignored them, completed his studies and become an economist.

conclusion

(404 words)

3.1 *This task is the classic argumentative essay. Start with an introduction, followed by the main part in which you find arguments and end in a conclusion, where you voice your personal opinion. In a comment you can stick to one line of argumentation (pros or cons) or weigh both sides. You are also expected to refer to the excerpt from the novel. Before you start writing your comment, think of possible reasons for and against such a decision.*

Arguments based on the excerpt:

Follow own ambitions	**Follow parents' advice**
– *studying economics helps Amar cope with his neurosis*	– *doctors are in demand everywhere*
– *he feels rather American, so he sees economics as his own way of life*	– *can even work anywhere in the world*
– *his parents' wish is rooted in Iraqi traditions, although they are liberal*	– *it would make his parents proud of him, he could share experiences with them and keep in touch with his Iraqi ancestry*
– *time for s. o. to break with the traditions*	

Arguments based on personal experiences/opinion:

Follow own ambitions	**Follow parents' advice**
– *you don't want to have your life planned right from the beginning (independence) you have a right to a fulfilling life*	– *parents may know what's good for you (life experience)*
	– *parents can help you through your studies/find an internship, job, etc.*

- *not pursuing your own dreams makes you unhappy*
- *you may not be good at what your parents suggest, so you won't be good at that job*

Amar's parents want him to become a doctor like them and his brother Sami, but he probably already decided in high school that he rather wants to be an economist. **introduction**
topic of comment

I can perfectly understand him and if I were in his shoes I would have made the same decision. **main part**
personal opinion

His mother and his father are right: doctors have a future-proof job. They are looked for everywhere and could effectively work anywhere in the world. It would also have made his parents really proud of him if he had taken up medical studies and would have strengthened his family bonds. Maybe Amar would have gotten rid of the feeling that he is the odd-one-out. It would have kept him in touch with his Iraqi ancestry, too. If he had become a doctor, he could have profited from his parents' experiences, there could have been an exchange of knowledge and expert opinions. It would no doubt have been the easier way. No arguing about life plans, no disappointment, no reproaches. **why to follow parents' advice**

doctors wanted

profit from parents' experiences

But would it have made Amar happy? I don't think so. From what we know about his character traits, studying economics surely helped him cope with his neurosis. The job of a doctor, on the other hand, might have worsened it. When you live in fear of how your present behaviour affects your future, knowing too much about diseases and their causes can make you nervous or anxious, whereas being able to manage your finances can leave you relaxed and self-assured. **why to follow your own ambitions**

Amar's neurosis

Amar seems to feel American, so he has internalized the idea of the American Dream, the pursuit of happiness everyone is entitled to. He, too, has the right to a fulfilling life. Even parents do not always know what is best for their children. What good are you in a job that you just take up because your mum and dad want you to? You may have difficulties motivating yourself when studying, you may even fail exams. Admittedly, you might get more support from a family that has followed the same course, they could even help you find an internship or a job later, but all that cannot fight the feeling of unhappiness or dissatisfaction with the work you are doing only for your parents' consent. his Americanness

right to fulfilling life

difficult to motivate yourself in a job you don't like

In the end, I believe that Amar's decision was right. I hope that all parents respect their children's life plans and support them rather than blackmailing them into a job they are not passionate about. **conclusion**

(410 words)

3.2 *A speech is similar to an argumentative essay. Here you, too, have to refer to pros and cons, as you are supposed to "discuss" the topic. The big difference is that you have to talk to people in front of you, so your text needs to be more interactive and probably also more entertaining.*

The typical features of speeches are metaphorical language, parallelism, direct address and rhetorical questions.

You are expected to take Klobuchar's quote into consideration and also define the American Dream to show the link between the two.

Yes, everyone can achieve the American Dream:
– *former presidents have made their way to the top through hard work (Bill Clinton, Obama)*
– *you yourself have to set you the goal, the American Dream does not mean that the state gets you to the top*

No, it is not for everyone:
– *BLM movement proves that minorities are still barred from achieving the Dream*
– *people who advance in life in spite of being part of a minority group are still often privileged when it comes to their economic and academic situation*

Appeal: *American Dream was not originally about money, but about cooperation.*

My fellow students,	**salutation**
We are all a step short of our adult life. We will soon be graduating from our colleges and universities and start our working life and our careers. The privilege of the right to the pursuit of happiness is often connected to the idea of the American Dream. Vice President, Kamala Harris, whose mother was born in India and whose father comes from Jamaica, is the first female Vice President as well as the first Black* and Asian-American Vice President. At her inauguration in 2021 Senator Klobuchar said: "When she takes the oath of office, little girls and boys across the world will know that anything and everything is possible."	intro to topic link between Harris and American Dream Klobuchar's quote
Anything and everything. Is this really true? It seems so. When you have a look at former presidents like Bill Clinton or Barack Obama, who have come a long way and made it to the top through hard work, dedication and the belief in the American Dream, it seems that the USA is the country of unlimited opportunities.	first pro argument
It is part of the American Dream that you have to set yourself the goal to rise to the top. The American Dream is not about asking the state to offer you all those opportunities. If you do not have the motivation and the will to succeed, you won't. It is possible in the USA to go from rags to riches, but there is no silver platter you can choose your career from. You go for it, and then you will make it!	second pro argument

At least in theory. In real life, movements like Black Lives Matter show that the American Dream is not achievable for everyone. Large groups of people are still being discriminated against, kept in poverty and barred from higher education. When you struggle daily to make ends meet, how can you rise to the top? first con argument

It is an important development that a woman like Kamala Harris can become Vice President today, but even she, like Barack Obama, was born privileged as both their parents came from an academic background. second con argument

The American Dream today needs to be more like working together, supporting each other, granting everyone a life of dignity. That is how everyone will have the chance to improve. appeal to listeners to make a change

We have to know our privileges and understand that we have not achieved the goal of equality that would enable everybody to achieve the American Dream. Let's do our best to not only reach our own goals, but to help others advance in life, too! **conclusion**

Thank you. *(420 words)* saying thank you

Aufgabenstellung 1.2

1 *This task wants you to sum up, i. e. concentrate on certain issues of the text and not summarize the whole content. It is also up to you whether you want to start with the introductory sentence containing the text type, title, author, source, etc.*
What you have to find out about is the challenges Obama mentions and the advice he gives. Draw a table or list the two categories after having underlined them in the text.
Challenges:
– *classes, tuition, online classes, video conferences amount to unusual times*
– *they had to find their way around in a troubled world, some of them being the first ones in their family to graduate from college or university*
– *pandemic, recession, inequality = extra burden for Black communities (racism)*
– *status quo needs fixing*
– *democracy demands cooperation, mutual help*
– *young generation in charge of change*
Advice:
– *get rooted in communities of real people (not just be online)*
– *be aware of positive/negative feelings in communities*
– *find allies to support your work, dreams*
– *support others and their fight for equality, against discrimination, etc.*
– *act as the role models H.B.C.U. have made you*
– *fight for democracy, show courage*

In the excerpt from his 2020 H.B.C.U. Commencement Speech Barack Obama focuses on the challenges the graduates have been facing and will probably face in the future. **introductory sentence**

In a world of a pandemic and on-going recession, studying in and outside classes seemed more difficult for them, since remote learning via Zoom could not fully compensate for a normal campus life and money may have been short for tuition. *(reference to unusual times of the pandemic and remote learning)*

Additionally they had to face the inequality and the extra burdens Black communities have been familiar with for centuries. Black people were hit harder by the pandemic and are in danger of being killed by racism in everyday situations. *(racism)*

To overcome the aftermath of these unusual times, every one of them has a personal responsibility to make the world a better place. The 2020 graduates are the generation in charge of that change. As they are part of a generation that is very aware of the existing injustice, they can take the responsibility and help democracy flourish. *(young generation in charge of making a change)*

Obama gives his listeners three pieces of advice, the first being that they must always be rooted in communities with real people and listen to their positive and negative feelings. The digital world cannot mirror reality well enough. *(**first piece of advice:** be analogue rather than digital)*

His second piece of advice revolves around working together. He tells them to find friends and allies, and also support others who are discriminated against in their attempts to fight for important issues like equality or against discrimination. *(**second piece of advice:** find friends and allies and be an ally)*

He finally makes them aware of the fact that as H.B.C.U. graduates they are role models now and will be judged by their actions and courage in the struggle for change. *(**third piece of advice:** act as role models)* *(272 words)*

2   When analysing a non-fictional texts, refer to its structure and its language. Typical stylistic devices used in speeches are direct address, parallelism, comparisons, rule of three and also metaphors.

It is usually enough to concentrate on a few repeatedly employed means or a really dominant one. Also define what function a device has (e. g. attracting attention, appealing to emotions, assuming agreement, etc.).

A range of means employed in Obama's speech (among others):

– direct address (you, your, etc.)
– word field of praise, compliments, pride and patriotism (cf. for example ll. 3, 5/6, 14, 32, 74/75)
– current examples of inequality/discrimination (cf. ll. 19/20)
– famous Black role models (cf. ll. 40–42)
– rule of three (cf. ll. 10, 48/49)
– structure of speech (from challenge to advice)
– metaphors, comparisons, imperatives, contrast, enumerations
– word field of change and (e. g. "seeds of change", l. 39; "strategy", l. 53)
– direct appeal to action (e. g. "stand up for and join up with everyone who's struggling", l. 63)

Obama's 2020 H.B.C.U. Commencement Speech shows a variety of stylistic devices, most prominent of which is putting the graduates in focus by constantly addressing them directly: "so many of you" (ll. 1/2), "You should be very proud" (l. 6), etc. Although he is also part of the Black community, there is no "we" or no addressing the parents, tutors or professors. This gives the graduates a feeling of importance and uniqueness.

introducing the most prominent stylistic device (direct address)

effect on listeners

The same effect is also employed by the word field of compliments, pride and patriotism. They have "chose[n] to follow in the fearless steps of [famous Black] people" (ll. 39/40) and "overcame a lot to get [t]here" (l. 2). They "had to stretch to afford tuition" (l. 3) and have "earned this moment" (ll. 5/6). Their graduation year is not one in "normal times" (l. 14), which is making them extraordinary. Obama calls them the generation that "has woken up to the fact that the status quo needs fixing" (ll. 21/22). He is sure that "if the world's going to get better, it's going to be up to [them]," (l. 29) and that is why "this is [their] moment – [their] generation's world to shape." (ll. 32/33) They "have to remember that [they] are inheritors of one of America's proudest traditions." (ll. 75/76) This may create a superior feeling in the graduates, but will also put a lot of pressure on them. They seem to be the only ones who are able to overcome the problems and challenges Obama mentions and to find a solution to the global problems of our time.

word field (praise)

effect on listeners

The responsibility he loads onto them is supported by the many examples from the Black community he refers to. He lists renowned politicians like Martin Luther King or writers like Toni Morrison (cf. l. 41) and – at the same time – tells them that they "are all role models now" (l. 76). But it is not only the famous names, it is also the common victims of discrimination and injustice like Ahmaud Arbery, whose death should not be forgotten. To end racist violence is "one of the big unfinished goals in this country" (l. 69) which the graduates are now expected to complete.

current examples of discrimination / famous role models of the Black community

effect on listeners

Next to typical devices like comparisons ("Nobody shines quite like a senior on the yard in springtime", ll. 10/11), contrast (e. g. "we think not just about ourselves, but about each other", ll. 24/25) and the rule of three ("rooted in academic rigor, community, higher purpose", ll. 9/10) it is also the structure of the speech itself that helps appeal to the graduates. In the beginning, Obama speaks in high terms of them, then enumerates the challenges they had to face only to go on talking about the ones that still lie ahead of them. Then he offers the three pieces of advice, and so leaves it to them to realize that they are now in charge of the necessary changes.

(494 words)

list of other devices

quote from the text

Obama's intention

3.1 *When writing a blog entry, make sure you have a headline and be aware that you are talking to your peers. Your style may be colloquial. Since the article is published on-line and can be read by anyone, try not to be too informal though.*

The task wants you to discuss, which means you have to consider both sides – pros and cons. At the end of your blog entry, invite other people to comment and give your name.

You are expected to start by referring to Obama's attitude:
- *Obama has high hopes in young generation*
- *young people have enough role models and road maps to continue the fight for democracy*
- *they are well-prepared by schools, universities, etc.*
- *they are already fighters for a better world*

Arguments that Obama is right:
- *fight for justice/remake of the world has been going on for a long time (Fridays for Future)*
- *lots of politicians, artists, activists could serve as role models*
- *we are living in a connected world where protests can be shared and spread easily*
- *adult world has become aware of global problems that younger generation has long been aware of*

Arguments that he may be wrong
- *people may be aware of problems and even willing to fight but are too lazy to start actions*
- *still hard for grass-root-protests to change politics*
- *reality/current events stand in the way of changes (e. g. war in Ukraine grounds phasing out fossil fuels to a halt)*
- *big players like China, India rather think and act locally rather than globally*

I am a warrior for justice
catchy headline

When you read this, do you see yourself mirrored in this phrase? Well, that's what I want to find out today.
introduction

It was Barack Obama, former US president, who labelled our whole generation this way. In a speech to college graduates from 2020 he said that "no generation has been better positioned to be warriors for justice and remake the world", and he means us.
reference to Obama's quote

Well, it seems Obama has high hopes for young people like me. But what exactly has put us into this position?

First of all, it is the fact that previous generations have been providing us with road maps and role models for decades. With all that knowledge in mind, shouldn't it be much easier for our generation to continue that fight? We seem to be so well-prepared to make necessary changes in society. Have we not been taught at schools, universities, by our parents, etc. about the long way to freedom, to justice, to equality? And haven't we proved to be fighters for a better world when you look at Friday for Future protests?
pro-arguments

At school, they told us about the Civil Rights Movement of the 1960s, about Rosa Parks and Martin Luther King. We also learnt about countries in Africa or Asia that freed themselves from the colonial powers which had ruled them for centuries. Just remember Mahatma Gandhi. There were artists who fought for peace and equality, think of John Lennon, for example. We can profit from their experiences and use them as a basis for our own goals. examples from past / present

We are even one step ahead of our past heroes. Our digital world, the world wide web makes organizing protests or supporting each other much easier than it used to be. It only took a few months before the whole world knew about Greta Thunberg and her *Skolstrejk för Klimatet*. Contrary to the 20th century when those brave people met a lot of resistance, the whole adult world now has become aware of the global environmental problems and at least is trying to take action against it. So we have to admit that Obama is right: we are in an excellent position to rebuild the world. conclusion: Obama is right

But isn't there always a "but"? Yes, I'm afraid there is. Although nearly everyone accepts the fact that we are facing major problems, it is still as hard as it was back then to convince people of changing their ways. Most countries are still emitting huge amounts of CO_2, the use of plastics is not restricted enough worldwide, we are producing much too much waste. Just ask people in charge in our parliaments, in the United Nations or in organisations like Greenpeace. They will agree. And reality often stands in the way of changes too. Take the war in Ukraine. Apart from all the grief and destruction it brings, it also grinds the phasing out of fossil fuels to a halt. Sometimes, this can disillusion even the strongest warrior. con-arguments

examples

Still, let us not be desperate! I am ready to be a warrior for justice! We want to live on this Earth of ours for many more decades, so let us accept Obama's challenge and take up the fight! **conclusion** appeal to readers

What do you think about this issue? I am eager to learn of your opinion. Feel free to leave a comment. asking for comments

Looking forward to hearing from you. saying good-bye,

Samira   *(564 words)* name

3.2 *In order to work on this task successfully, you need to analyze the cartoon and refer to its message before you start discussing distance learning. There is no need to fully analyze it, but a short description to show its relevance to the topic would be necessary.*

Description:
– *graduate in typical graduation gown/tasselled cap*
– *sitting in front of a computer*

- *is invited to click for speech and diploma*
- *thinks to himself that it is just not the same*

Message:
- *digital university lacks unique feeling of graduation*

Benefits of distance learning:
- *free schedule/personalized structure of day*
- *you choose what you learn at what pace*
- *you really need to think, no one there to answer questions for you*
- *by writing down a lot, you will automatically memorize it*
- *improves computer skills*
- *no bullying, shy/introverted students will benefit*
- *relaxed environment*

Challenges of distance learning:
- *you need to have/buy the equipment*
- *poor internet access*
- *no one there to motivate you*
- *no direct contact/interpersonal relationships*
- *work longer than school day because you got lost in a task*
- *distraction by other devices*
- *completely new topics difficult to study*

Distance learning is a word that has made its way into our vocabulary in times of the corona pandemic. The given cartoon features the problems that come with it. It shows a graduate in their typical graduation gown, with the tasselled cap sitting in front of a laptop. He is invited to click to hear his graduation speech and to print his diploma, which is why he is telling himself that things are just not the same in remote learning. The message derived from it is clearly that working or studying from home in a digital classroom leaves teachers and students lacking from what they would experience in the analogue world. *(introductory sentence / description of the cartoon / message of the cartoon)*

At first glance, distance learning seems to be the must-do in a computerized society. You can learn at your own pace, and you choose when to study what and to what extent. No getting up in the morning to get to school early. You can tailor the timetable according to your personal needs. Along the way you acquire computer skills in word processing as well as editing films or uploading data of all formats. You can study in a relaxed environment that you know, you are close to food and drink and a place to chill out, if necessary. Are you an introvert? Have you even been bullied by classmates? Well, then distance learning seems to be perfect for you. *(benefits of distant learning)*

What we should not neglect is that you really have to think for yourself. No other student to answer the teacher's questions for everyone else in class. By writing something down you will also notice that you memorize content much better.

But when you have a closer look at distance learning, there are quite a lot of challenges, as most students found out after weeks at home. First of all, you need to have the equipment to work from your own place. Excellent internet access is also really important. Both can be quite expensive. A lot of students also find it difficult not to allow themselves to be distracted by text messages from friends, siblings, parents, etc. Motivating yourself can also become a big issue in distance learning. When there is no one to help you solve problems, no classmate to talk to directly, no teacher you can call to come to your desk, studying can become really hard. Quite a lot of students also stated that they got lost in tasks when searching the net for answers, so their digital school day was even longer than the analogue one.

challenges of distance learning

So all in all, I am sure that distance learning cannot compensate for or substitute studying at school with real people around you. It may be an additional tool for certain tasks and a way to learn about how jobs are done in the working world, but the school of the future will never be a digital one. *(479 words)*

conclusion + personal opinion

Prüfungsteil 2: Sprachmittlung

Aufgabenstellung 2.1

As far as the type of task is concerned, a mediation is very much like a summary. Both tasks ask for extracting the general ideas and presenting them in a compact way.
In the given extract you are expected to tell "your" readers about the general idea of the game.
Rules:
– mixture of game and saving the environment
– character of the game (changing personal consumer habits, becoming more sustainable, environmentally friendly)
– what you have to do (stick to an eco-friendly lifestyle in five different categories; gain/lose points for good/poor examples, collect as many points as possible within twelve weeks or 222 points in a shorter time frame)
– the aim of the game (to question your consumer habits in five categories to avoid losing to your friends)
– outcome (more environmental awareness, aspect of gaming makes it easier to accept new lifestyle)
Players:
– three childhood friends with an academic background
– in their 30s
– living in different cities
– have noticed that they have not made any progress in being more environmentally friendly

Gaming for a better world headline

Three friends, Chris, Cyril and Nils, all in their early 30s and with an introductory part
academic background, combine playing and saving the environment.
They felt the need to contribute to a better world, and so they came up
with the idea of *Moral Games*. But how does it work?

It all started four years ago, when the three friends, who have known main part
each other since childhood, wanted to change their consumer habits three friends, in their 30s
and become more sustainable and environmentally friendly after ad-
mitting to themselves that they haven't made any significant progress reason why they created the game
in those matters. So they created *Moral Games*, which works as fol-
lows: there are five different categories in which every player can win
or lose points; eating meat, eating fish, plastic consumption, organic the five categories
and fair-trade products and food waste.

At the beginning of every new week all players start from scratch. If the rule of how to gain / lose points
you want to win points, you will need a perfect week. Have you manag-
ed seven meat-free days? Great, 10 points added to your scoreboard.
On the other hand, points will be deducted when you eat fish fingers
or a steak. If you neglected fair labour principles, that's minus 10 % of
the price of the product you bough.

The exact number of points won or lost is negotiated by the whole number of points to win the game
team. Anyone who reaches 222 points first – which takes a minimum
of six weeks – or whoever has most points after twelve weeks is the
winner and the "Moral King". What can you win? The king will be winner's reward
treated to a dinner in a restaurant by the team members. He will also
wear a massive silver ring. The losers will have to donate one euro for
every extra point the winner has over them. At the end of the year they donating money to charity
balance their account. If you travelled by plane, you have to pay a "sur-
charge". In the end all of them donate their money to charity.

The game has also had a positive impact on their friendship. Although positive impact on friendship
they are living in three different cities now they contact each other
daily due to the game.

I think this really is a great idea. I am already looking around for players to join my team. What is your opinion about *Moral Games?* Tell me in the comment section below. **asking for comments**

Take care.

Paul

(387 words) **name**

Aufgabenstellung 2.2

This task is a very common one for mediation. "Summing up" again means you point out the most important facts for your friend, who has to deliver a speech on the given topic. So your email may provide the arguments for the debate. That makes you an "expert" in this matter and that is why you can come up with examples, statistics, etc. to allow his address to be more vivid.

One point you have to concentrate on is the connection between digitalization and climate change:

- *computer work is not environmentally friendly*
- *data storage and delivery needs big server farms that depend on power for cooling*
- *worldwide more and more data are sent, which is constantly increasing energy consumption*
- *all in all internet usage produces as much CO_2 as air traffic in Germany*
- *saving CO_2 by reducing online work, deduplication of data, deleting older files*
- *big computer centres have to be made more energy-efficient*

Also pay attention to the email format/style (personal address, some small talk in the beginning, reference to the article, greetings).

Hi Ian, **personal address**

How is it going? How is life as a sixth former? Well, mine is quite busy at the moment. I've been studying for the final exams for weeks and hoping for some easy tasks. Maths will be quite an issue, I'm afraid. small talk

Anyway, did I get that right, you are going to deliver a speech at the United Nations!? How come? You must be really excited. reference to friend's request

I also like the topic. No-one actually thinks about how climate change is fuelled by digitalization. I wouldn't have known either, to be honest, so I checked on the net for the facts. And, shame on me, did you know that this search has already produced 0.2 grams of CO_2? This email will add another two grams, so it seems we are right in the middle of your topic.

I have found all these pieces of information in an article on the website of one of our state television channels, so it's a reliable source. It compares the carbon dioxide output of the internet usage to the annual air traffic in Germany. Believe it or not, it's the same amount of this greenhouse gas! And experts warn that our internet habits may cause double the tonnes of CO_2 within the next ten years. Isn't that frightening? The author of the article, Elisabeth Schmidt, actually thinks that instead of reference to article

example: CO_2 emissions

flight shame we should rather be talking about click shame. Sending emails, streaming videos, searching things on the web – all these things produce CO_2.

So far, I have actually thought that writing emails instead of sending letters would save resources like water and paper and protect the environment. But the billions of servers in the gigantic server farms worldwide need cooling and power. More and more of those server parks have been built, increasing energy consumption by 40 %.

But what can we do to reduce our energy demand? It's simple: delete old emails, unsubscribe from newsletters, store photos and videos on external storage devices rather than in the cloud, deduplicate data, i. e., don't send photos around that will be sent on to others, so that in the end it's not only one but 50 photos on 50 different computers using 50 times the amount of energy.

There is also hope for the big server farms. In one institution in Hanover, they have refurbished theirs and have cut down their CO_2 emission by 750 tonnes. That's great, isn't it?

I hope I've given you some facts and figures to help you write a thrilling speech. The world has to do something to make click shame more popular.

Tell me how it went, I'm eager to get to know what New York is like.

See you,

Elizabeth   *(455 words)*

Margin annotations:
- computer usage not really environmentally friendly
- example server parks
- actions to reduce CO_2 emissions
- deduplication
- examples of refurbished server farms
- expressing hope that info would be suitable
- ending letter
- name

---

* We have decided to capitalize "Black" and "White" to signal that they are not natural categories but social ones (for more background information on this topic see e. g. https://www.theatlantic.com/ideas/archive/2020/06/time-to-capitalize-blackand-white/613159/).

Prüfungsteil 1: Leseverstehen und Schreiben (70 %)

Der Prüfungsteil 1 besteht aus zwei Aufgabenstellungen, von denen Sie eine zur Bearbeitung auswählen.

Aufgabenstellung 1.1 – Tasks

Themenschwerpunkte: *Saving the planet; Aims and ambitions*

1 Outline the Cairngorms Wolf Project and its aims. (30 %)

2 Analyze how the author presents the meeting between the locals and the members of the project. (30 %)

3 Choose <u>one</u> of the following tasks:

3.1 *"That's all well and good for nature, [...] but it's costing me land I could be grazing sheep on. Agriculture is the third-largest employer in rural Scotland. You threaten that and you threaten the entire community."*
(ll. 49–51)
Comment on the farmer's position. (40 %)

OR

3.2 You are a member of the Global Youth Community, an internet platform by and for young people to exchange ideas and collaborate on different projects.
Write an entry for the forum blog in which you assess to what extent local projects can make a difference in solving global problems. (40 %)

Text (excerpt from the novel)

Once There Were Wolves
by Charlotte McConaghy

In this excerpt from the novel, a team of biologists has arrived in the Scottish Highlands, among them the female protagonist Inti Flynn.

1 The school auditorium has no heating; the air within feels even colder than it does outside. My fingers are turning numb as I sink into a backrow seat beside Niels and Zoe. There is a woman in the audience holding a sign that reads CIGARETTES AND WOLVES, KILLERS THAT COME IN PACKS and a kid waving one that says WILL
5 THERE BE ANY DEER LEFT WHEN I GROW UP? I roll my eyes.

On the stage sit a row of people. Evan is among them, our spokesperson, chosen not only because he is articulate and charismatic, but because he's the only one in our core team who is Scottish, and this, we've been told, is likely to land better with the locals. […] I am a bad-tempered Australian who finds it hard to hide contempt and
10 sucks at public speaking. Next to Evan sits Anne, the warrior who singlehandedly got this project through Parliament and also a massive pain in my ass. I don't know who the rest of the people up there are, I suppose prominent members of the community. In the crowd I know there are members of the farmers union, the gamekeepers union, and the Hillwalkers group, plus dozens of landowners from the entire Cairngorms region –
15 all of whom have opposed our project. And despite my teasing with Anne, I do understand why. There are no members of corporate agriculture here tonight. These people are mostly local farmers living under massive financial pressure, and a perceived threat to their hard-earned livelihoods is a frightening thing. It's Evan's job to try and ease some of that fear.

20 One of the men on the stage stands to speak, white-haired and pairing his traditional tartan kilt with a more casual knit pullover. "Most of you know me but for any who don't, I'm Mayor Andy Oakes," he says. "This meeting's been called to give you some necessary information and for you to voice your concerns and hopefully have them appeased. Here to speak to us tonight is Anne Barrie, head of the Wolf Trust, in coop-
25 eration with Rewilding Scotland, and Evan Long, who's one of the biologists with the Cairngorms Wolf Project."

Anne gives a little thank-you speech that could not be more brownnosing if she tried, then she yields the stage to Evan to explain the situation: that there are now three pens holding a total of fourteen wolves within the Cairngorms National Park and that
30 come the end of winter the wolves will be released from these pens to live freely in the Scottish Highlands. They are here specifically for a rewilding effort in a broader attempt to slow climate change, and on an experimental basis.

"What we have here in Scotland," Evan says, "is an ecosystem in crisis. We urgently need to rewild. If we can extend woodland cover by a hundred thousand hectares
35 by 2026 then we could dramatically reduce CO_2 emissions that contribute to climate change and we could provide habitats for native species. […]"

I look around at the faces I can see; most appear somewhere between pissed off, bored, and plainly confused.

Evan continues. "Deer eat tree and plant shoots so that nothing has a chance to
40 grow. We are overrun with deer. But wolves cull that deer population, and keep it
moving, which allows for natural growth of plants and vegetation, which encourages
pollinating insects and smaller mammals and rodents to return, which in turn allows
the return of birds of prey, and by keeping the fox population in check the wolves also
allow medium-sized animals to thrive, such as badgers and beavers. Trees can grow
45 again, creating the air we breathe. When an ecosystem is varied, it is healthy, and everything benefits from a healthy natural ecosystem."

A man from the crowd stands. He's wearing a crisp white shirt and tie and holds
his tweed flat cap in his hands. His gray handlebar mustache is a sight to behold, even
from my angle. "That's all well and good for nature," he says in a deep, resonant voice,
50 "but it's costing me land I could be grazing sheep on. Agriculture is the third-largest
employer in rural Scotland. You threaten that and you threaten the entire community."

There are a few rumbles of agreement.

"It is unacceptable to me," he goes on, "that animals could be introduced that would
destroy the Highlander way of life. I want to see a thriving, vibrant community that
55 supports its people. To me there's nothing sadder than a glen with no sheep and no
people. People are the lifeblood of any area."

A whistle, a smattering of applause. I stare at the back of the farmer. This world he
describes, empty of wild creatures and places, overrun instead by people and their agriculture, is a dying world.   *(798 words)*

McConaghy, Charlotte. "Once There Were Wolves." Orion Magazine. Aug. 4, 2021. Accessed Nov. 10,
2022 from https://orionmagazine.org/article/once-wolves/

Annotations
l. 14   Cairngorms: a mountainous region and national park in the Scottish Highlands
l. 27   brownnosing: derogatory: pleasing someone of authority in the hope of improving one's standing

Aufgabenstellung 1.2 – Tasks

Themenschwerpunkte: *Aims and ambitions; Saving the planet; Overcoming prejudice in society; The impact of the media on society*

1 Outline the information on Dara McAnulty and his writing. (30 %)

2 Analyze the way the author presents Dara McAnulty as a writer and his way of dealing with the challenges he faces. (30 %)

3 Choose <u>one</u> of the following tasks:

3.1 "Inspired by Greta Thunberg, […] he leads a school strike to highlight inaction against climate change." (ll. 48/49)
Using the quote and Dara McAnulty's experience as depicted in the article as a starting point, comment on the need for courageous role models who inspire young people to become active against climate change. (40 %)

OR

3.2 You have been invited to deliver a speech at the "International Youth and Nature Conference" and want to show your listeners the cartoon below while introducing your topic. Taking the message of the cartoon into consideration, write a speech assessing the potential of experiencing nature for personality development and ways in which digital tools can be used in this context. (40 %)

By permission of Gary Varvel and Creators Syndicate, Inc.

Text (excerpt from the article)

A Young Naturalist Inspires With Joy, Not Doom
by Alex Marshall

1 [...] [Dara] McAnulty, 17, is fast becoming one of Britain and Ireland's most acclaimed nature writers for work that is brimming with his passion as well as open about his autism. His debut book, "Diary of a Young Naturalist," published last year by Little Toller in Britain and released last month by Milkweed in the United States, won the
5 Wainwright Prize, Britain's biggest award for nature writing.

Reviewers have heaped it with praise. "It really is a strange and magical experience," Christophe Hart wrote in The Daily Mail, before comparing McAnulty's writing to that of the poet Ted Hughes.

Robert Macfarlane, a fellow nature writer whose books include "Underland" and
10 "Landmarks," said in a telephone interview he had been shocked by McAnulty's writing after first stumbling across it online four years ago. "I remember thinking, 'What is this voice?'" Looking through McAnulty's eyes reveals a world that "sparkles differently," Macfarlane said. [...]

McAnulty, in an interview at his home, said he had been obsessed with nature for
15 as long as he could remember. Along with his brother and sister, he spent days as a child "climbing trees, rustling about, doing things most parents would never allow their children to do." His mother, a former music journalist, and his father, a conservationist, nurtured that passion, even if school bullies took exception to it.

One day, while he was struggling in primary school, the Royal Society for the Pro
20 tection of Birds visited to talk about reintroducing red kites to Northern Ireland. "I listened, for the first time, in a long time," he wrote, and it made him want to fight for nature as well as play in it.

But he only started writing about it because of his autism. "I need to write, to process what's going on," he said, "otherwise everything's just banging around in my
25 brain causing damage in there."

McAnulty started his own blog when he was 12. His early posts were simple profiles of animals, with titles like "Magical Moths!" But when he was 14, Little Toller asked if he wanted to write a series of posts for its website. Once McAnulty started, he realized what he was writing could be a book.

30 "Diary of a Young Naturalist" is divided into the year's seasons. In Spring, McAnulty's writing is filled with the joy of being outside. On a trip to Northern Ireland's Rathlin Island, whose cliffs are a kaleidoscope of bird life, he tries to take in one species after another – such as "a fulmar, dozing and waiting, a queen on her throne," and puffins, "diminutive inspectors," flying from burrow to burrow.

35 The diary entries are also frank about how autism affects McAnulty's life. "Dandelions remind me of the way I close myself off from so much of the world," he writes, "either because it's too painful to see or feel, or because when I am open to people, the ridicule comes."

In Summer, his family prepares to move to a new house. He becomes overwhelmed
40 by thoughts of change and of losing his favorite landscape, until one day he breaks

down. "I'm submerged right now, completely under," he writes. He begs his parents
to dig up their plants and bring them along.

"For most of the book, I'm not in a good place," McAnulty said, which he didn't
realize at the time. "I don't think you realize how dark something is until you turn back
45 on the lights."

He said he never considered leaving any of those experiences out. "It's a diary. If
there's pieces of me missing, I'm going to come off as not being human, and it'll feel
weird and awkward," he said. "Half of my decisions in the book wouldn't make sense
if I didn't mention that I'm autistic, and the feelings wouldn't unless I mentioned that
50 I was bullied."

The book is ultimately uplifting. In Autumn and Winter, McAnulty's pain is eased
as he moves to a more supportive school. Inspired by Greta Thunberg, the Swedish
environmental activist, he leads a school strike to highlight inaction against climate
change. He goes to London to help deliver a "people's manifesto for wildlife" to the
55 British government. He speaks at the first Irish meeting of Extinction Rebellion, a
group whose members regularly get arrested. All those efforts build on previous con-
servation work, such as raising money to track and save raptors, his favorite birds. […]

His next book, "Wild Child," scheduled to be published in Britain this month by
Macmillan Children's Books, encourages children to seek and protect the natural
60 world. He's already planning another book, too, he said, about his wanderings around
Ireland, connecting nature with myth. Once that's done, he was unsure what would
happen, but "writing will never disappear from my life," he said. "I need it." […]

(791 words)

*Marshall, Alex. "A Young Naturalist Inspires With Joy, Not Doom." The New York Times. July 7,
2021. Accessed on February 7, 2022 from https://www.nytimes.com/2021/07/07/books/dara-
mcanulty-diary-of-a-young- naturalist.html.*

Annotations

ll. 3/4	Little Toller: independent publisher of books about nature, wildlife and landscape
l. 8	Ted Hughes: (1930–1998) English poet, translator, and children's writer, frequently ranked as one of the twentieth century's greatest writers
l. 33	fulmar: seabird
l. 43	not in a good place: *here:* not well, depressed
l. 57	raptor: meat-eating bird

Der Prüfungsteil 2 besteht aus zwei Aufgabenstellungen, von denen Sie eine zur Bearbeitung auswählen.

Aufgabenstellung 2.1 – Task

Themenschwerpunkte: *Overcoming prejudice in society; Aims and ambitions; The impact of the media on society*

As an intern at an American newspaper, you have been asked for information on diversity initiatives in Germany.
Write an email to the editor in which you present the "Neue deutsche Medienmacher*innen" (NdM) and their campaign #WeatherCorrection.

Text (Auszug aus dem Artikel)

Wetter migrantisch: Tief Ahmet, Hoch Dragica
Von Andrea Dernbach

1 Ahmet hatte schon seinen Einsatz. Demnächst dürften Bartosz und Cemal, Bozena und Chana über Deutschland kommen. Sturm und gutes Wetter tragen ab sofort und vorerst keine traditionsdeutschen Namen mehr: Auch der Wetterbericht bekommt Migrationshintergrund. Die ersten Tief- und Hochdruckgebiete erhalten 2021 türkische, rumäni-
5 sche, polnische oder arabische Namen, also die der am stärksten vertretenen Herkunftskulturen. Dem Turnus folgend gibt es zwölf Monate lang Männernamen für die Tiefs, Frauennamen für die Hochs.

Der Grund für den migrantisch-meteorologischen Jahresbeginn: Die Neuen deutschen Medienmacher*innen haben die Patenschaften für die ersten Wetterlagen im
10 neuen Jahr übernommen, das deutsche Wetter „gekapert", wie es auf ihrer Website heißt. Die NdM sind ein Zusammenschluss von Journalistinnen und Journalisten aus Familien mit und ohne Einwanderungsgeschichte, die sich für mehr Vielfalt im Journalismus einsetzen.

„Wir leben in einem Einwanderungsland. Trotzdem tragen die Wetterhochs und
15 -tiefs fast immer nur Namen wie Gisela und Helmut. Zeit, dass sich das ändert." Deutsche hießen „schließlich auch Ahmet, Chana, Khuê und Romani". Und bis das endlich bei allen angekommen sei, werde man „nicht aufhören, Wirbel zu machen".

Es ist nicht die erste Spaßguerilla-Aktion der NdM vor dem durchaus ernsten Hintergrund eines erheblichen Diversitätsproblems im deutschen Journalismus: Während
20 inzwischen ein gutes Viertel der deutschen Bevölkerung Migrationshintergrund hat (26 Prozent), gilt das lediglich für fünf bis zehn Prozent der Belegschaften in den Redaktionen. Tendenz nur langsam steigend. Weil das aus NdM-Sicht auch auf den Journalismus durchschlägt, der so entsteht, haben sie etwa für die „unterirdischste" Berichterstattung eines Jahres den Anti-Preis „Goldene Kartoffel" ausgelobt – und dies

25 nicht nur mit deren Wachstum unter der Erde begründet: Die Kartoffel sei auch das
deutscheste Gemüse überhaupt, habe aber gleichzeitig eine lupenreine südamerikani-
sche Migrationsgeschichte. [...]

Nun also die Aktion #wetterberichtigung, mit der die NdM symbolisch auf die re-
ale Vielfalt in den drei deutschsprachigen Ländern aufmerksam machen wollen. Mit
30 dabei sind die Schwesterorganisation „Neue Schweizer Medienmacher*innen" und ös-
terreichische Initiativen – auch Idee und Umsetzung kamen aus Wien, von den Krea-
tiven Goran Golik und M. Alexander Trybus. Das Geld für die Aktion – auch Wetter-
patenschaften kosten – kam durch Sponsoring zusammen.

Die Wettertaufen sind übrigens eine sehr berlinische Angelegenheit: 1954 machte
35 sich am Institut für Meteorologie der Freien Universität die damalige Studentin und
spätere ZDF-Meteorologin Karla Wege dafür stark, das US-Modell zu übernehmen.
Dort hatten seit dem Zweiten Weltkrieg die pazifischen Taifune Namen. Gab es mehrere zugleich, ließ sich so besser der Überblick behalten.

Erst nach der Einheit nahm auch der Rest Deutschlands Orkane namens Wiebke
40 und Vivian wahr. Berlin vergibt die Namen seither für alle weiter; der Deutsche Wet-
terdienst war einverstanden. Seit einer kleinen Debatte Ende der 1990er Jahre darüber,
ob nicht Frauen diskriminiert werden, heißen jährlich wechselnd mal die Tiefs und mal
die Hochs nach Männern, dann wieder nach Frauen.

Ausgerechnet in geschlechterpolitischer Hinsicht sahen sich nun die diversitätsbe-
45 wegten NdM zu einem Rückschritt gezwungen: Sie sind Patinnen für etliche Männer,
aber nur für drei Frauen: „Wir wollten den gesamten Januar übernehmen", erläutert
die Vorsitzende Ferda Ataman. „Aber im Januar gibt es nun mal nicht so viele Hochs."

Deshalb dürfen vorerst nur die Hochs Bozena, Dragica – Erinnerung an die jugo-
slawischen „Gast"arbeiterinnen und -arbeiter – und Chana ran. Danach übernimmt
50 wieder eine Elke. Tiefdruckmann Kasper hat seinen Einsatz erst nach zehn Migranten
– von Ahmet und Bartosz bis Jussuf und Irek. *(532 Wörter)*

*Dernbach, Andrea. „Tief Ahmet, Hoch Dragica". Der Tagesspiegel. 5. Jan. 2021. Zugriff am 28.
Jan. 2021 von https://www.tagesspiegel.de/politik/wetter-migrantisch-tief-ahmet-hoch-
dragica/26771256.html*

Annotation
Z. 18 Spaßguerilla-Aktion: provokative Aktion, um auf politische Anliegen aufmerksam zu machen

Themenschwerpunkte: *Aims and ambitions; Overcoming prejudice in society*

The "Young Migrants Blog" has asked its readers to post success stories about migrants. Write a blog entry, outlining the information in Carola Tunk's article about immigrants who founded companies in Germany, about the problems they face, and about possible solutions to these problems.

Text (Artikel)

Jedes fünfte Start-up in Deutschland wurde von Migranten gegründet
Von Carola Tunk

1 Was haben der Impfstoffhersteller Biontech, der Lebensmittellieferdienst Gorillas und die Reiseplattform Omio gemeinsam? Sie alle kommen aus der Start-up-Szene und wurden von Menschen aus Einwandererfamilien gegründet. Die neue migrantische Gründerszene ist gut ausgebildet, risikobereit und stärkt den Standort Deutschland, wie
5 eine Studie zeigt. Doch der bürokratische Dschungel, Sprachbarrieren und mangelnde Finanzierung machen es Gründerinnen und Gründern mit ausländischen Wurzeln nach wie vor schwer. Branchenvertreter fordern deshalb Erleichterungen.

Rund jedes fünfte Start-up in Deutschland wurde zuletzt von Migranten der ersten oder zweiten Generation gegründet, wie aus einer Sonderauswertung des Deutschen
10 Start-up-Monitors hervorgeht. Der „Migrant Founders Monitor" des Bundesverbands Deutscher Start-ups und der Friedrich-Naumann-Stiftung analysiert die Lage von 354 Start-ups, die von Menschen aus Familien mit Einwanderungsgeschichte gegründet wurden.

Demnach bringen vor allem im Ausland geborene Gründer öfter einen Uni-Ab-
15 schluss mit als der Durchschnitt. Fast jeder Dritte strebt den Verkauf des Start-ups für mindestens 100 Millionen Euro an – im Schnitt planen das nur rund 20 Prozent. Und der hohe Anteil an Gründern mit Migrationserfahrung in der Frühphase des Unternehmensaufbaus spreche für eine aktuell hohe Dynamik, heißt es.

„Menschen mit Migrationshintergrund haben eine überdurchschnittliche Bedeu-
20 tung für die deutsche Start-up-Szene, nicht nur als Gründerinnen und Gründer, sondern auch als Schlüsselbeschäftigte beispielsweise in IT-Start-ups", sagt die Chefökonomin der staatlichen Förderbank KfW, Fritzi Köhler-Geib. Der Co-Vorsitzende des Start-up-Verbands, Christian Vollmann, betont: „Gerade die Bereitschaft, Risiken einzugehen und groß zu denken, sind Dinge, die in Deutschland oft noch fehlen und die wir
25 als Standort im internationalen Wettbewerb brauchen."

Naren Shaam kommt aus Indien und gründete 2012 in Berlin die Reiseplattform Omio. Den Befund der Studie, dass migrantische Gründer eher risikobereit seien als jene aus Familien ohne Einwanderungsgeschichte, erklärt er mit dem sozialen Sicherheitsnetz in Deutschland. Das sei andernorts, wie etwa in Indien, nicht selbstverständ-
30 lich und nur den Reichen vorbehalten. „Risiken einzugehen ist also Teil der Kultur",

sagt er. Im vergangenen Sommer sammelte das Unternehmen nach eigenen Angaben 100 Millionen Dollar (83 Millionen Euro) frisches Kapital ein.

Als er nach Deutschland kam, habe er kein Wort Deutsch gesprochen und niemanden gekannt, erzählt Shaam. Grundlegende Dinge, wie ein Bankkonto zu eröffnen, hät-
35 ten sich angefühlt „wie ein Berg, den du besteigen musst". Auch die Start-up-Studie nennt bürokratische und sprachliche Hürden als große Herausforderung für Gründer mit ausländischen Wurzeln. Bei vielen Formularen, etwa bei der Unternehmensgründung oder bei Steuerunterlagen, sei Deutsch die einzige Option, sagt Vollmann. Da müsse die Politik ran. „Es muss einfach alles auch auf Englisch zur Verfügung stehen!"
40 Der Start-up-Beauftragte der Grünen im Bundestag, Danyal Bayaz, sieht auch die Politik stärker in der Pflicht. Wirtschaftlicher Erfolg und Vielfalt seien zwei Seiten derselben Medaille, sagt er. „Dazu braucht es auch mehrsprachige Angebote bei der Beratung und für die Finanzierung." Außerdem müsse mehr Sichtbarkeit für erfolgreiche Gründer geschaffen werden.
45 Gerade die Finanzierung ist für viele Jungunternehmen ein Problem: Mit 1,1 Millionen Euro konnten Gründer aus dem Ausland im Mittel weniger als halb so viel Fremdkapital aufnehmen als im Bundesdurchschnitt (2,6 Millionen). Und die durchschnittliche Mitarbeiterzahl liegt mit 10,2 unter dem Durchschnitt von 14,3. Vielen fehle hierzulande das nötige Netzwerk, sagt Vollmann, der als sogenannter Business
50 Angel selbst in Start-ups investiert. „Da müssen wir als Szene gegensteuern."

Hinzu kommen mangelnde Kontakte über die Start-up-Szene hinaus. So haben Start-ups laut Studie durchschnittlich sieben Kooperationen mit etablierten Unternehmen – migrantische Gründer der ersten Generation jedoch nur zwei. […] Lösungen könnten etwa Netzwerkveranstaltungen oder professionelle Gründerberatungen sein.

(554 Wörter)

Quelle: Tunk, Carola. „Jedes fünfte Start-up in Deutschland wurde von Migranten gegründet."
Berliner Zeitung. 3. Mai 2021. Zugriff am 30. November 2021 von https://www.berliner-zeitung.de/
news/jedes-fuenfte-start-up-in-deutschland-wurde-von-migranten-gegruendet-li.156725

Annotation
Z. 10 Migrant Founders: Begriff, den die deutschen Autoren des „Migrant Founders Monitor" verwenden, der aber so im Englischen nicht gebräuchlich ist
Z. 11 Friedrich-Naumann-Stiftung: parteinahe Stiftung, die Angebote zur politischen Bildung bereitstellt und Stipendien vergibt

Aufgabenstellung 1.1

1 *An outline is a summary. Here you are to sum up what the text says about the Cairngorms Wolf Project and its aims. Mark the important information in the text and structure it before you write your solution. By doing this, you will make sure that you include all the necessary aspects and leave out what is not important for the task.*

Cairngorms Wolf Project
– *project to reintroduce wolves to the Scottish Highlands*
– *authorised by parliament*
– *14 wolves currently held in pens will be released*
– *strong opposition from farmers, who fear for their cattle and are under financial pressure, as well as from landowners and the gamekeepers union*

Aims
– *control overpopulation of deer and foxes*
– *deer eat plants and tree shoots and thus destroy forests*
– *by reintroducing wolves biodiversity is increased*
– *ultimate goal is to reduce CO_2*

The Cairngorms Wolf Project aims to reintegrate wolves into the countryside of the Scottish Highlands. It is an experimental project authorised by parliament and run by a team of biologists in co-operation with other environmental organisations. 14 wolves, currently in captivity, will be released into the wild in the spring in order to control the overpopulation of deer and foxes. *(reintroduce wolves / authorised by parliament / control overpopulation)*

Lacking a natural enemy, deer overrun the woods, eating all the small plants and tree shoots that would otherwise bind CO_2 and mitigate climate change. In addition, the reduction of the fox population would allow other small animals to thrive in the wild. The presence of wolves acts as a balancing element, reducing the overproliferation of other animals and re-establishes a biodiverse ecosystem. *(more plants and tree shoots, less CO_2 / biodiversity)*

The project is opposed by landowners, local farmers and gamekeepers, however, who worry that the wolves will destroy their agricultural livelihood by eating their sheep and deer for hunting. *(opposition)*

(152 words)

2 *It is obvious that the members of the project and the majority of the local population stand in opposition to one another. For your analysis you have to find elements in the text that prove this. The mayor is an exception to this as he is a local who supports*

the ecological project and who is trying to mediate between the two positions. You can refer to the following aspects:
- narrative perspective: first-person narration from the perspective of an environmental activist
- temperature of the room matches the cold reception of the group by the locals
- locals are introduced as emotional and sensationalist (signs in bold letters)→ narrator rolls her eyes at them (cf. ll. 3–5)
- narrator is portrayed as a bad-tempered Australian who finds it hard to hide contempt; she is understanding but slightly condescending towards the locals
- mayor stands in between the two groups; a local who supports the activists' project; tries to mediate; this is represented by his clothes, which represent both worlds
- the reader feels with the narrator: sympathy for worries of the locals but their dreamland is a "dying world"

The story is told through the eyes of one member of the team of biologists. The author sets the scene for the atmosphere in the room by describing the temperature: "The school auditorium has no heating; the air within feels even colder than it does outside. My fingers are turning numb" (ll. 1/2). This is a portent of the cold reception from the locals who are opposed to the narrator and her team, but the lack of heat also indicates that this local area is poor. The protest signs around the room are written in capitals suggesting that the local arguments are sensationalist and emotional rather than fact-based: "CIGARETTES AND WOLVES, KILLERS THAT COME IN PACKS ... WILL THERE BE ANY DEER LEFT WHEN I GROW UP?" (ll. 3–5). The narrator "roll[s her] eyes" when she sees the signs (l. 5). This juxtaposition demonstrates the conflict between the scientists and local farmers.

narrative perspective

cold temperature = cold atmosphere

protest signs = sensationalist and emotional

conflict between scientists and locals

The team of biologists is described as very diverse. They have chosen as their spokesperson the member who would appeal most to the audience: "he's the only one in our core team who is Scottish, and this, we've been told, is likely to land better with the locals" (ll. 7–9). The narrator describes herself as "a bad-tempered Australian who finds it hard to hide contempt and sucks at public speaking" (ll. 9/10). This attitude is shown when she rolls her eyes at the signs. The relationships within the team are also complex: the team includes Anne, for example, whom the narrator describes as "the warrior who singlehandedly got this project through Parliament and also a massive pain in my ass" (ll. 10/11).

diverse team

spokesperson

attitude of the narrator

relationship within the team

The opposing group is shown sympathetically, demostrating the narrator's understanding of their anger and worries when she says that they have all "opposed our project […] I do understand why" (ll. 15/16). According to her, "[t]hese people are mostly local farmers living under massive financial pressure, and a perceived threat to their hard-earned livelihoods is a frightening thing"

angers and worries of locals

(ll. 16/17). However, they are described as a little simple-minded. Their signs are viewed with contempt by the narrator (cf. l. 5) and during Evan's presentation they seem "somewhere between [...] bored, and plainly confused" (ll. 37/38). It is obvious that despite showing some understanding for them, Inti Flynn thinks their concerns are just "a perceived threat" (l. 17) and that "Evan [can hopefully] ease some of that fear" (ll. 18/19).

simple-minded locals

The mayor is introduced first with a description of his appearance: "pairing his traditional tartan kilt with a more casual knit pullover" (ll. 20/21). This combination of traditional and contemporary clothing reflects his split position of siding with his constituents but also believing the current scientific proof that the environment is at risk. The author initially creates suspense as to which side the mayor will take, but it soon turns out that he is on the side of the environment: "This meeting's been called to give you some necessary information and for you to voice your concerns and hopefully have them appeased" (ll. 22–24). Due to the word "appease" the message is clear that the project will go through despite the protests. The reader is pulled into an ambivalent situation, siding with the scientists and the facts, but then becoming more empathetic with the locals, who are the ones who will suffer as a result and see the project as "a perceived threat to their hard-earned livelihoods" (ll. 17/18). They protest that "[a]griculture is the third-largest employer in rural Scotland. You threaten that and you threaten the entire community" (ll. 50/51). The stark contrast between the farmer's idyllic description of the Highlands as a "thriving, vibrant community" (l. 54) that would be sad "with no sheep and no people" (ll. 55/56) and the description of the same scene by the narrator as a "world [...] empty of wild creatures and places, overrun instead by people and their agriculture" (ll. 57–59) as a "dying world" (l. 59) shows that some differences between the opposing groups cannot be overcome.   *(690 words)*

mayor stands in the middle

expressed by clothing

supports environmentalists

ambivalent situation

sympathy for farmers

idyllic perception of the farmland contrasted with narrator's opinion ("dying world")

3.1 *If you comment on a quote, it can be useful to explain the quote in your own words. In this task you can agree or disagree with the statement. It is not necessary to find points for both sides. Possible aspects for your solution are:*
   – *The conflict between preserving the environment and industry has evolved over time.*
   – *People in local areas have to be included in the development of new industries and opportunities.*
   – *We have to compensate them for negative consequences of measures that help reduce climate change.*
   – *In the long run it is necessary to prevent global warming because otherwise not only will the farmers' livelihood be at stake but our world will become uninhabitable.*

The man makes a good point. If farmers in the Scottish Highlands can no longer raise sheep, for instance, which is the only thing they might know, what will they do instead? He does not dispute that there are environmental problems, but he questions how he and others like him will be able to make a living if they have to stop their traditional way of life.

The quote expresses the inherent conflict between the environment and mankind. The economy has been set up without regard for and often at the expense of the environment. Industries like agriculture use a lot of resources and are mainly unsustainable, but they offer jobs and a livelihood to people in rural areas and put food on our plates.

The problem is that no one is suggesting a solution to the farmers. Therefore, they are angry. Even if new opportunities arise through environmentally-friendly policies, how will they fit in? Will they be able to transition to a new livelihood? If there were more talk of compensation, public support for jobs lost, or retraining, they might soften their resistance and open their minds to the possibility of change.

Everyone is interested in preserving, saving and improving the environment, but some will suffer more than others. For true sustainability we have to include those people in the process.

(222 words)

3.2 *Here, the type of text is an entry for a forum blog, so your text should have a heading. Your style can be colloquial as you are addressing young people, but do not make it too informal as you are writing about a serious topic. You could include some of the following aspects:*

opportunities local projects offer:
– *improve immediate environment*
– *people have the experience that it is possible to make a change and maybe continue on a broader level*
– *showing results on social media can spread the idea*

limitations local projects face:
– *most projects require financing*
– *you have to find volunteers*
– *your project might meet opposition*

Local greenery, global benefits

Local projects are an ideal way to make people aware of global problems. Take our neighborhood for example. We have raised money to buy small trees and distributed them among members of the community. Those individuals then take the initiative to plant and water their tree. Neighbors with a green thumb are willing to

---

introduction
explanation of the quote

main part
very old conflict between environment and industry

new opportunities and compensation for farmers

conclusion

heading

introduction
positive example from your own experience

offer advice on looking after the trees. Thus the whole community is able to witness the effect of trees on the temperature and humidity around them, as well as the positive psychological effects of green spaces in an urban environment.

We see this as a very motivating activity, empowering young and old alike to improve their immediate environment. This will hopefully increase their awareness of how easy it is to plant and take care of a tree. The manifold positive effects of a greener environment will build on themselves, so that people will plant more and more trees, flowers and plants to beautify the area and improve the air quality. Some, we hope, will go even further and campaign politicians for district or even citywide public greening projects. By showing the positive results on social media, we can help public greening to go a long way.

why local projects make a difference

motivation

larger projects

spread ideas via social media

The project depends on financing and local commitment, of course. We have raised money from local individuals and businesses that are interested, and to inform them about the project we had volunteers knock on doors and distribute leaflets. This may not always work in every community: poorer communities may not be able to raise enough funding to develop the project to any noticeable degree, for example. In addition, volunteers are needed to initiate the door-to-door campaign. Here, social media could play a limited role. It might also be hard to convince sceptical neighbors of the global benefits of planting trees locally.

problems local projects face

funding

lack of volunteers

political opponents

However, once the green ball gets rolling, the positive results will be hard to ignore.

conclusion

(320 words)

Aufgabenstellung 1.2

1 *The text offers a lot of information on Dara McAnulty and the challenge is to summarise it without repeating yourself. As his book is a memoir, it is difficult to distinguish between author and writing, but that is not necessary in order to complete the task. You should include the following aspects in your solution:*

general information:
– *17 years old, autistic*
– *grew up in Northern Ireland*

childhood:
– *spent a lot of time outside in nature*
– *bullied in school*
– *supported by his parents*

writing career:
– *started a blog when he was 12*
– *won the Wainwright Prize, a prestigious award for his first book* Diary of a Young Naturalist, *which describes his experiences in nature and as an autistic child who*

is bullied; it is split into four parts each describing one season; praised by fellow authors
- *his second book, which encourages children to appreciate and protect the environment, will be published soon*
- *he is planning a third book on nature and myth in Northern Ireland*

activist work:
- *raised money to track and save birds*
- *led a school strike to call attention to political inaction against climate change*
- *went to London to deliver a "people's manifesto for wildlife"*
- *spoke at the first Irish meeting of Extinction Rebellion*

Dara McAnulty is a seventeen-year-old popular nature writer, who has just won a prestigious British award for his first book, *Diary of a Young Naturalist*. He has been praised by critics and fellow authors, who find his writing unusual and special. Dara, who has autism, spent his childhood in nature and began writing about his experiences. His parents have always supported his love for nature. When he was twelve, he started writing a blog and then posting regularly on a publisher's website. He soon realised it could be turned into a book. *Diary of a Young Naturalist* is divided into seasons, containing close observations of the wildlife and nature Dara encounters. What is unique about his writing, however, is his openness about his autism and bullying, and that he describes his feelings and experiences very frankly.

successful teenage writer

childhood

writing career

wildlife and nature

autism and bullying

Dara has been very active politically. At a young age he raised money to protect a species of bird, and later, he led a school strike to call attention to environmental inaction, went to London to deliver a "people's manifesto for wildlife" and spoke at the first Irish meeting of Extinction Rebellion.

environmental activist

He has just finished his second book, which encourages children to appreciate and protect the environment, and he is planning a third one on nature and myth in Northern Ireland. He says writing is a necessary part of his life that he will always pursue it.

upcoming books

(234 words)

2 – *The author mentions how renowned McAnulty is, referring to the prize he has won, quoting famous critics who appreciate his work and naming different well-known publishing companies that publish his work.*
- *He describes how McAnulty's inspiration for his work comes from his childhood.*
- *He outlines how McAnulty uses writing as a coping mechanism to deal with his autism.*
- *By referring to Greta Thunberg, another famous activist, who has Asperger's syndrome, he stresses how powerful people with autism can be and lends credibility to McAnulty's activism.*

The author begins by listing the accolades the 17-year-old writer Dara McAnulty won a for his first book, in order to prove that this is an extraordinary case: "McAnulty, 17, is fast becoming one of Britain and Ireland's most acclaimed nature writers […]. His debut book […] won the Wainwright Prize, Britain's biggest award for nature writing. Reviewers have heaped it with praise" (ll. 1–6). The author of the article names well-known people and institutions to validate the story's authenticity as well as to demonstrate the level of attention the young man is receiving: "Little Toller in Britain and […] Milkweed in the United States" (ll. 3/4), "the Wainwright Prize" (ll. 4/5), "Christophe Hart" (l. 7) and "Robert Macfarlane" (l. 9).

McAnulty's intense childhood relationship with nature is presented. The author writes that "he had been obsessed with nature for as long as he could remember" (ll. 14/15) and that "he spent days as a child 'climbing trees, rustling about'" (ll. 15/16). Marshall mentions the encouragement McAnulty receives from his parents. It is significant that his mother used to be a (music) journalist and his father is an environmentalist, who both do "things most parents would never allow their children to do. His mother, a former music journalist, and his father, a conservationist, nurtured that passion" (ll. 16–18).

The author then introduces McAnulty's reason for writing, asserting that "he only started writing […] because of his autism. 'I need to write, to process what's going on,' McAnulty says" (ll. 23/24). The author uses quotes to reveal McAnulty's unique, engaging writing style, such as "a fulmar dozing and waiting, a queen on her throne," (ll. 33/34), but also the honesty McAnulty is willing to express: "'Dandelions remind me of the way I close myself off from so much of the world,' he writes, 'either because it's too painful to see or feel, or because when I am open to people, the ridicule comes. […] For most of the book, I'm not in a good place'" (ll. 35–43).

The author mentions another autistic person to show how powerful people with autism can be in fighting for what they think is important. He writes that McAnulty was "[i]nspired by Greta Thunberg, the Swedish environmental activist" (ll. 52/53). By doing so, the author lends credibility to the extent of McAnulty's commitment, listing his various activities: "he leads a school strike to highlight inaction against climate change. He goes to London to help deliver a 'people's manifesto for wildlife' to the British government"

Margin notes:

prove McAnulty's quality as a writer

Wainwright prize

well-known people and institutions praise his work

childhood as inspiration for writing

autism as reason for writing

unique, engaging writing style

honesty

reference to Greta Thunberg

credibility to political activism

(ll. 53–55) and even meets with risky groups – "Extinction Rebellion, a group whose members regularly get arrested" (ll. 55/56).

To illustrate McAnulty's focus, the author then mentions further books McAnulty is in the process of writing, which are also connected to nature: "[h]is next book, 'Wild Child,' […] encourages children to seek and protect the natural world" (ll. 58–60) and "[h]e's already planning another book […] about his wanderings around Ireland, connecting nature with myth" (ll. 60/61). This ambition is then modified when McAnulty explains the real reason he writes: "'writing will never disappear from my life,' he said. 'I need it'" (l. 62).

various upcoming book projects → ambitious writer

(547 words)

3.1 *As you have to write a comment in this task, you can choose whether you want to argue that role models are important or that they are not necessary. It is much more difficult to find good arguments for the second position. You can also include arguments from both sides, but you should come to a convincing conclusion.*

Arguments in favour of role models	Arguments against role models
– *raise awareness for important topics* – *show that it is possible to make a change* – *give examples of successful activism using (social) media to be heard*	– *many activists face criticism in public; this may deter young people* – *opinion of someone in the public eye could overshadow activists' own perspective or hinder them from developing their own view of climate issues* – *young people could be recruited to take part in semi-illegal, even violent acts as part of a radical group*

Greta Thunberg has been an inspiring role model for many young people troubled by climate change and the inaction of authorities to mitigate it. Motivated by her example, Dara McAnulty moved beyond writing and overcame his autism and bullying to become politically active in several arenas. He has organised a school strike, helped deliver a manifesto to the British government, spoken to a famous activist organisation and raised money to save an endangered species.

introduction

reference to quote

Greta Thunberg as a role model for Dara McAnulty

Role models like this are excellent examples for others to stand up and defend causes they believe in.

main part

By talking about the problem in public they make young people aware of the problems that have led to and come with climate change. Media coverage of environmental activists can be a call to others to join their movement, or start their own. As we can see by the Fridays for Future demonstrations, many young people are demanding action on climate change.

raise awareness of the problem

With today's social media power, the word of activists like Greta Thunberg can spread instantly. Witnessing concrete individual examples of successful political activism will motivate others to take action regarding current and looming environmental problems. With a little creative thinking, anybody can attract public attention to issues of climate change, in spite of setbacks or difficulties. Thus the youth of today do not need to feel powerless against governments or institutions that are indifferent to or even endangering their future.

(margin: show it is possible to be heard)

That said, sometimes global attention and public criticism of individuals fighting against climate change can intimidate other young people into not getting involved. Therefore, it is important that we all support young climate activists to protect them from undeserved criticism. Change is necessary and we have to start now.

(margin: conclusion)

(283 words)

3.2 *Keep in mind that it is not necessary in this task to actually describe the cartoon. The task explicitly says that you show the cartoon to your listeners. It is, however, necessary to elaborate on the meaning of the cartoon. Typically, you would start your speech by greeting your audience. As the audience might not know you in this case, you can start by briefly introducing yourself and the topic you are going to talk about. To make your speech more interesting, include typical elements such as rhetorical questions, the rule of three, speaking to your audience directly and so on.*

Hi everyone. My name is Jan Dove and I'm here today to talk about personality development through interaction with nature and how digital tools can assist in this process.

(margin: introduction)

Look at this cartoon. What do you see? A mother is showing her child the world outdoors, but the child only sees it as a substitute for something he saw on the computer. The child doesn't see a difference between the digital world and the physical world around him/her. This is a little overdramatic, of course. Even if they spend more time on screens, children still play outside. But it does raise the question of how we can combine experiencing nature and living in a digital world so that children can have the best of both worlds.

(margin: main part / reference to cartoon)

Let's face it, children can run circles around their parents when it comes to digital devices. However, those who remember a time before the internet and social media keep telling us that the youth of today is often missing out on the real world and is spiralling into a virtual universe instead. They claim that experiencing the world online or via computer games is alienating people from their natural environment.

(margin: problems of digital tools / alienation from natural environment)

But there is a solution – a compromise – if you will. Digital tools can be used to heighten the experience of the outdoors and thus lead young people out of the house.

different ways to use technology

Let me remind you of the manifold benefits of experiencing nature. For one, physical activity outdoors improves health and encourages a balanced lifestyle. The myriad impressions on the senses promote happiness and lead to an increased appreciation of the environment and thus the need to protect it. Thus, we become acutely aware of the emergency we're facing regarding climate change. In addition, nature allows us to slow down from the constant digital information overload.

benefits of experiencing nature

That notwithstanding, digital tools can provide more insight into the workings of nature. Using certain apps, you can learn about the natural environment, plants, insects and yourself. GPS along with activity apps and maps can create new challenges by intensifying outdoor games. With social media, everyone can join activist groups or create new groups that fight for climate change and spread the word quickly to others to attend a protest or demonstration, for example.

examples of positive ways to use tools

However, it can be difficult to find the right balance when you incorporate digital media into a child's experience of nature. It may distract them from their environment if they rely too heavily on digital tools rather than develop their physical senses and knowledge. On the whole, though, I think it is essential for children to combine digital tools with the natural environment so that they learn to experience the real world and the virtual world in combination.

conclusion

Thank you!

(456 words)

Prüfungsteil 2: Sprachmittlung

Aufgabenstellung 2.1

Your task here is to "present" the information given in the German text. This means that you are not supposed to include your own opinion. Just summarise what it says in the text about the project. You should present the information in the form of an email. As you are an intern who is writing to an editor, you should use a formal style. Include the following information:

- *The New German Media Makers (NdM) are a collective of journalists, some of whom are from an immigrant background, who are trying to make journalism more diverse.*
- *While 25% of the German population come from an immigrant background, this is only true for 5–10% of the editorial staff.*
- *In 2021, the collective acquired the sponsorship of several high and low pressure areas in Germany for January.*

- *In Germany it is possible to give names to high and low pressure areas if you sponsor them.*
- *The names were usually very traditional German names.*
- *The organisation gave them names from the five largest groups of minorities found in Germany.*
- *By using this lighthearted topic, the organisation is trying to raise awareness regarding a more serious topic: Germany is an immigration country and this should be represented in the media.*

Subject: Diversity initiatives in Germany **subject**

Dear Catherine, **form of address**

Thank you very much for this task. I immediately thought of a project I read about on Instagram recently. **introduction**

There is an interesting initiative among journalists in Germany to name weather fronts according to the population groups that most represent immigrants. Instead of assigning only German names, as has been the practice since the trend was adopted from the USA, the New German Media Makers are calling for better representation of the current German population. This group of journalists from diverse backgrounds has created a system that, this year, will assign low pressure systems male and high pressure systems female immigrant names. With this initiative, they want to point out that while 25 % of the German population are from immigrant backgrounds, only 5–10 % of the editorial staff come from minority groups. This will symbolically emphasize the serious problems in achieving inclusive journalism, and will continue until everyone gets the message. The *#WeatherCorrection* campaign is co-operating with similar organisations in Austria and Switzerland, and is financed by donations. **main part** / information on the campaign

I hope you can use some of the information for your article. **closing phrase**

Best wishes, **sign off**

Elena *(192 words)*

Aufgabenstellung 2.2

The task already tells you which information you have to look for in the text: who are the founders, what are the problems they encounter and what would be possible solutions? You could use three different colours to highlight the necessary information in the text. You can also use the aspects to structure your solution.

immigrants who have founded companies:
- *examples of companies: Biontech, Gorillas, Omio*
- *well-educated, ambitious founders*
- *willing to take risks, as they come from countries which do not have a good social security system → taking risks is part of their culture*
- *good for German economy*

- *one in five start-ups in Germany is founded by a first- or second-generation immigrant*
- **problems they face:**
  - *bureaucracy; e. g. difficulties opening bank accounts, filling out forms, German tax system*
  - *language barriers*
  - *lack of funding*
  - *no business network in Germany, fewer employees*
- **possible solutions:**
  - *forms should be available in English*
  - *governments should offer consulting for financing in different languages*
  - *make successful founders from immigrant backgrounds more visible*
  - *networking events for founders*
  - *professional consulting for funds*

One in five start-ups has a migrant founder

headline

Do you know what Biontech, Gorillas and Omio have in common? They were founded by immigrants. Did you know that one in five companies founded in Germany is started by either first- or second-generation immigrants? Immigrant founders are more well-educated than average and ambitious. They are also more willing than Germans to take risks because they come from countries where there is less social security to fall back on. They are very important for the German economy.

introduction
information on founders

Yet immigrant founders in Germany encounter many setbacks. They often do not speak German well or at all, while most bureaucracy – banking, forms and taxes – is in German and thus a hurdle. They do not have as much access to financing as German companies, and do not have as strong a network either. They therefore have fewer connections to established companies.

main part
problems they face

Solutions could include making official forms bilingual, so that they are in English as well as German. The government could provide multilingual staff to inform those who do not speak sufficient German about financing and help them navigate the bureaucracy. Networking events and professional coaching services could be organized by the start-up scene. Finally, there should be more publicity for founders of successful start-ups who are migrants.

possible solutions

If Germany wants its start-up community to flourish, it needs to address the diverse and multilingual needs of its founders. *(233 words)*

conclusion

Prüfungsteil 1: Leseverstehen und Schreiben (70 %)

Der Prüfungsteil 1 besteht aus zwei Aufgabenstellungen, von denen Sie eine zur Bearbeitung auswählen.

Aufgabenstellung 1.1 – Tasks

Themenschwerpunkte: *Aims and ambitions; Overcoming prejudice in society*

1 Outline the information about Manuel and his performance. (20 %)

2 Analyze how atmosphere is created in this excerpt. (40 %)

3 Choose <u>one</u> of the following tasks:

3.1 "We've all had this dream […]. The dream in which, to the world's surprise and our own, we turn out to be best." (ll. 70/71)
Using the quotation and Manuel's example as a starting point, assess to what extent educational institutions can help young people realize their potential. (40 %)

OR

3.2 You are taking part in a TEDYouth event on equality and social justice with live speakers and discussions for young people.
Write a speech, commenting on different ways to overcome prejudice in society. (40 %)

Text (excerpt from the novel)

Trust Exercise
by Susan Choi

In this excerpt, Latino student Manuel is auditioning for the school musical, "Guys and Dolls", an American musical romantic comedy from 1950.
Among the audience are his charismatic drama teacher, Mr Kingsley, and Sarah and Ellery, two of his classmates.

1 Manuel had come onstage, an apparition. Perhaps it wasn't Manuel. He wasn't dressed like Manuel, in the slightly too-small and slightly too-youthful striped T-shirts you could tell, just from looking, had been bought from the sale rack at Sears, or maybe

from the Purple Heart Thrift Store, by Manuel's unknown mother, after being dis-
5 carded by whoever had bought them at Sears. The shirts Manuel wore every day had
pills, and faint, ancient stains of the kind that defeated all efforts, and they squeezed
his upper arms and his neck. For pants, Manuel wore corduroys that had almost no
cord left. And regardless of weather conditions, Manuel never took off his jacket, the
same fake-wool-lined corduroy jacket they'd first seen him in, and that seemed to them
10 now as permanent as a turtle's scuffed shell. The onstage Manuel was missing this
traditional garb, though not dressed any better. He wore a pair of black slacks that were
shiny with age, and a grayish-white button-up shirt that, despite being short at the
sleeves, was tightly buttoned at the cuffs, emphasizing the bony excess of his wrists.
The feet were encased in hard black leather shoes that looked too small, and the usual
15 bushy brown hair was combed back from the face exposing large, startled eyes, unfamiliar to all, beneath an equally novel, creased brow. A sheaf of paper was gripped in
the hands. The Manuel-apparition looked like a waiter, an unhappy and poorly dressed
waiter.

Sarah realized with amazement he was dressing, as well as he could, for the part.
20 *Guys and Dolls* would of course call for old-fashioned menswear: leather shoes, slacks,
a button-up shirt. Not one other boy, for the sake of the audition, had made the slightest
alteration to his everyday clothes. They'd all auditioned in their Levi's and polos and
dumb slogan T-shirts. [...]

Manuel again turns that mesmerizing color of a live coal. At length he says, barely
25 audibly, "I am going to sing the 'Ave Maria' of [a bunch of syllables Sarah can't
hear]." Strings seem to be tied to his elbows, equally pulling on him from both sides,
so that, in his tensile, motionless state, he might fly to pieces. Then the stage-left string
breaks, and he lurches toward Mr Bartoli, extending his music. Mr Bartoli pages
through it, nods. "Shall I begin?" he asks.
30 Manuel wrings his hands in a fretful grandmotherly way, abruptly drops them to
his sides. Mr Kingsley, still standing, his back to the rest of the house, says, "Manny,
I know you can do it."

He speaks as though he and Manuel are entirely alone. Yet no one in the house
fails to hear him, to the very last row.
35 It's possible for silence to change quality. The silence had been enforced, the silence of quashed merriment. Now it's the silence of genuine puzzlement. Mr Kingsley
never uses nicknames or pet names. To indicate an altered attitude he sometimes calls
them, instead of their given names, Ms or Mr and then their last name. This denotes
bemusement, disapproval, and much in between, but whatever the case there is always
40 a distance implied. "Manny" observes no such distance. "Manny" doesn't even ob-
serve that there might be some forty-odd people elsewhere in the room.

Mr Kingsley sits down again. The back of his head, with its limited features, its
expensive haircut, and the ends of his spectacles' temples hooking over the backs of
his ears, is nearly as expressive to them as his face – it radiates a peremptory certitude.
45 "Come on. You know what I want. Give it to me." If the back of his head can say this,
just imagine the front. [...] Manuel – Manny? – seems to be in wordless communication with this hidden front of Mr Kingsley's head. He gazes into it, receives something

from it – he looked different when he first came onstage, and he somehow looks different again. With what might almost be called self-possession he nods to Mr Bartoli.
50 Mr Bartoli raises his hands, brings them plunging back down. Manuel sucks air into his lungs.

To this point in her life, Sarah has associated opera with Bugs Bunny in braids, PBS, overweight men wearing tunics, shrieking women, and shattering glass. She's never understood, certainly because she's never seen a live opera but also because
55 she's never heard a half-decent performance, not even in part, on TV, that opera, in fact, is the highest redemption of longing. […]

Manuel sings. His Spanish accent, which he drags like a weight on his uncertain journeys amid English words, is a bona fide now. Who else among them could sing this, even if they were blessed with the voice? Who else among them is blessed with
60 the voice? Manuel sings, it seems, to horizons beyond the light booth. His eyes are cast up, anxiously, as if he's aware he is barely retaining the fickle attention of God. So plaintively does he exhort this remote audience that Sarah glances back over her shoulder, expecting to see ranks of angels, their feet floating just off the ground. Instead she sees the faces of her classmates, rapt with unself-consciousness, the joyful respite from
65 the problems of self. […]

Her body twists forward again as if slapped, as Manuel, like a fountain, upraises his arms and their glorious burden, his final note, into the air. As if they awaited this gesture, the house detonates: clapping, whistling, foot-stamping, Ellery leaping up to shout, "Hombre!" Onstage Manuel, streaming with sweat, grins while wringing his
70 hands. We've all had this dream, Sarah thinks. The dream in which, to the world's surprise and our own, we turn out to be best. *(941 words)*

Choi, Susan. *Trust Exercise*. New York: Henry Holt and Co., 2019, 41–43

Annotations
l. 3   Sears: an American chain of department stores
l. 4   Purple Heart Thrift Store: non-profit organization helping families who are in need
l. 6   pill: ball of loose fibres on clothes
l. 25   Ave Maria: musical version of the Latin prayer to the Virgin Mary used in the Catholic Church
l. 28   Mr Bartoli: pianist who accompanies the students during their audition
l. 52   Bugs Bunny in braids: a cartoon character's parody of German opera
l. 53   PBS: Public Broadcasting Service (PBS) is an American public non-profit television network
l. 58   bona fide: *here:* something authentic, very suitable
l. 69   hombre: *Spanish:* man, sometimes used informally in English

Themenschwerpunkte: *The impact of the media on society; Saving the planet; Aims and ambitions*

1   Outline the features of climate fiction and the reasons why cli-fi has become so popular. (30 %)

2   Analyze how the author conveys her attitude towards cli-fi and its potential impact on readers. (30 %)

3   Choose <u>one</u> of the following tasks:

3.1   "In times of intense worry and rampant uncertainty, [cli-fi novels] almost seem to hold out the promise of a how-to manual – how to handle crisis, how to deal with calamity, how to simply muddle through." (ll. 32–34) Using the quote as a starting point, assess to what extent reading literature helps people in their search for direction in life. (40 %)

OR

3.2   Using the information on the novel "Dreamland" from the book cover and the article to illustrate your point, write a blog entry for www.goodreads.com in which you discuss whether reading cli-fi in schools contributes to raising students' awareness of environmental issues. (40 %)

'Liquid grace and glinting sparkle'
THE OBSERVER

'A beautiful book'
BRIT BENNETT

'Read this now'
GQ

'A writer we will all want to read again and again'
MONIQUE ROFFEY

DREAMLAND

ROSA RANKIN-GEE

Source: https://www.simonan dschuster.co.uk/books /Dreamland/ Rosa-Rankin-Gee/978147 1193842. Accessed September 27, 2022.

Text (Excerpt from the article)

The rise of apocalyptic novels
by Hephzibah Anderson

1 Imagine you're enjoying much-needed time away with your family, staying in a luxurious Long Island holiday rental, miles from anywhere. Then comes a late-night knock at the door and strangers bearing news of a sinister power outage in New York City. The internet has gone down, phone service has been severed, and when you switch on
5 the TV, every channel shows the same blank screen. Your children are asleep down the hallway, and you've no way of knowing what's going on, or even whether these people are telling the truth.

Hooked? You wouldn't be alone. It's the premise of *Leave the World Behind* by Rumaan Alam, a propulsive, penetrating new novel about race, class, and climate
10 change. Because while the true nature of what's going on remains obscure – could it be a terrorist attack, the actions of a rogue state? – clues scattered throughout hint heavily at a climate event. Not only did this profoundly unsettling novel make the shortlist of the US National Book Award, it's also become a bestseller.

Comfort has been at a premium during the current pandemic, and it hasn't always
15 come from expected sources. Never mind cosy home-baking and box sets: readers have turned not just to beloved classics but also to the often-dystopian genre known as cli-fi-novels in which environmental devastation is a driving force, catapulting protagonists into an apocalyptic "after" or else pinning them in the fast-vanishing "before", with disaster bearing down, inaction endemic and anxiety soaring.

20 Short for climate fiction, cli-fi is a relatively new term for a trend whose long roots extend back to sci-fi. Think J.G. Ballard's *The Drowned World* or Ursula K. Le Guin's *The Lathe of Heaven,* both written at a point in history when frequent wildfires and regular flash floods belonged to the realm of the speculative. In the past couple of decades, contributions from titans of literary fiction, including Margaret Atwood and
25 Cormac McCarthy, have brought cli-fi into mainstream storytelling. Worsening scientific projections are keeping it there. […] This trend isn't about to lose momentum anytime soon, either – novels poised for release in the coming months include Rosa Rankin-Gee's *Dreamland*, depicting Britain in 20 years' time, a place of rising sea levels and populist tides.

30 It might seem masochistic to turn just now to tales of havoc and wrenching loss, yet these cautionary narratives also offer catharsis, a degree of hope, sometimes humour. In times of intense worry and rampant uncertainty, they almost seem to hold out the promise of a how-to manual – how to handle crisis, how to deal with calamity, how to simply muddle through. […]

35 Climate fiction feels less and less like fantasy, its fever-dream visions increasingly begging questions not of "if" but "when". Even so, it wouldn't be entirely prudent to look to its pages for practical tips on how to survive an apocalypse. Not that they aren't there. Lie low until the initial mayhem subsides. Follow the animals for safe drinking water. Always be ready to run.

40 As a child, Rankin-Gee took dystopian novels very seriously. "As soon as I read *Z for Zachariah*, I packed my Karrimor backpack with odd tins of food, spare underwear

and some rope. I was ready to go at any minute," she recalls. Her own novel, *Dream-land*, which will be published in April, stars Chance, a heroine born just four years from now. Sea levels are rising, but it's also hotter. "That's the scary part," she tells
45 BBC Culture. "Many elements of my future in *Dreamland* are not future at all – they are things that have already happened."

Plenty of cli-fi novels, she notes, jump-cut to the moment after the catastrophe has occurred, giving protagonists the benefit of hindsight. "I wanted to write the 'during'. The characters are not nostalgists, they don't have a great deal to romanticise. At the
50 same time, they're not bleak or despondent – they're just continuing to live with what they're faced with."

Though quick to point out that this isn't a book intended to yield clues on how to survive, Rankin-Gee believes that "in the writing and reading there can be a stoic work-ing through of things. And that sense we look for in all books, film, art – connection,
55 that we are not alone." It's one of the recurring themes of cli-fi: not only are we not alone, we're vastly stronger together. Even with zombies and monster rats on the ram-page. […]

There is a necessary limit to the succour that cli-fi can offer. While it shows us that even in the midst of a global pandemic, things could always be much worse, the prob-
60 lem is that our being distracted from it hasn't made looming environmental collapse go away. For Rankin-Gee, there's a worry that a genre that eyes humanity's extinction risks "normalising" climate breakdown, painting pictures so bleak that we're left with an unintended – and wholly false – sense of reassurance. "Then I remember the climate deniers, and the fact that a basic normalisation is still a crucial part of confronting the
65 problem," she says.

Optimism is a different matter. As Alam insists, "I have to find optimism, you've no choice but to go on." He finds it in the next generation, in the ability of children to see with clarity rather than turning away, to act decisively rather than pretend that buy-ing the recycled coffee filters will have an impact. That same belief in the future is
70 embedded in his novel, a book that – like so many other excellent examples of not only this genre, but of literature in general – reminds us of something else, just as vital to survival: there is always a place for art, no matter how grave the crisis.   *(941 words)*

Anderson, Hephzibah. "The rise of apocalyptic novels". BBC Culture. January 11, 2021. Accessed January 11, 2021 from https://www.bbc.com/culture/article/20210108-the-rise-of-apocalyptic-novels

Annotations

l. 11   rogue: aggressive or defying international agreements

ll. 24/25   Margaret Atwood, Cormac McCarthy: award-winning writers, well-known for their dystopian novels

ll. 40/41   *Z for Zachariah:* novel about a teenage girl who believes herself to be the survivor of a nuclear war

Der Prüfungsteil 2 besteht aus zwei Aufgabenstellungen, von denen Sie eine zur Bearbeitung auswählen.

Aufgabenstellung 2.1 – Task

Themenschwerpunkte: *Aims and ambitions; Saving the planet*

You are going to take part in an international youth conference about sustainable business ideas. To prepare for the discussions, participants share an example from their own country on the conference website.
Write an article for this website in which you present "Lieferrad DA".

Text (Auszug aus dem Artikel)

Der Spargel kommt per Lastenrad
Von Astrid Ludwig

1   Lange schon hegte das Professoren-Trio die Idee für einen Lieferservice der anderen Art. Einen, der die Umwelt schont, den örtlichen Handel stärkt, Mitarbeiter fair bezahlt und trotzdem rentabel ist. Doch die Wirtschafts- und Logistikexperten Johanna Bucerius und Axel Wolfermann von der Hochschule Darmstadt und Kai-Oliver Schocke
5   von der Frankfurt University of Applied Sciences fanden niemanden, der bereit war, das auch auszuprobieren. Dann aber kam Corona. „Als wir gesehen haben, wie schlecht es dem Einzelhandel geht, haben wir den Lieferservice selbst gestartet", berichtet Bucerius. Beim hessischen Wirtschaftsministerium beantragten die drei Forscher Fördergeld. Sie bekamen rund 100.000 Euro, mit denen E-Lastenräder ange-
10 schafft und Gehälter für das studentische Team aus Hilfskräften und Kurierfahrern gezahlt werden konnten.

     Seit dem Sommer rollen die schwarzen Lasten-Bikes mit dem gelbblauen Aufdruck „Lieferrad DA" durch Darmstadt. Sie bringen Blumen, Bücher, Wein, Lebensmittel, die nicht gekühlt werden müssen, Kleidung, Kosmetik oder auch Medikamente
15 von den Einzelhändlern direkt nach Hause zu den Kunden. „Es lief gut an", sagt Axel Wolfermann – dank Werbung über soziale Medien sowie Kontakten zur Stadt und örtlichen Wirtschaft. Ein Spargelbauer im Stadtteil Arheilgen machte den Anfang. Bei manchem Geschäft fragten die Studenten auch persönlich an.

     Mittlerweile nutzen rund 50 Einzelhändler in Darmstadt den unentgeltlichen Lie-
20 ferservice. Darunter auch große Händler wie das Modekaufhaus Henschel und die Buchladen-Kette Thalia. Armin Pourhosseini, Mitbegründer des Naturkosmetik-Shops „Woodberg", hat sich nach eigenen Worten bewusst für den klimaschonenden Raddienst entschieden. […] Umweltschutz gehört für ihn zum Geschäftsmodell. Für seine Naturprodukte nutzt er recyceltes Verpackungsmaterial, bei Versand und Bezahlung

25 bietet er Kunden Modelle an, die Ökoprojekte unterstützen. Rund vier von zehn Bestellungen aus Darmstadt lässt er von Lieferrad DA zustellen.

Die studentischen Radkuriere haben gut zu tun. Wöchentlich fahren sie zwischen 100 und 150 Pakete aus. „Weihnachten ging es deutlich nach oben, da waren es rund 300 Pakete pro Woche. Das war Rekord", so Wolfermann. Am Valentinstag nahmen
30 die Ausfahrten ebenfalls zu, und Ostern werde sicherlich eine weitere Herausforderung, vermutet Bucerius. Bis Ende 2020 brachte „Lieferrad DA" montags bis freitags insgesamt 1 068 Pakete an die Haustüren. Die zwei studentischen Kuriere radelten mehr als 3 000 Kilometer durch die Straßen Darmstadts.

Die Kunden bestellen bei den Händlern, die die Aufträge an das Studententeam
35 weiterleiten. „Wird bis 12 Uhr bestellt, liefern wir am selben Tag aus", sagt Florian Treiber. Der Dreiundzwanzigjährige, der Logistikmanagement an der Hochschule Darmstadt studiert, ist für die Tourenplanung zuständig. Er pflegt die Bestellungen in die Tourensoftware ein, prüft, ob Händler wegen vieler oder schwerer Pakete mehrfach angefahren werden müssen, checkt Öffnungszeiten, rechnet Pufferzeiten ein und über-
40 nimmt die Datenanalyse. Weil Kundendaten sensibel sind, stellt die Hochschule dafür einen gesicherten Laptop zur Verfügung. Treiber ist für die Kuriere erreichbar, „falls ein Kunde nicht da, die Adresse falsch oder der Akku leer ist". Vor Weihnachten ist er sogar selbst als Fahrer eingesprungen – ein lehrreicher Blick auf die andere Seite. „Das Projekt ist ohnehin eine super Einstiegsmöglichkeit in die Logistikbranche", findet der
45 Student. Und das ohne Druck und schlechte Bezahlung, über die Paketzusteller immer wieder klagen. Die Lieferrad-Kuriere und Hiwis werden pro Stunde honoriert, nach den Sätzen der Hochschule. Studenten mit Bachelorabschluss erhalten rund 15 Euro. „Sie werden zudem in das Forschungsprojekt einbezogen, bringen ihre Erfahrungen ein", ergänzt Bucerius. Der Lieferdienst ist auch Gegenstand mehrerer Bachelorarbei-
50 ten.

Das Professoren-Trio ist zufrieden mit dem Projekt. Zum Jahresende ist zwar die Förderung ausgelaufen, doch eine Fortsetzung ist in Sicht. Noch ist die Hochschule Darmstadt Betreiberin und der Lieferdienst gebührenfrei. Doch es soll eine neue Rechtsform gefunden werden, damit Lieferrad DA als Verein oder GmbH Gewinne
55 generieren kann. Denn die Forscher wollen auch herausfinden, unter welchen Bedingungen ein derartiger Lieferservice rentabel bestehen kann. Bei voller Auslastung betragen die Kosten je Lieferung derzeit rund vier Euro. Der Einzelhandel, sagt Wolfermann, habe Interesse an dem Lieferdienst, aber angewiesen ist das Projekt auf zusätzliche Kunden wie die Stadt, kommunale Betriebe, Unternehmen oder Wochenmarkt-
60 Beschicker. Andere Kommunen haben schon Interesse am Aufbau eines ähnlichen Lieferdienstes bekundet. […] *(640 Wörter)*

Astrid Ludwig, „Der Spargel kommt per Lastenrad", in: https://www.faz.net/aktuell/rhein-main/hochschule-darmstadt-der-spargel-kommt-per-lastenrad-17258331.html

Annotationen
Z. 13   DA: Autokennzeichen von Darmstadt
Z. 46   Hiwi: studentische wissenschaftliche Hilfskraft

Themenschwerpunkte: *Overcoming prejudice in society; The impact of the media on society; Aims and ambitions*

Your friend in California is working on the project "Representation Matters", which focuses on minorities in the media. He/She has asked you if this issue plays a role in Germany.

Write him/her an email in which you outline the information on the situation of minorities in the German film industry and ways to improve it.

Text (Auszug aus dem Artikel)

Studie „Vielfalt im Film" Du hast den Farbfilm vergessen!
Von Christiane Peitz

1 Melden allein genügt nicht. Zu diesem Ergebnis kommt die von Citizens for Europe erstellte Studie „Vielfalt im Film", an der insgesamt 38 Einrichtungen beteiligt sind, von ProQuote Film über die Schwarze Filmschaffende Community und die Filmuniversität Babelsberg bis zur Antidiskriminierungsstelle des Bundes. Wie divers, fair und
5 inklusiv geht es vor und hinter den Kameras im deutschsprachigen Raum zu?

Eher wenig, so die Studie: Sie belegt, so die Soziologin und wissenschaftliche Leiterin Deniz Yildirim, nicht nur eine strukturelle Diskriminierung von Frauen, People of Color, queeren oder trans Menschen und Personen mit Beeinträchtigungen. Sie macht auch klar, wie wenig sich ändert, wenn Betroffene sich wehren. Zwar melden
10 zwei Drittel von ihnen eine erlebte Diskriminierung erst gar nicht, weil sie berufliche Nachteile befürchten. Aber die 172 Personen, die den Mut dazu aufbrachten, machten zu großen Teilen negative Erfahrungen: Meldungen blieben häufig ohne Konsequenzen, manchmal verschlechterte sich die Lage sogar.

Die am Mittwoch vorgestellte Studie basiert auf einer anonymen, freiwilligen Be-
15 fragung im Zeitraum von Juli bis November 2020, die sich an die 30 000 Nutzer:innen von Crew United richtete. Teilgenommen haben 18,3 Prozent. Crew United ist die größte deutsche Branchendatenbank, und die Parameter der Teilnehmenden (Alter/ Wohnort/Geschlechtsidentität etc.) entsprechen in etwa denen aller Datenbank-Nutzer:innen: Die Studie mit 5 455 ausgewerteten Fragebögen kann also als weitgehend
20 repräsentativ gelten.

Die Zahlen sprechen für sich: Über 1 600 der Befragten gaben an, Diskriminierung selber erlebt zu haben, wegen ihrer sexuellen Orientierung, ihrer Geschlechtsidentität, dem Alter oder rassistischen Zuschreibungen. Acht von zehn der sich äußernden Frauen wurden in den letzten zwei Jahren im Arbeitskontext sexuell belästigt, drei
25 Viertel davon mehrfach. LGBTQ-Personen reden am Set meist nicht offen über ihre sexuelle Orientierung oder ihre Geschlechtsidentität, anders als im privaten Umfeld, manche Agentur rät sogar zu Zurückhaltung. Und wenn sie sich outen, erleben sie oft Heterosexismus oder übergriffige Anmache [...].

Bei den Filmen selbst sieht es nicht besser aus: Mehr als drei Viertel der Befragten
30 finden, dass etwa arabische, muslimische und Schwarze Menschen oder auch Personen
mit niedrigem sozialem Status überwiegend stereotyp dargestellt werden. Dabei ist die
Vielfalt längst da: Im Schauspiel-Department von Crew United finden sich allein
knapp 20 Prozent LGBTQ-Personen und 16 Prozent Schwarze Menschen und People
of Color – Diversität und Multiperspektive im Film wären also kein Problem, die
35 Schauspieler:innen müssten nur entsprechend besetzt werden.

„Meine Straße ist bunt. Meine Stadt ist bunt. Deutschland ist bunt. Wo ist das Bunte
in Film und Fernsehen?", fragt denn auch der Schauspieler Gustav Peter Wöhler auf
der Webseite des Bündnisses.

Bessern kann sich das nur, wenn die Politik in die Verantwortung genommen wird
40 und die Branche sich außerdem selbst verpflichtet, ist das Bündnis überzeugt. Gegen
die Wirkungslosigkeit von Diskriminierungs-Meldungen könnten ähnliche Einrichtungen helfen wie Themis als Vertrauensstelle gegen sexuelle Belästigung und Gewalt.
Skadi Loist von der Filmuni Babelsberg hält beim Abbau von Diskriminierung neben
Quoten auch Diversity-Checklisten bei den Förderinstitutionen für sinnvoll. In Groß-
45 britannien ist die Berücksichtigung von Diversität bereits Voraussetzung für staatliche
Subventionen.

Als der Schauspieler und Produzent Tyron Ricketts wegen einer entsprechenden
Verankerung im hiesigen Filmfördergesetz bei der Behörde von Kulturstaatsministerin
Monika Grütters vorstellig wurde, lief er jedoch gegen Mauern, wie er bei der Online-
50 Präsentation der Studie berichtete. Der Filmemacher Dieu Hao Do setzt unter anderem
auf Sensibilisierungsworkshops, auf mehr Diversität auch in Redaktionen und Jurys.
Daniel Gyamerah, Bereichsleiter bei Citizens for Europe, empfiehlt der Branche eine
Einrichtung wie das Projektbüro Diversity Arts Culture, das den Berliner Kulturbetrieb
berät und Konzepte entwickelt.

55 Manchmal hilft auch der Markt. Tyron Ricketts verweist darauf, dass der US-Film
oder internationale Streamingportale schon deshalb diverser sind, weil sie ein vielfältiges Publikum auf dem Weltmarkt erreichen wollen.

Übrigens, gerade erst publizierte McKinsey eine Untersuchung mit dem Ergebnis,
dass die US-Filmindustrie ihren Jahresumsatz um zehn Milliarden Dollar steigern
60 könnte (7 Prozent!), wenn sie mehr Schwarze Künstler beteiligen würde. [...]

(619 Wörter)

Peitz, Christiane. „Studie ,Vielfalt im Film' Du hast den Farbfilm vergessen!". Der Tagesspiegel.
25. März 2021. Zugriff am 19. November 2021 von https://www.tagesspiegel.de/kultur/studie-vielfalt-
im-film-du-hast-den- farbfilm-vergessen/27037722.html

Annotationen

Titel Du hast den Farbfilm vergessen! – Anspielung auf ein erfolgreiches Lied in den 1970er-Jahren

Z. 1 Citizens for Europe: Gemeinschaft von über 500 Organisationen, die sich für ein partizipatives, vielfältiges und demokratisches Europa einsetzen

Z. 28 Heterosexismus: sexistische Einstellung, die Heterosexualität als überlegene Ausrichtung von menschlicher Sexualität ansieht und andere sexuelle Orientierungen ablehnt

Z. 42 Themis: unabhängige Vertrauensstelle gegen sexuelle Belästigung und Gewalt in der Kultur- und Medienbranche

Z. 49 Monika Grütters: CDU-Politikerin, von 2013 bis 2021 Staatsministerin für Kultur und Medien

Aufgabenstellung 1.1

1 *"Outline" is the keyword to tell you what type of text you are being asked to create. In contrast to a summary, you would not need an umbrella sentence containing the title, author, source etc. Instead you can start right away.*
The task gives you a good hint as to how to structure your text.
Information about Manuel
– *is taking part in the audition for a school musical*
– *usually dressed in cheap, worn-out, second-hand clothes, but has dressed up for the occasion*
– *Hispanic background*
– *sings Ave Maria*
Information on his performance
– *very shy, nervous, reluctant in the beginning*
– *needs his teacher's encouragement to start*
– *performs extraordinarily well, which greatly surprises the audience*
– *is frenetically applauded by his schoolmates after his performance*

Manuel is a young Latino who is auditioning for a role in the school musical. | audition for school musical

In contrast to all the other students, he has dressed up to match the 1950s setting of the play. Manuel is known for wearing rather cheap, threadbare clothes bought from local charity organisations or discount markets, indicating that he comes from a poor background. His clothes are still cheap and ill-fitting but suit the musical, which shows he has put some effort into his preparations for the audition. | cheap clothes but dressed up

Consequently, he feels quite nervous when he announces he is going to perform "Ave Maria". After a little encouragement from Mr Kingsley, his drama teacher, he starts singing. To everyone's surprise he turns out to be an excellent singer and even his Spanish accent now contributes to the authenticity of his performance. | nervous / needs encouragement / turns out to be excellent singer

At the end, the audience applauds Manuel frenetically, while the artist, still sweating with the strain, is happy but takes it in modestly. | is applauded by audience

(158 words)

2 *If you want to find out more about the atmosphere in a story, you can analyse the room, the light, the sounds and the appearance of the people depicted in the excerpt. The narrative perspective also has an effect on the atmosphere.*

Perspective:
– *third-person personal narrator*
→ *reader does not know more than Sarah/the audience; this increases suspense*

Description of Manuel's appearance:
– *contrast between appearance on stage ("an apparition" l. 1; "Perhaps it wasn't Manuel. He wasn't dressed like Manuel" ll. 1/2) and usual outward appearance (cf. ll. 2–10)*
– *body language indicates insecurity (cf. ll. 24, 30)*
→ *thanks to the choice of words the audience expects something out of the ordinary; his outward appearance (ill-dressed, insecure) would indicate that he would fail, but from the beginning it is clear that there is something special about him*

Sounds:
– *to start with Manuel is "barely audibl[e]" (ll. 24/25); the teacher speaks to him in an unusual manner (cf. ll. 31–41) → increases the tension as everyone is watching them*
– *during the scene Mr Kingsley and Manuel "seem[] to be in wordless communication" (ll. 46/47) → makes reader want to know more*
– *when Manuel sings, the narrator refers to his accent first (cf. l. 57) and then to the good job he did on stage*
– *when the "house detonates" (l. 68) the tension is released*

Place:
– *stage → limited space, Manuel can't escape, increases his nervousness; with his words the teacher creates an intimate scene "as though [the two] are entirely alone" (l. 33)*

Structure:
– *some passages diverging from the main action/interruption in plot*
– *growing expectations*

Stylistic devices:
– *different register at the end (l. 68) → more respect for Manuel*
– *rhetorical questions (ll. 58–60) → silent agreement expected*

The atmosphere created in the excerpt is rather tense at the beginning, but this tension is released in the end and makes way for an electric atmosphere, in which everybody feels excited. **thesis**

This change is described by a third-person personal narrator. Sarah, Manuel's classmate, is as much surprised by his performance as the reader. We only know what she knows or what she is telling us. This gives us a feeling of being part of the audience. narrative perspective

When Manuel comes on stage, the tense atmosphere is created by the expectant attitude of the audience. He is characterised as "an apparition" (l. 1). The choice of words here and in the phrases: "Perhaps it wasn't Manuel. He wasn't dressed like Manuel" description of Manuel's appearance (ll. 1/2) gives the boy a mystical touch. The contrast between the "stage" Manuel and the "real" Manuel raises expectations. Manuel is expected to fail. This is also indicated by the narrator's description of his body language. He "turns the [...] color of a live coal" (l. 24) and "wrings his hands in a fretful [...] way" (l. 30).

body language

His outward appearance also contributes to it. His ill-fitting clothes that "squeeze[] his upper arms and his neck" (ll. 6/7) and the "corduroy jacket [...] that [seems] as permanent as a turtle's scuffed shell" (ll. 9/10) support the feeling that Manuel is too weak, too much out of place to be a great performer.

clothes

To start with Manuel is "barely audibl[e]" (ll. 24/25) when speaking, which shows his lack of self-confidence. When his teacher tries to encourage him, "no one in the house fails to hear him, to the very last row" (ll. 33/34), although the teacher speaks "as though [the two] are entirely alone" (l. 33) . The way Mr Kingsley addresses his student is unexpected, so that the tension in the hall increases even more and all eyes are on Manuel. There is a limited space now, in which only Mr Kingsley and Manuel interact. Manuel "seems to be in wordless communication with this hidden front of Mr Kingsley's head" (ll. 46/47) and he "somehow looks different again"(ll. 48/49). The tension is at its peak.

Manuel is very quiet at the beginning

limited space

This point of highest suspense, in which Manuel "sucks air into his lungs" (ll. 50/51), is interrupted by a passage in which Sarah, the narrator, recalls her experience of opera. To the reader, it painfully increases the desire for relief by finally finding out how well Manuel will perform.

The structure of the text, how Sarah presents the events to us, maintains the reader's attention. Sarah does not immediately describe the beauty of his voice, but instead first mentions that "Manuel sings [with a] Spanish accent" (l. 57), which she describes as a "bona fide" (l. 58), a very sophisticated word. This is in clear contrast to the words used to describe Manuel at the beginning, with his worn-out shirts with "pills, and faint, ancient stains" (l. 6). She continues with two rhetorical questions: "Who else among them could sing this [...]? Who else among them is blessed with the voice?" (ll. 58–60) The anaphora that comes with them supports the fact that Manuel is performing excellently.

structure

Manuel's voice

choice of words

rhetorical questions

The tension, which is reflected in the silence of the audience, is finally released by the opposite: noise. When he "upraises [...] his final note, into the air" (ll. 66/67), "the house detonates". (l. 68)

tension is broken by clapping audience

(568 words)

"Assess" means you have to write an argumentative text here. You are expected to structure your text well (introduction, main part, conclusion) and discuss both sides. You will also have to express your personal opinion.

Argument based on the excerpt:

– *Manuel, a student who is underestimated, is encouraged by his teacher and manages to perform extremely well*

Arguments based on personal experience/opinion

Pro: educational institutions can help	*Con: educational institutions can't help*
– *teachers are trained to see students' potential*	– *teachers' work overload*
– *teachers are supposed to encourage and support children*	– *too many students to really acknowledge every single one*
– *educational staff should know about ways of getting support from other organisations*	– *strict rules regarding how/what to teach, so individual skills might not play a role*
– *coaches in clubs can easily boost their team members' self-confidence*	– *parents' responsibility must not be ignored*

Manuel has made it; a star is born. He dares to perform in front of a large audience, although it takes a lot of effort, and he ultimately succeeds. What a boost to his self-confidence that must be. | **introduction**

However, have we not all dreamed of such a "Manuel moment" to occur in our lives? And do we not all deserve that? | **reference to quote**

Let us have a look at the father of Manuel's success: Mr Kingsley, apparently. He encourages Manuel to be the best he can be. He believes in Manuel and knows what his student needs to perform excellently, even though he comes from a poor background where the struggle to make a living is more important than being a good singer. Kingsley sees Manuel's potential behind his underprivileged circumstances. | Manuel's example

What better place is there than all the different educational institutions to give each and every child "one moment in time" like that, as Whitney Houston once sang? | **main part**

The problem is that most teachers moan about their workload and that in classes of up to 30 students there is hardly any time to look after every single one. Teachers are often also set a list of rigid rules about what to teach and when to teach it, not to mention all the tests they have to give the students to find out about their reading or writing abilities and so on. Some parents may also feel as if their privacy is being encroached upon when they have to apply for scholarships and reveal their financial difficulties, for example. | **cons** heavy workload large classes rigid curriculum parents

I still hope every child has a Mr Kingsley in their school career. It should be in teachers' DNA to encourage and support their students. They are trained to see the students' specific talents and by encouraging them they can help them succeed. They also know | **pro** teachers' support see talent where to get resources and can help find one of the many different programmes offered by firms and organisations that help students realise their potential, such as START, for example, which helps students from an immigrant background. It may take some effort to fill in all the forms and so on, but it is worth it. Of course, all of this does not only apply to school teachers, but to coaches from sports clubs or trainers from other extracurricular activities as well, who can help athletes, musicians and other artists to find their place in life.

get resources

other educational staff can help students succeed in sports or the arts

Sometimes students – especially those from poorer backgrounds – need to be pushed a little to take part in different competitions. That is what teachers, coaches and other educational staff can do to boost young people's self-confidence. *(435 words)*

conclusion

3.2 *When writing speeches, make sure that you actively address your audience. This is the best way to attract and maintain their attention. A well-structured text will also be of help, since it can be more demanding to follow spoken language than following written language. Rhetorical devices help to make your speech more memorable. Which elements you should use depends on the context. Alliteration, anaphors, rhetorical questions, repetition, the rule of three, antithesis and metaphors are safe choices. Be careful when using irony or sarcasm as it can make you sound harsh or bitter, which might not fit the context, which is the TEDYouth event in this case.*

The task does not explicitly say that you have to consider two sides, so you can fully concentrate on how to overcome prejudice rather than what makes it difficult to do so.

How to overcome prejudice:

political change (levelling the field):
– opportunities in education: free of charge, compulsory daycare for every child between 3 and 6, comprehensive schools
– laws and regulations: hate speech on the internet
individual change (becoming an ally):
– learning about diversity
– help people who are discriminated against
– talk to biased people

In the country where I come from, your chances of higher education depend heavily on how much money your parents earn and whether you come from an immigrant background. Although this has been known for decades, no one is ready to change anything.

introduction
personal story

But that is no longer acceptable! Not in Germany or anywhere else in the world. We have the opportunity to change this and to overcome prejudice in our society.

addressing audience

In the US, for example, the rate of high school drop-outs is much higher among black teenagers. In France, the number of university

examples of social injustice

graduates is significantly lower in the banlieues, the poorer sub-urbs around Paris; in Britain young Indians and Pakistanis have been discriminated against for decades and have often been push-ed to live on the outskirts of the big cities.

Just imagine what potential has been wasted in the process! Think of all the children who never had the chance to live up to their potential because of other people's prejudices.

consequences of social injustice

Let's tell our governments to increase the fight for social justice and equality. What can they do? They can make access to educa-tion completely free of charge. Legislation should be passed to get every child between the ages of three and six into daycare. We need comprehensive schools that allow students to stay after school for extra-curricular activities, extra tuition or joint projects. We are the future of the world, so start investing in us, not indust-ries that blow tax payers' money on polluting our planet or ex-hausting its resources.

government

education equality

We also need stricter regulations to abolish discrimination. Hate speech has become a massive problem on the internet. We need strict laws and institutions which also have the technical capacity to prosecute offenders who insult or threaten people on the Web. Many of the prejudices against minorities can be found in com-ments sections and on social media. By enabling the police and public prosecutors to prosecute people for hate speech, we prevent prejudice from spreading further.

stop hate speech

But what can we as individuals do to become true allies?

individual

The first thing we can do is to listen. We have to learn about the different forms of discrimination that affect people and we have to start to believe that what minorities experience is real.

learn about discrimination

Then we can turn around and have a look at the people around us. Stand up for anyone who is bullied or discriminated against by others! We have to say loud and clear that we will not accept dis-crimination and we will not turn a blind eye to injustice.

speak up

At the same time we should not build up walls. If you see someone discriminating against somebody, talk to the offender and try to find out their motives and how they can overcome their prejudices. While some people seem completely lost in hatred, most people are not even aware of what they are doing. By staying in contact and helping them learn more about minorities, we can hopefully change their hearts and minds.

stay in contact

I do hope that in the days to come we will see lively and fruitful discussion on how to deal with discrimination and return to our home countries with new knowledge and the motivation to fight for equality.

conclusion

Thank you.

(538 words)

Aufgabenstellung 1.2

1. *When it comes to non-fictional texts, the first task, in which you are supposed to show that you have understood the text, usually involves writing an outline. You concentrate on the important facts, leaving out the details. Frequently, the task asks for specific aspects of the text. In this exam you have to concentrate on the features of climate fiction and find out what the text says about the reasons for its popularity.*

   Features:
   - *take place before or after an apocalypse: destruction of the environment*
   - *people react to aftermath or threat of a disaster*
   - *relatively new term rooted in sci-fi (science fiction genre)*
   - *sometimes does not seem to be "fiction", as climate change is already happening*

   Reasons for popularity:
   - *famous authors have started to write cli-fi novels*
   - *worsening scientific projections make climate fiction more relevant*
   - *the stories offer catharsis, degree of hope, sometimes humour*
   - *they seem to provide tips on how to survive*
   - *message: we are not alone → necessity of working together*

The comparatively new term "cli-fi" has its roots in science fiction literature. The plot of cli-fi stories takes place before or after catastrophic events that result from the destruction of the environment. It shows how people react to the (imminent) disaster. Due to the fast developments in climate change many of the scenarios described sound rather like events that are already happening instead of fictional events in the future.

features
catastrophic event

destruction of environment

very realistic

Climate fiction has become increasingly popular among readers all over the world. Many famous authors have switched to that genre, which might be contributing to its high sales figures. Another reason why it has grown into the mainstream is obvious: science has proven that we are failing again and again in the attempt to cope with environmental issues and, therefore we are looking for advice to help us survive if disaster strikes. Cli-fi novels seem to offer hope that we will succeed. They also show the necessity of working together to do so and thereby offer us a sense of community. *(170 words)*

reasons for popularity

best-selling authors

guide for real events

hope

community

2. *After reading the article, you are bound to have an idea of whether the author recommends cli-fi literature or not. Therefore, watch out for quotes, examples and rhetorical questions, which are usually employed to support someone's opinion. The structure of the arguments (more pros, more cons etc.) also gives you a hint.*

   Thesis: *author's attitude = positive, recommends reading cli-fi*

Stylistic devices/structure	Function/effect
– starts article with example of storyline (ll. 1–7)	– attracts attention
– rhetorical question (l. 8); speaks to the reader directly	– does not expect an answer – "Hooked?" (answer is "yes")
– informal language/register (ll. 8, 15, 30, 41/42); personal approach	– on an equal footing with audience, like talking to a friend
– examples of book reviews (l. 13); snippets from interviews (ll. 53–55, 63–65)	– proves importance/success of the novels; quotes support her theories
– personal story from an author (ll.40–42)	– closer relationship to readers, more credibility
– mentioning best-selling authors (ll.24/25)	– high credibility, "guaranteed" success
– structure of arguments: mainly positive, only one negative towards the end, which is followed by a positive argument at the end	– reassurance that both sides have been considered
– choice of words: positive connotations; sophisticated words (ll. 32–34) vs. informal register	– leave a lasting impression; shows detailed work on topic; author's opinion is reliable

The author's attitude towards climate fiction is a very positive one. The structure of her article, the choice of words and the general tone show that she recommends reading it.

thesis

Anderson starts her article by retelling the storyline of a cli-fi novel. The request that the readers "[i]magine […] enjoying much-needed time away […], staying in a luxurious Long Island holiday rental" (ll. 1/2) is a vision the readers are more than ready to conjure up in their mind's eye. This ends in Anderson's rhetorical question of whether they are "[h]ooked" (l. 8). A question like this requires no answer, so she expects the reader's unspoken agreement. The effect is clear: Anderson has attracted the reader's attention.

main part
retells storyline of a novel

rhetorical question

The informal register also creates a personal approach. She seems to be talking to her readers as if she were talking to her friends, speaking in a chatty tone, reminding them of the pandemic years and its "cosy home-baking and box sets" (l. 15). When she starts referring to shortlists or quotes from interviews with authors like Rankin-Gee, however, her register is more formal. She presents plain facts and uses sophisticated words like "catharsis" (l. 31) and "calamity" (l. 33). This gives her article strong credibility.

choice of words: informal tone

versus

scientific vocabulary

In the second part of the article, Anderson starts to support her arguments with quotes from an interview with the author Rosa Rankin-Gee and a quote by Rumaan Alam, the author whose story Anderson retells at the beginning of the article. By adding Rankin-

quotes
personal story

Gee's personal story to the text, Anderson proves that cli-fi novels are often read as "how-to manuals" (l. 33): "as a child, Rankin-Gee took dystopian novels very seriously. [She had even] 'packed [her] Karrimor backpack with odd tins of food'" (ll. 40/41) to be prepared for possible disasters.

Anderson also structures her arguments well. First, she explains why it is worth reading cli-fi (prediction of actual climate events, cf. ll. 22/23, 35/36; "catharsis" l. 31; "how-to manual" l. 33). Then she comes up with one counterargument (the risk of "'normalising' climate breakdown", l. 62). This adds to her reliability. The reader sees that she has researched the topic well and considered all sides of the issue. However, she ends her article with a positive aspect ("Optimism is a different matter," l. 66) which proves that it is still worth reading cli-fi literature.

structure of the arguments: counterargument

This matches the generally positive tone of the article, which shows in the many words that have positive connotations ("Comfort" l. 14; "degree of hope" l. 31; "the promise of a how-to manual" l. 33; "succour" l. 58). They leave a lasting impression on readers who are looking for ways to deal with the threat of the climate crisis.

choice of words: positive connotations

All in all, the way Anderson structures the text and describes cli-fi novels makes us want to know more and readers are likely to buy one of the novels recommended in the article.   *(488 words)*

conclusion

3.1 When a task contains a quote, you are expected to rewrite or explain it in your own words first. Read the task carefully. Sometimes you have to refer to further aspects mentioned in the text, and sometimes the quote is merely a starting point for you to come up with your own arguments. In this task, you have to broaden the perspective. You are supposed to assess the extent to which literary texts can help us when it comes to important decisions in our lives. While the climate crisis may be a part of your solution, you must also consider other aspects of our lives where we may be looking for direction.

understanding the quote: when times are hard, novels dealing with current issues seem to offer (simple) solutions to real problems or may give tips on how to get through the crises safely

Literature can help in the search for direction	Fictional context cannot provide help
– how-to manual: model for how to deal with certain situations; catharsis has always been used to educate readers or audiences – broadens horizons: offers insight into different perspectives	– fiction is meant for pleasure, not to serve as a manual – literature oversimplifies matters: solutions offered may not work in real life

- *basis for conversation: may have*
  effect on real-life politics

- *novelists are daydreamers, not*
  scientists/economists/politicians
  (textbooks may provide better
  knowledge)

The papers are full of bad news: war in Ukraine or Yemen, hunger and starvation in Sudan, polluted rivers in Asia and deforestation in Brazil. The world's problems are complex and there seems to be no solution ahead. Politicians do not seem to be ready to deal with all these calamities either. Therefore, turning to fiction may be one way to look for solutions to all the problems.

introduction

When reading about how fictional characters handle crises, you feel like you are being given a blueprint for reality. And yes, literature can indeed contribute. Think back to your childhood, when you learnt from Red Riding Hood not to linger on the way. Later in our lives, stories became more complex. Ever since the time of Ancient Greece, drama has been used to offer people direction by cleansing them from certain emotions through catharsis. Shakespeare's Macbeth is too greedy, Lessing's Saladin is prejudiced, Schiller's Luise too naïve. But we have concluded that we will do better. They live through all those ordeals to wake us up and prevent us from making the same mistakes.

main part
pro
stories teach children lessons

catharsis

However, literature goes further than that. It does not only present us with situations that are similar to our own. By reading stories we broaden our horizons and gain insight into different situations in life. What is it like to be of another race or gender or to live on the other side of the world? Hopefully, this teaches us to be more tolerant and kind.

broadens horizons

When best-selling books pick up important topics such as climate change or technological development, they can also increase awareness of a certain topic. *The Circle* by Dave Eggers is a good example of this. It warns us about the immense influence of media companies. The book explains why the huge power of Google or Apple jeopardises our freedom and it contributed to the discussion among journalists, politicians and the public on why we urgently need regulations when it comes to data policies on the internet.

increase awareness of a topic

However, we have to keep in mind that fiction is not meant to be a manual. In most cases we are not supposed to learn from it, but to dive into its stories and find pleasure in the reading process. While climate fiction is of course a warning to focus on the climate crisis, at this point only cynics and preppers would read novels on scenarios involving the world ending as how-to manuals. Similarly, we do not read novels about murders and serial killers to find advice on how to murder somebody. Literature is trying to feed

con
purpose is pleasure not being a manual

our excitement and it is not meant to find easy or practical solutions.

After all, yes, we read about the characters, yes, we feel for them, but they remain fictional nonetheless. It is not real life and often you cannot simply apply the measures taken in literature to current problems in the real world. Literature oversimplifies situations. Just because you read a book about someone who is queer for example, it does not mean you know what it is like to be queer. Maybe not even the author of the book is queer. While it broadens our horizons, it is only a small element in the overall picture that you can grasp.

oversimplification

Similarly, when it comes to cli-fi or sci-fi novels, most novelists are neither specialists and nor scientists, so their solution strategies may be pure fantasy nonetheless. They can increase awareness of a topic, but if we are looking for real solutions, we need to listen to the experts. And when it comes to our personal lives, a reading companion or actual how-to manual might be more useful than a piece of fiction.

authors are not experts

To sum up, I am sure literature can help you to find your direction in life, but in a real crisis you need to dig further to find real solutions to initiate change.   *(647 words)*

conclusion: personal opinion

3.2 *This is quite a complex task because you have to consider three different aspects: the information on the book from the cover, the information from the article and the type of text for your solution, which is a "blog entry". Note that you are not expected to analyse the visual when it is part of task 3. It is quite sufficient to mention it in reference to the task. While the task only asks you to sum up the information on the book* Dreamland *from the article, you can also use the article to find arguments about whether it is a good idea to read cli-fi in class. Remember that a blog entry is an informal text form in which you also express your personal opinion.*

Information from book cover:

– *Text:*
  - *positive reviews*
  - *recommendation as must-read*
  - *recommended by quality paper (The Observer), successful writers (US: Brit Bennett, GB: Monique Roffey) and a lifestyle magazine (GQ)*
– *Illustration:*
  - *large sun in the background*
  - *tanker or skyline behind rough sea*
  - *flock of birds crossing the sky*
  - *modern block of flats, seemingly flooded by water*
  - *couple on top holding hands*

Information on the book in the article:
- *novel shows Britain 20 years from now; rising sea levels and populist tides; temperature is hotter; main character is a teenage girl called Chance*

Does reading cli-fi in class raise students' environmental awareness:
- *Arguments against:*
  - ***students may not be interested:*** *no interest in sci/cli-fi literature at all, could be too extreme, too gloomy*
  - ***environment is not the only topic in class***: *several books to be read*
- *Arguments in favour:*
  - ***most important topic of our time:*** *destruction of the environment; many stories do not seem to be fantasy, things are already happening*
  - ***ideas for change:*** *sometimes offer solutions for how to deal with environmental problems, characters might serve as role models*
  - ***emotional support:*** *offer optimistic perspective; authors hope next generation will find options; allows us to talk about fears; may lead to feeling of togetherness*

Britain could be plunged underwater by 2100   headline

Hello bookworms out there,

Welcome back to my blog on 'good reads for school'!   addressing reader

Have you devoured Dave Eggers' *The Circle* and *Every* and talked it over in class as I suggested? Have you also discussed how far our social networks have come to match the scenarios created in the novels? Are you ready for more? Then hear this: cli-fi is the new sci-fi!   **introduction:** reference to previous blog articles

"Cli-fi?" you may ask. Yes, climate fiction, as you've probably guessed, is the latest trend in the genre.   introducing "cli-fi"

The novel I have read has just recently been published: *Dreamland* by Rosa Rankin-Gee. What people on islands (like the UK) fear most – rising sea levels – has become reality in the future Britain depicted in the book. The main character, a teenage girl called Chance, grows up in this world in which climate disasters fuel populist tendencies.   example: *Dreamland*

information from the article

On its cover you can see a couple standing on a block of flats which seems to be half submerged by the rough sea rolling in from the left. The scenario is lit by a huge sun, which reminds us that the weather is getting hotter. You can't help shivering when you see how lost the two are in this world. It's exactly what meteorologists and climate experts are predicting! But there is a ray of hope: they are holding hands!   information from the cover:

cover design

The cover also reveals that famous authors like Brit Bennett and Monique Roffey, quality newspapers like *The Observer* and even the popular lifestyle magazine, *GQ*, would really recommend it.   reviews

Well, yes, I'm sure there will be students who don't like cli-fi books. Some may say that it's pure fiction and they'd rather listen to what real scientists tell us. We'd better start doing something other than reading novels and discussing them hypothetically. Some might even find them too gloomy, as the scenarios are a little too close to what is happening in reality.

Added to that, there are many more topics that need to be talked about in class. We could read more classics like Shakespeare or Austen or we could spend more time on important topics such as race relations or immigration.

However, climate change is increasingly becoming the primary topic of our time. The world has woken up to the crisis that we have created for ourselves. Many of the scenarios described in cli-fi are no longer future scenarios. The poles are melting, warm regions are dealing with fires and droughts and the rest of the world is dealing with storms and floods of an intensity that we have not experienced before. Sci-fi novels could be a wake-up call.

Cli-fi novels could provide ideas that – although coming from outside the scientific world – could show us how to tackle environmental problems.

Reading and discussing cli-fi literature in class could also help students cope with their fear of the future and give them a feeling of togetherness. When the situation seems so bleak that we want to give up, it can offer a certain optimism that we can still make a change.

All in all, I'd love to deal with cli-fi in class!

When I read *Dreamland* I couldn't put it down, and when I had read it from cover to cover I knew novels like that needed to be part of our school curriculum. Tell me what you think and if you'd read *Dreamland* in the comment section below.

Live long and prosper. *(571 words)*

Prüfungsteil 2: Sprachmittlung

Aufgabenstellung 2.1

You are supposed to write an article for a project website. This means you have to include the following parts: heading, introduction, main part and conclusion. Your style should be formal, but as those being addressed are mainly young people, some colloquial language is also allowed. As no additional questions narrow down the content needed for your article, the whole text must be summarised with a special focus on the project's sustainability.

The following issues are important:

introductory paragraph:

What is "Lieferrad DA?

– a delivery company that delivers products within the city by bike

What makes "Lieferrad DA" a perfect example of sustainable entrepreneurship?

– protects the environment

– good for local business

– fair wages for employees

– goal: profitability

characteristics of the project:

– founded by three university professors

– COVID pandemic as the perfect opportunity to start a bike delivery service

– ministry provided funds

– marketing via social media and through personal contacts

– staff (both administrative and drivers) made up of students

– customers order directly from retailers, who inform "Lieferrad DA", who are responsible for the delivery

success of "Lieferrad DA":

– in high demand (among both bigger and smaller retailers); sustainability is an important factor for many businesses

– peak times around holidays

– very employee-friendly: students are paid quite well and can gain experience in their field of business (e. g. logistics)

future outlook:

– new subsidies in sight

– so far, the delivery service has not generated money, but new and profitable business models are planned

– hope that new clients will be gained

– expansion to other cities

A green idea with a bright future   headline

Sustainable entrepreneurship combines protecting the environment with supporting local businesses, paying fair wages and still being profitable. This is what "Lieferrad DA", a bike delivery service founded in Darmstadt, a town near Frankfurt, is all about.   introduction

Inspired by the COVID pandemic and with the help of a government grant, three university professors working in the fields of business, logistics and applied sciences set up the company in the summer of 2020 and started delivering all sorts of goods to people's doorsteps. From the start, they advertised on social media and made use of their good relationship with both the town administration and local businesses to succeed. Customers can order directly from the retailers participating. These are in contact with "Lieferrad DA", who then handle the rest of the delivery process.   main part / characteristics of the project

The service is in high demand with both big and small businesses using it. During peak times in particular, such as Christmas or other holidays, the students, who make up most of the workforce, deliver several hundred parcels a week. Still, working conditions at "Lieferrad DA" are better than with most other delivery services. The employees are not only paid the university's standard hourly wage, but are also given the chance to work behind the scenes and incorporate their work experience into their academic studies and future careers. success of "Lieferrad DA"

So far, the company's services are free of charge. For the future, profitable business models are planned although new subsidies are also in sight. With what is hopefully growing client base and a planned expansion to other cities, the project will continue to set a good example of sustainable entrepreneurship. *(275 words)* conclusion
future outlook

Aufgabenstellung 2.2

You are asked to write an email to a friend in California, so address them by name, do a bit of small talk at the beginning and refer to their task (project "Representation Matters"). Then start outlining the content of the article. You should also pay attention to issues that only native speakers would understand (Bund, Monika Grütters etc.). You should either explain them or not mention them at all.

The following issues are important:

Situation of minorities:

– *films/TV programmes not diverse*
– *minorities are still facing discrimination based on sex, gender identity, race, sexual orientation or having a disability; sexual harassment = largest problem; heterosexism*
– *reporting it makes no difference/even backfires, therefore victims do not report discrimination*
– *poll of users of CrewUnited shows that 1/3 of the users who responded have experienced discrimination*
– *members of LGBTQ community often hide this aspect of their identity at work*

Ways to improve it:

– *make active use of diverse data base*
– *pass legislation*
– *introduce confidential counseling, workshops*
– *subsidies depending on diversity of cast*
– *film market/audience/sales figures may regulate diversity*

from: Lisa_Blume@email.com
to: JimKnox@geemail.com e-mail
addresses

Hi Jim form of address

How's it going? Haven't heard from you in ages. Seems you have to work quite hard for school this term. Well, it's the same here. introduction

You're working on a Representation Matters project? How cool. The topic of gender-inclusive language is a matter of hot debate in Germany too, so when your email came I asked myself: do the German media focus on minorities?

reference to project

The clear answer is "no". It seems to be even worse. A study addressed 30,000 users of CrewUnited, the biggest data base in Germany for movie and TV staff. They represent the average employee as far as age, gender identity, and residence are concerned. The result was that there is constant discrimination based on sex, gender, age or race, and against people with special needs.

main part
study reveals discrimination

Eight out of ten women have experienced sexual harassment. LGBTQ people are advised not to talk about their sexual orientation, and when they do, they often face heterosexism or sexual assault.

sexual harassment

To make matters worse, they all learnt that reporting those offenses would not help. Often, this also leads to them being bullied. Most people asked also complained about the stereotypical appearance of Arabs, Muslims, and people of color or of a lower social status.

reporting discrimination leads to bullying

But what could be done to represent more minorities in the media? Well, for once CrewUnited already has 20 % LGBTQ and 16 % BIPOC in their data bases. So where's the problem?

possible solutions

This is also a question of passing legislation of course. If you want to have your production subsidized, make sure that it's diverse. The movie industry could control itself. You could also establish confidential counseling centers or issue checklists that could help you avoid discrimination. Last but not least, editorial staff and juries should be more diverse and more aware of the issue after being trained in workshops.

legislation
self-control

counseling centers

And every one of us can contribute as well. Just don't watch or buy movies or TV productions without diversity. Money and profit have regulated a lot in recent years.

Well, I hope I was able to help you on with your project a bit further. I think affirmative action is needed to make people rethink their attitude toward diversity.

market regulation

Good luck for your presentation! Do tell me how it went.

closing phrase
sign off

Take care,
Lisa

(380 words)

Um Ihnen die Prüfung 2024 schnellstmöglich zur Verfügung stellen zu können, bringen wir sie in digitaler Form heraus.

Sobald die Original-Prüfungsaufgaben 2024 freigegeben sind, können sie als PDF auf der Plattform **MySTARK** heruntergeladen werden. Ihren persönlichen Zugangscode finden Sie auf der Umschlaginnenseite vorne im Buch.

Aktuelle Prüfung

www.stark-verlag.de/mystark